TAKE BACK THE ECONOMY

Take Back the Economy

An Ethical Guide for Transforming Our Communities

J. K. Gibson-Graham
Jenny Cameron
and Stephen Healy

University of Minnesota Press
Minneapolis • London

Illustrations throughout book created by Adam Turnbull.

Published by the University of Minnesota Press
111 Third Avenue South, Suite 290
Minneapolis, MN 55401-2520
http://www.upress.umn.edu

Library of Congress Cataloging-in-Publication Data
Gibson-Graham, J. K.
Take back the economy : an ethical guide for transforming our communities / J. K. Gibson-Graham, Jenny Cameron, and Stephen Healy.
Includes bibliographical references and index.
ISBN 978-0-8166-7606-4 (hc : alk. paper)
ISBN 978-0-8166-7607-1 (pb : alk. paper)
1. Community development—Australia. 2. Community development—Moral and ethical aspects. I. Cameron, Jenny. II. Healy, Stephen. III. Title.
HN850.Z9C638 2013
307.1'40994—dc23 2013000919

Printed in the United States of America on acid-free paper

25 24 23 22 21 20 19 10 9 8 7 6 5 4 3

For Julie and in her memory

Contents

Acknowledgments

Taking back the economy is not a task for a loner. The job calls for concerted action by many. Thankfully we know that there are already many on the job. This book could not have been written without them.

In the late 1990s Julie Graham and Katherine Gibson, writing as the authorial voice J. K. Gibson-Graham, suggested, in *The End of Capitalism (As We Knew It),* that we didn't need to wait for the revolution; we could smash capitalism by working at home in our spare time. It wasn't till a decade later, with diverse movements across the globe chanting cries of "Other Economies Are Possible!" and "Life after Capitalism," that our cheeky feminist proposition was finally old news.

In *A Postcapitalist Politics,* J.K. laid out a vision of a community economy as a space of ethical negotiation and decision making. Much of the thinking for this book was generated in the context of community-based action research projects conducted with Jenny Cameron in Australia and Stephen Healy in the United States. Over the decades the four of us have been connecting and plotting around kitchen tables, at community meetings, in university lecture halls, and via the Internet to take back the economy any way we could. In 2008, with the encouragement of Jason Weidemann from the University of Minnesota Press, we decided to write a manual that would help connect a broad range of economic experimenters, activists, students, and researchers. Working now as an expanded authorial collective, we launched into what we thought was a project of popularizing these ideas. We had no idea that our journey would take us far away from our familiar starting point, out into uncharted territory.

During the four years it has taken this book to emerge, it has developed a life of its own under the direction of influences and forces we can only just make out. Multiple collectivities have sustained us with their energy, resources, and creativity. The Community Economies Collective has been a constant source of theoretical nourishment and comradely care. Its web of loving connection surrounded us when Julie Graham died in April 2010, supporting us to proceed with what was at that time a very sketchy manuscript. Julie's presence lives on in our collective's memory in countless ways—in our regular discussions, when we ponder the bizarre differences between English and American punctuation codes, and when we have lost the plot and need to channel her clarifying conceptual capacities. All members of this thirty-some-strong international collective have offered feedback, suggestions, and examples that have enriched this work.

Our ongoing conversation with Julie is not the only one with someone no longer living who has directed our journey. We would like to acknowledge three inspirational thinkers with whom we have continued to converse since their recent deaths. Val Plumwood has pushed us to engage with the ecological world and to extend ethical thinking to include earth others. Jane Jacobs has led us toward a closer engagement with ecological dynamics. And Eve Sedgwick has continued to whisper "reparative, reparative" in our ears as we have contemplated action and possibility. Our debt to these women is heartfelt, not least because they help us accept that death does not sever our interdependence with others.

Some very specific communities and organizations have guided our journey, variously educating us in the work of habit cultivation, popular education, and ethical deliberation. We would like to thank the Cooleyville community; Empower Biodiesel Cooperative Solidarity and Green Economy; Newcastle community gardens; the recovery and twelve-step movements; Latrobe Valley Community Partnering initiatives; the Town Farm Road hummingbirds; Alliance to Develop Power; Nuestras Raíces; Jagna and Linamon Community Partnering initiatives; the Te Maiharoa family, especially Ramonda; Valley Alliance of Worker Cooperatives; the Association for Economic and Social Analysis; Ex-Prisoners and Prisoners Organizing for Community Advancement; the Tait crowd; and the Picnic Point cockatoo colony, among many others.

Our institutions have offered us material and collegial support. The University of Western Sydney provided Katherine with generous research support. It funded Julie on an Eminent Research Visitor Fellowship for three months in 2010 and Stephen on a four-month fellowship that took him to Australia for a crucial period. Study leave from the University of Newcastle gave Jenny a concerted block of writing time away from the interruptions of teaching and administration. Worcester State University has supported Stephen's absences.

Above all, we would like to thank a vast array of individuals who in different ways have made this book possible. Thanks first to all who read the manuscript or interacted around it at various stages, made suggestions or corrections, and helped with clarification and examples: our reviewers George Henderson, Roger Lee, Brian Marks, and Sallie Marston and our activist friends, colleagues, and students—Violeta Anahi Castillo Angon, Chris Cavanagh, Janelle Cornwell, Louise Crabtree, Mark Creyton, George De Martino, Esra Erdam, Carly Gardner, Michael Garjian, Ilene Grabel, Caroline Graham, Joseph Haider, Rose Heyer, Ann Hill, Matilda Hunt, Leo Hwang-Carlos, Michael Johnson, Sharon Livesey, Sarah Lutherborrow, Yahya Madra, Julie Matthaei, Ethan Miller, Janet Newbury, Ceren Oszelcuk, Robert Pekin, Jamie Pomfrett, Gerda Roelvink, Annie Rooke-Frizell, Lee Roscoe, Deborah Bird Rose, David Ruccio, Boone Shear, Kevin St. Martin, Lillian Tait, Abby Templer, May-an Villalba, Ted White, and Susan Witt.

Special thanks to Kate Boverman and Ethan Miller, who have pulled out all the stops to help bring this book to life, offering detailed research and editorial assistance and searching theoretical engagement. Our illustrator, Adam Turnbull, has provided wonderfully creative input, and our designer, Daniel Oschner, has transformed our amateurish layout into a masterpiece. Above all, thanks to our editor, Jason Weidemann, for his unstinting encouragement and ability to see what we were aiming for.

Finally, to all those who are taking back any little bit of the economy with an eye to our future on this precious earth, we acknowledge and thank you for your efforts. You are our ultimate inspiration.

Take Back the Economy

Why Now?

This book rests on the following premise: our economy is the outcome of the decisions we make and the actions we take. We might be told that there's an underlying logic, even a set of natural principles, that direct how economies operate, but most of us can see that the decisions and actions of governments and corporations have a lot to do with how economies shape up. Encouraged by the idea that we can build the economies we live in, individuals and communities across the globe are taking economic matters into their own hands to help create worlds that are socially and environmentally just. *Take Back the Economy* is inspired by these efforts.

When we explore the ways that people are taking back the economy to make it work for societies and environments, we find they are thinking deeply about shared concerns and experimenting with ways of responding. These concerns are as follows:

- What do we really need to live healthy lives both materially and psychically? How do we take other people and the planet into account when determining what's necessary for a healthy life? *How do we survive well?*
- What do we do with what is left over after we've met our survival needs? How do we make decisions about this excess? *How do we distribute surplus?*
- What types of relationships do we have with the people and environments that enable us to survive well? How much do we know about those who live in distant places and provide the inputs that we use to meet our needs? *How do we encounter others as we seek to survive well?*

- What materials and energy do we use up in the process of surviving well? *What do we consume?*
- How do we maintain, restore, and replenish the gifts of nature and intellect that all humans rely on? *How do we care for our commons?*
- How do we store and use our surplus and savings so that people and the planet are supported and sustained? *How do we invest for the future?*

The message we are getting loud and clear right now is that we've not paid sufficient attention to these concerns. In fact, we've downright ignored them. Even though we live on a finite planet, we have plundered the earth's nonrenewable energy resources and overused and destroyed renewable ones. Even though we live in a society with others, we've focused on individual desires and preferences, and a few have grown massively rich at the expense of many others.

When we think about the scale of the problems facing our planet home, it is daunting. It seems as if the damage we've wrought and the ways of thinking that underpin our profligate economies are insurmountable. We can find evidence for this all around us. But everywhere we turn, we can also find individuals and communities innovating with ways of thinking and acting to address the challenges of our times. If we are to take back the economy for people and the environment, each of us can join in this effort to help address concerns about survival, surplus, encounter, consumption, commons, and futures.

Consciously and realistically build for oneself, and one's community and nation, *sources of hope*.

Thomas Princen, *Treading Softly: Paths to Ecological Order*

Take Back the Economy is for individuals and communities who want their decisions and their commitments to each other and the earth to shape the economies we live in. The book is not a pie-in-the-sky program for revolution, nor is it a step-by-step guide to reforming what we have. It is a simple but radical set of thinking tools for people who want to start where they are to take back their economies—in countries rich or poor, in neighborhoods or in nations, as groups or as individuals.

THINKING BIG

Imagine planet Earth as the astronauts see it—a wonderful blue-and-white sphere floating in the firmament—and, on closer inspection, an oasis of green-and-brown land masses and blue water bodies. This is our life-support system, fed by unlimited solar power, in which inputs and outputs circulate and change form and energy is expended and conserved, all without the totality changing its mass. It is one big garden, if you like, where we toil—farming the soil, producing food and shelter and all manner of goods and services that we need to live on. It is our commons—what we and all other living species share (and should maintain and safeguard).

Let's zoom down from our vantage point in space and focus a bit more closely on the earth below. Now we see cities and rural settlements housing people organized in smaller, more differentiated, human-made support systems we call societies and economies. For a moment let's think of these as gardens again, in which nature provides resources and energy, people labor to survive, inputs and outputs circulate, and wealth is produced and distributed.

These human support systems are like the community gardens we find in so many parts of the world. If we look at one community garden, we find gifts of nature (sunlight, rain, land, and soil); the application of seeds, tools, and fertilizer; and the volunteer efforts of community gardeners. All these inputs interact in the productive activity of gardening. As vegetables grow, some are eaten by the gardeners so they can sustain themselves and continue to work in the garden. Seeds are dried and kept for the next year's crop. Stems and leaves are composted and used to replenish nature's soil. The products of the garden flow back to the producers and the environment to ensure the ongoing survival of the gardeners and the garden.

When nature is kind and gardeners work hard, they are rewarded with a plentiful harvest. There is a surplus, even after vegetables are eaten by the gardeners and their families, seeds saved, and compost tended. The gardeners decide to give some of the vegetables away. They give to their extended families and to neighbors who live near the garden, and they fill bags and boxes to donate to the local food bank.

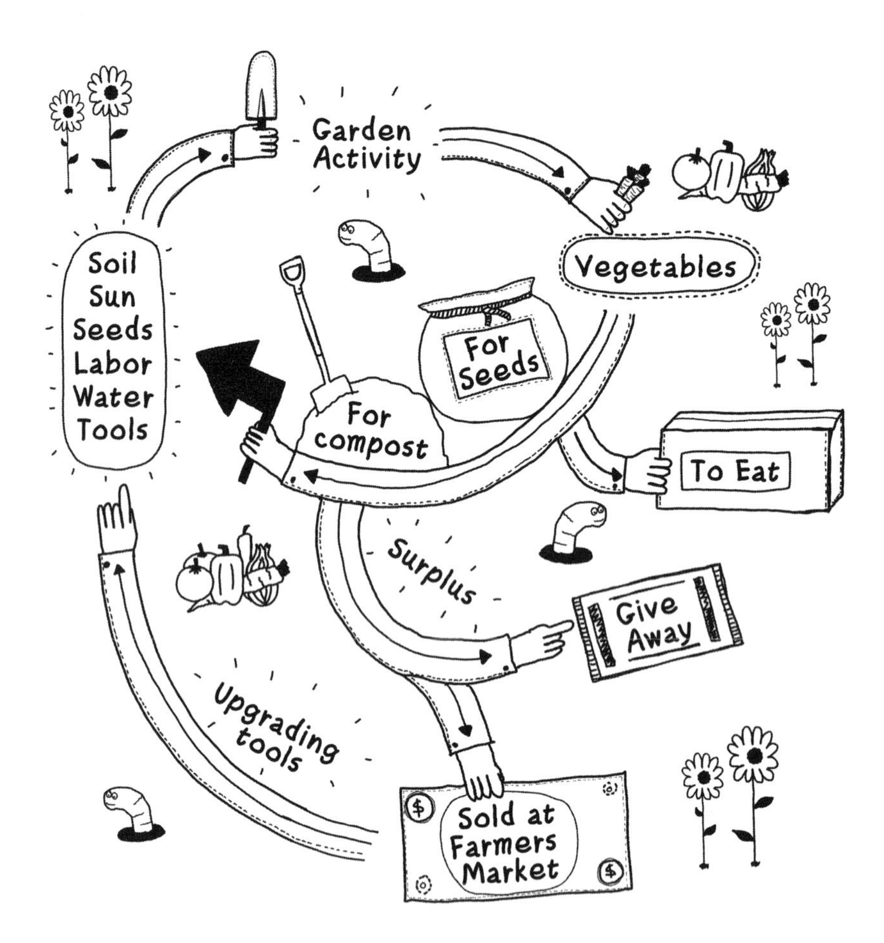

These gifts build goodwill and contribute to the community-building goal of the garden. The gardeners also decide to sell some of the surplus at the local farmers' market, and they use the money raised to buy new equipment that will make the next round of production easier and more productive.

The community garden offers a simple vision of interdependence among the gardeners, other people, and the natural world. The gardeners make decisions about the forms this interdependence will take. They decide how they will

- share the commons—drawing from it, maintaining it, and replenishing it;

- produce together what is needed for individual and collective survival;
- consume resources and encounter others in the process of meeting individual and collective needs;
- produce and dispose of the surplus (which is given to friends, neighbors, and the food bank or sold to raise funds to buy more tools); and
- invest in the garden (by taking so-called waste and composting it so it can be returned to the soil as nourishment for future crops).

Economies are basically no different from this garden—each economy reflects decisions around how to care for and share a commons, what to produce for survival, how to encounter others in the process of surviving well together, how much surplus to produce, how to distribute it, and how to invest it for the future. These decisions are made under varying conditions of plenty and scarcity.

When we put simple visions of the economy "garden" next to the image of the planetary "garden," we see what we are up against. In the economy garden we now live in, we consume more than we can replace, use surplus inequitably and unsustainably, destroy our commons, and threaten species survival. We have become incapable of maintaining our finite life-giving planet garden. And it's become obvious that our planet home can no longer support economic systems that ignore environmental restoration and societal care.

Hopefulness is risky, since it is after all a sign of trust, trust in the unknown and the possible.

Rebecca Solnit, *Hope in the Dark: Untold Histories, Wild Possibilities*

We have hope, however, that change is possible and that there are steps we can take to turn things around.

THINKING ETHICALLY

When we reflect on the thinking that currently guides our economic actions, we see that a few key beliefs predominate. One is that growth is good. Across the globe, growth at any cost is the mantra. Economic growth, we're told, is the means to improve the fortunes of all. Another key belief is in the value of private enterprise, which is privileged as the means by which individuals can apply their energy and creativity to generate wealth, perhaps even great wealth, for themselves and their families. In turn, private enterprise is underpinned by the value that is given to private ownership, with the private ownership of resources, land, and property of all kinds enshrined in legal systems.

But these beliefs have a cost. And the cost is borne most heavily by people and ecosystems that have little voice. Along with degradation of the planet, social and economic inequalities continue to grow. Current economic approaches aren't working. The beliefs by which we have been living economically are bankrupt. Even people who win at the game are beginning to suspect that there is a price that is not worth paying. We have lost, and maybe never had, a moral compass to guide economic actions so that they reflect care and responsibility for one another, for other living beings, and for our environment.

We face a dilemma—whether to follow our present course to the bitter end, acting as if there is no alternative, or to try something new. The times call for ethical action. This means thinking and acting in the economy with concern for others along with ourselves. It means thinking in terms of "we," "us," and "our." It means not putting an end to personal choice, responsibility, or freedom but rather acknowledging that our individual decisions affect others, just as their decisions and actions affect us. As much as anything else, ethical action is a practice of adopting new habits—habits of reflecting on our interconnections with others, approaching the new with an inquiring mind and an appreciative stance, trusting others as we jointly encounter a future of unknowns and uncertainties, and learning to allay our fears and conjure creativity. There are no easy solutions to the problems that confront us, and there are no guaranteed outcomes, but by thinking ethically we can expand our capacity to act.

For us, taking back the economy through ethical action means

- *surviving* together well and equitably;
- *distributing surplus* to enrich social and environmental health;
- *encountering others* in ways that support their well-being as well as ours;
- *consuming* sustainably;

- *caring for*—maintaining, replenishing, and growing—our natural and cultural *commons;* and
- *investing our wealth in future generations* so that they can live well.

An economy centered on these ethical considerations is what we call a *community economy*—a space of decision making where we recognize and negotiate our interdependence with other humans, other species, and our environment. In the process of recognizing and negotiating, we become a community.

THINKING SMALL

What has stopped us from taking back the economy and building strong community economies before this? Our answer is that most people don't see themselves as significant actors in the economy, let alone shapers of it. In wealthy countries we are told that we're consumers and are asked to increase our consumption to help grow the economy. Certainly our role as shoppers and consumers is uppermost in media representations. And often we relate to people we don't know according to their visible consumption—the cars they drive, their hair and clothing styles, their toys and trophies. People's overall level of prosperity and "worth" is communicated by their consumption.

But consumers have a limited economic role—they can decide to consume more, consume less, or consume differently. Sure, many people are responding, voluntarily or not, to the challenges of the time by reducing their consumption or changing their consumption habits, and this has to be part of our taking back the economy. But we want to introduce many more strategies.

We all do more than consume. Many of us work to earn money to survive and also grow some of our own food or care for one another directly. We participate in organizations and enterprises that cater to our needs or help us live well. Some of us start businesses in which we can be our own bosses. Some employ workers and decide what they should do. We work for money, for nonmonetary satisfaction, and out of obligation. We save money and invest in houses, our children's education, or the stock market. We join unions or political campaigns and try to influence the way economic laws are enacted and enforced. The economy is a diverse social space in which we have multiple roles.

It is also a space in which we are integrated with others in many different ways. In household economies we connect with our nearest and dearest to negotiate who does what for household survival and well-being. In neighborhoods and villages we connect with friends, acquaintances, and strangers through buying and selling, working and employing. In national and global economies we connect with distant others through trade and investment. At all these scales we interact with our environments in complex relations of use and care.

When we see ourselves as economic actors with multiple roles, we can start to envision an exciting array of economic actions. When we take responsibility for our economic lives and for interconnected others, we can begin to shape the economies in which we live. *Take Back the Economy* introduces the ethical thinking that can help us frame the ways we might want to shape our economies and start to take them back, bit by bit.

This book is for students, community members, interest groups, nongovernmental organizations, unions, governments, and businesses that want to create community economies. Each chapter starts by discussing the dominant understanding of a different part of the economy—the typical way that we think about work, business, markets, property, and finance. This mainstream conceptualization is followed by a story that shows how real people are taking back the economy as a space of ethical decision making. We then reframe the dominant understanding in light of the community economy concerns we have identified in this introduction—surviving well, distributing surplus, encountering others, caring for commons, and investing for the future. In each chapter the discussion also touches on the community economy concern with consuming sustainably.

Throughout each chapter we use visual tools to prompt our ethical thinking. The tools help us to see our lives and our worlds from a different angle and through a new frame.

Each chapter (except chapter 1) concludes with examples from

HOW TO USE THIS BOOK

Whether you're working alone, you're an activist and community organizer, or you're a member of a group, here are some pointers to help you use this book.

Work in Groups

We have written this book with groups of people in mind—students and teachers, communities and congregations, unions and associations—reading, thinking, and acting together. We believe that when people work in groups, their different ways of thinking and seeing are fertile ground for the imaginative and creative work of taking back the economy. Therefore, if you are reading this book by yourself, you might want to create opportunities to talk to your friends, family, work colleagues, and neighbors about the ideas the book provokes. If you are already part of a group, we encourage you to think about the ways that your group could read and use the book together. You might be able to form a study group or a reading circle. You might be able to use the material in a teaching situation. Or the visual tools included could be the basis of workshops and discussion groups.

Start Anywhere

Each chapter stands on its own. If you or your group has a particular focus or initiative, start with the chapter closest to your interest.

Make a Record

As anyone who has done activist work or started a community group or enterprise knows, the outcomes are far from certain: success isn't guaranteed, and unexpected swerves and surprises are inevitable.

We like to think of taking back the economy as one big uncontrolled and multipronged experiment. If it is an experiment, perhaps we should take a page out of the book of our friends who work in fields like biology or chemistry. They understand that knowledge advances through keeping a record of the steps and missteps that occur in the course of their experiments. As we experiment with taking back the economy, we should make an effort to record our journey. Therefore, we encourage you to

- take notes to document your discussions and your actions;
- modify and augment the tools that are presented in this book;
- make sketches, take photos, devise diagrams, and make audio or video recordings of events or particular developments; and
- take time to reflect on what is and isn't working.

Share Your Results

All knowledge advances through sharing results. The experimenters want their experiments repeated. When an experiment is successfully repeated elsewhere, its validity increases. Therefore, we encourage you to share your experiences with others. For example, you might

- produce a newsletter, zine, or blog;
- make an online video or audio recording; or
- write to us so we can learn about and share what you are doing with others.

across the globe of the ways that people are working collectively to take back the economy and build community economies that support and nourish life.

THE GROUNDS FOR HOPE

One thing that gives us hope that we can change ourselves and the economy is that people *do* change. Look at the major transformations that have taken place in our lifetimes—the widespread adoption of recycling and the new ways we now feel and act around trash, as well as the changes in the status of women and what can no longer be said about or expected of them.

Perhaps most profoundly, the human species can change. Many people see world population growth as an insurmountable barrier to environmental health. But look at the way that rates of reproduction have varied at societal levels according to the microdecisions of households confronted with survival challenges and possibilities and in response to states' investment in health and education. People have changed themselves as new framings have become the norm. They have even welcomed legal recognition of new norms and behaviors, such as laws against domestic violence and the lowering of acceptable blood alcohol levels for drivers who drink.

Something else that gives us hope is the extraordinary proliferation of economic experiments that are being conducted all around us. From local community gardens all over the world to Argentina's factory takeovers, to the vibrant social economy in Europe, to African indigenous medicine markets, and to community currencies in Asia, economic experimentation abounds. There is no shortage of examples of alternative economic organizations and practices that are creating socially and environmentally sustainable community economies. In this book we are able to showcase only a few, but once we become attuned to the possibilities, we can find examples at every turn.

Nature also gives us hope. As we understand more about our role in changing the world's natural systems, we are also gaining greater knowledge about the reparative dynamics of ecosystems. Nature teaches us that

- diversity produces resilience,
- maintaining habitats sustains life, and
- changing one thing creates changes in others.

We can learn from these life-giving and life-shaping ecological dynamics. Perhaps we can mimic them in our economies. We can certainly choose to activate dynamics that support diversity, maintain survival systems that are working, repair ones that are not, and be aware that every change we make will have effects that need to be identified and assessed.

Long ago, small and seemingly inconsequential actions took place that eventually changed the world.

Paul Hawken, *Blessed Unrest: How the Largest Social Movement in History Is Restoring Grace, Justice, and Beauty to the World*

Most important, what gives us hope is that different economic dynamics can be activated by ethical choices. And small actions can have big effects, as the trim tab does on an ocean liner. A trim tab is a tiny flap that controls the rudder, creating a low-pressure area on one side that enables the rudder to turn. It takes only a movement of the tiny trim tab to steer a large and complex ship toward a very different destination than it was previously headed for. In society, too, small actions can initiate major changes. An idea can spread rapidly, reframing our sense of possibility and unleashing new capacities. A local project can be replicated on a global scale. As we have seen in the cases of the World Wide Web and YouTube, we are living in an age when self-organized movements can spread their knowledge and effects across the globe at lightning speed. Starting where we are, we are in a good position to begin taking back the economy. Are you ready?

1.

Reframing the Economy, Reframing Ourselves

WHAT *IS* THE ECONOMY?

If we are to believe the evening TV news, our lives are dictated by the state of the economy. Our fortunes rest with how well governments manage the economy and how much scope businesses are given to grow the economy. Economists have become the soothsayers of the modern world, predicting what will happen as interest rates rise and fall, currencies are valued and devalued, and export and domestic markets expand and contract. The economy, it seems, is an ordered machine that governs our lives.

It's even a machine whose interactions have been captured in working models. At the end of the nineteenth century, Irving Fisher designed and constructed a mechanical model of the economy using a system of water tanks, levers, valves, and pipes. By adjusting the spigots and water levels he could model the impact of economic changes, including falling or rising consumer demand and increased or decreased money flow.

Since then, economists have continued to tinker with machines and models to demonstrate the mechanics of economic interaction. One of the most famous machines was built by New Zealand economist Bill Phillips (of Phillips curve fame) in 1949.[1] The Monetary National Income Analogue Computer, or MONIAC, made its debut at the London School of Economics. Long before computer simulations could do it mathematically, the machine used water to mimic how money flowed through the British economy. By closing valves and pulling levers, the god-economist-operator could see the impact of interventions such as raising or lowering interest rates. Around fourteen copies of the machine were built and sold to institutions that included Harvard, Cambridge, and Oxford Universities; Ford Motor Company; and the Central Bank of Guatemala.

This image of the economy as a machine has prevailed throughout the twentieth century. The major actors are business entrepreneurs and investors who make products, profits, and wealth; the banks that adjust interest rates; and governments that slow down or hasten growth by exacting and spending tax revenues. Everyday people are included as income earners and consumers—generators of demand with appetites that need to be satisfied.

The machine is seen to operate best if it is largely left to its own devices. Interventions by concerned citizens, unions, environmentalists, and even governments pose a threat to its smooth and well-oiled operations. Importantly, these types of interferences are thought to jeopardize the growth mantra that drives this machine to greater and greater outputs.

The image of the economy as a machine has been so robust that even at the beginning of the twenty-first century, economists such as Jeffrey Sachs merrily declare, "The wonderful thing about markets is they self-organise. You don't really have to do very much. You turn a couple of dials and the whole national economy changes. . . . You can sit in a finance ministry or a central bank and make tremendous progress for a whole economy."[2]

Notice Sachs's confidence that progress automatically flows if the machine is minimally guided by an economist-operator. But is this confidence well founded? Increasing numbers of people have grave concerns about how this machine economy operates. It has a voracious and unsatisfiable appetite for natural resources. It is largely oblivious to the consequences of industrial production as it pumps out greenhouse gas emissions and other environmental pollutants that destroy the health of our ecological commons. It pays no regard to the widening gap between those with excessive material wealth and those with so little that bare survival is difficult. And it appears to have no way of regulating the destructive greed and gambler habits of its financiers—those tasked

with oiling and priming its key valves and spigots. For all the ease with which Fisher, Phillips, and Sachs might claim to be able to manipulate and adjust their levers and dials for the greater good, these intractable problems remain.

The more we go along with the idea that the economy is an engine that must be fueled by growth, the more we are locked into imagining ourselves as individual cogs—economic actors *only* if we work to consume. But there are many other ways that we contribute economically.

Clearly we do not live in a machine that is controlled by turning dials and adjusting valves. But there is work to do to fully reject the idea that the economy is a machine and recognize that it has no existence apart from us and the wider world we inhabit. This work is what we call reframing.

Reframing involves imagining the economy differently. It means taking notice of *all* the things we do to ensure the material functioning and well-being of our households, communities, and nations. It means finding ways of framing the economy that can reflect this wider reality. In such a reframed economy we might imagine ourselves as economic actors on many different stages—and as actors who can reshape our economies so that environmental and social well-being, not just material output, are addressed.

Across the globe, people are reframing the economy and their role in it in all sorts of ways. They are reframing growth by divorcing it from increased spending (or Gross Domestic Product) and linking it more directly to social and environmental well-being, using tools such as the Genuine Progress Indicator (GPI), the survey of Gross National Happiness, and the Happy Planet Index.[3] They are reframing the boundaries of the economy, showing that the value of products and services produced in homes and communities is comparable to what is produced in paid workplaces.[4]

This book gives examples of only some of these reframing actions. Our intention is to highlight the difference that reframing makes and what emerges when people take economic matters into their own hands. In this chapter we start with just two examples—the first involving one individual in the United States, the second involving thousands of women in India.

FASHIONING DIFFERENT FUTURES

In 2009, after ten years in the advertising industry in New York City, Sheena Matheiken decided to "reboot" her life and give something back to India, where she had been brought up.[5] She decided to do this in a way that was creative and engaging and that was based on transforming a simple daily routine. She pledged to wear one dress (actually seven copies of the same dress) every day of the year. A friend designed a reversible black cotton tunic modeled on one of her favorite dresses. And Sheena jazzed up this one black dress each day without buying anything new. Her challenge was to use only handmade or secondhand accessories gathered from thrift stores or donated as gifts. The Uniform Project™ was born.

For each of 365 days Sheena posted a photo of her "new outfit" on the Internet and donated US$1 to the Akanksha Foundation, a non-profit organization providing educational opportunities for children from poor households (in a country where thirteen million children don't have access to an education). Soon she gathered a legion of supporters and had attracted the attention of a somewhat alarmed fashion industry. By the end of the year she had raised over US$100,000 for Akanksha, helped over three hundred children gain access to education, received donations of a bizarre range of accessories, and been named one of *Elle* magazine's Women of the Year for 2009.

There's a renewed sense of possibility, collectively our individual actions can have macro impact. Everyday people can have real impact in the world.

Sheena Matheiken, TEDxDubai 2010

The Uniform Project™ recognizes that what we wear is an important aspect of our identity. Our clothes shape how we feel about ourselves and how we are treated by others. But the very human desire to look good, to feel both different and "in," feeds an environmentally voracious form of economic growth.[6] As we raise and lower our hems and switch high-waisted pants for low riders, double-breasted for single-button business suits, or platform shoes for Cinderella pumps, it's hard not to feel like pawns in a huge conspiracy to get us to consume, discard, consume, discard. The volume of unworn clothes in our wardrobes speaks heaps about our fickleness and disregard for the environmental impact of our actions.

Sheena's initiative shows another way forward. We don't need to be blind consumers to contribute to the economy. By participating in economic activities such as recycling and reusing, we can reduce our ecological footprint and avoid feeding a fashion industry that exploits workers. And we can improve the educational opportunities of Indian children directly through people-to-people economic connections. Using her flair and creativity, Sheena is refashioning fashion and reframing what it means to be part of an economy.

While Sheena is reducing her involvement with the global fashion industry (and encouraging others to do likewise through the ongoing Uniform Project™), thousands of poor Indian women are increasing their engagement with it via the SEWA Trade Facilitation Centre (STFC).[7] STFC was launched by SEWA (the Self-Employed Women's

Association), an extraordinary union of self-employed informal-sector workers in India. Since 1972 SEWA has been reframing poor women as economic actors who can command respect from their families, peers—and, most importantly, themselves—as well as police, city officials, politicians, and policy makers.

With 93 percent of the Indian labor force working in informal-sector jobs, unprotected by progressive labor laws, there is little opportunity for the vast majority of workers to share in the benefits of national economic growth. SEWA's membership, of over 1.2 million across seven states, has taken their economic destiny into their own hands, organizing hundreds of producer and marketing cooperatives, a cooperative bank, health care and child care services, a housing trust, training centers, and now STFC, a not-for-profit craft business.

STFC is based in rural Northern Gujarat, where conditions are harsh, drought is frequent, and families must regularly migrate from their villages to find food and work. Women wear clothing beautifully embroidered in traditional designs—even their bullocks sport colorfully embroidered covers. Today, thanks to SEWA's reframing and organizing activities, Gujarat women's embroidery adorns fashion garments worn in London, New York, and Sydney, and fifteen thousand families in northern India are well on the way to accessing a stable income. Gujarat women may think that black is an ugly color to wear, but they now bow to the market advice that New York women won't wear anything else and incorporate this new "color" into their designs.

Now I am able to earn a livelihood and support my family not only with the bare necessities of life, like food, clothing, and shelter, but am also able to educate my children, especially my daughter who is today studying in the second year of Primary Teacher Certification course.

Jamuben Khangabhai Ayar, artisan and craft leader, Dhokawada, Gujarat

As they embroider cloth for an international fashion market, the artisans are assured that 65 percent of the proceeds of any sale will return to them via STFC. This not-for-profit company in which they are the suppliers, managers, and shareholders cannot pay individual dividends. Instead, all surplus returns to the company to increase wage payments for the fifteen thousand artisan members and to expand the company's productive capacity.

For Sheena and SEWA, reframing is a prelude

to claiming a space in the economy in a new way. Sheena reframes the faddish fashion industry as a realm in which a commitment to reduced consumption and increased people-to-people connection can be practiced. SEWA reframes poor women artisans as skilled producers and shareholders in a company with a global reach, market savvy, and operational principles of social justice. Each is pursuing a pathway toward building a better world. In so doing, Sheena and SEWA are taking back the economy as a space of ethical decision making.

The stories of Sheena and SEWA are not without their contradictions. One woman is advocating reduced consumption of new clothes while thousands of other women in a very different location are banking on marketing their brand to well-heeled global consumers. Here we see in microcosm one of the biggest challenges of our times—how to take back the economy for people and the planet without resorting to a one-size-fits-all approach.

Clearly, there are no simple answers. We must approach each effort to reclaim the economy with open and curious minds, feeling hearts, and an orientation toward the experimental rather than the programmatic. Let's not rush too quickly toward the big picture and the big judgments.

Is there a way of addressing the challenges without thinking there is one truly best pathway forward? If the economy is not a machine that operates in a predictable way, we can't set a course and expect that things will systematically unfold. And if our earth is not a bottomless resource pit, we can't keep feeding it to a machine to be gobbled up and spewed out. We must find other metaphors, other frames of meaning, that inspire new ways of being and acting.

REFRAMING: A KEY CONCERN OF A COMMUNITY ECONOMY

Reframing starts with seeing something familiar in new terms. Think of the drawing that can look like a duck or a rabbit or the profile that can appear to be two heads or a vase. Reframing can achieve what's called a figure/ground shift and produce very different understandings that can lead to previously unthinkable actions.

Reframing the economy is a critical step in building community economies. By seeing the economy not as a machine but as the day-today processes that we all engage in as we go about securing what we need to materially function, it's clear that the economy is created by the actions we take. People are creating community economies based on ethical decisions to live well with other humans and with the world around them. Sheena is creating a community economy by acting on her recognition of the destructive environmental impact of the fashion industry and her desire to advance educational opportunities in a context in which too many miss out. The STFC is creating a community economy by acting on a commitment to the power of women to collectively act as economic decision makers and by providing opportunities for them to secure material well-being for their desperately poor families.

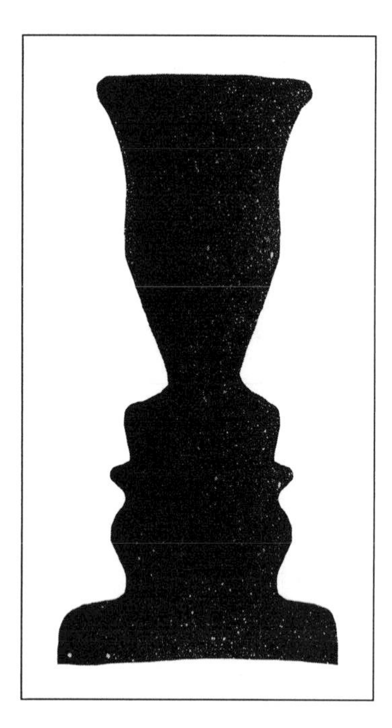

The practice of reframing is central to social and political transformation. Centuries ago, abolitionists fought to end the slave trade and slavery in general. Key to the campaign was the reframing of slaves as fellow humans who experienced unimaginable physical and psychic suffering as they were ripped from their families and communities, transported in chains across the seas, sold at auction like animals, and literally worked to death on plantations. The rhetorical question "Am I not a man and a brother?" may have ignored the slavery of women, but this reframing of slaves as human became a catchphrase that was taken up on both sides of the North Atlantic and helped to build widespread public support for the abolition movement. The catchphrase and the accompanying image of a kneeling slave even became a fashion item adorning everything from men's snuffboxes and women's bracelets to domestic crockery.

Social and political change might start with a handful of concerned citizens, but, through a process of reframing, familiar understandings are shifted and new norms of thinking and acting emerge (often supported by government legislation). Indeed, it is hard to think of a contemporary social and political transformation that has not used the strategy of reframing. Smoking, for example, has been reframed against the continued opposition of the powerful tobacco industry. Where once images of healthy outdoor characters, whether rugged North American cowboys or glamorous European skiers, adorned cigarette packs, now there are more likely to be images of diseased lungs or rotting teeth and gums (as increasingly required by government legislation across the globe).[8]

Fashion, which usually confines itself to worthless things, was seen for once in the honorable office of promoting the cause of justice, humanity, and freedom.

Thomas Clarkson, 1808, *The History of the Rise, Progress, and Accomplishment of the Abolition of the African Slave-Trade*

And new reframings are continually emerging. One that we use throughout this book is a recent reframing of the world's nations. We are all familiar with the idea of first and third worlds or of "developed," "underdeveloped," or "less developed" countries (LDCs). The effect of these names is to highlight what most countries of the world apparently lack ("development") and celebrate the sort of progress only a very small number of nations have achieved (with considerable negative consequences for the environment and for people in other parts of the world).

In the early 1990s, Bangladeshi photographer Shahidul Alam proposed a different terminology that has become widely adopted—that of majority (and minority) worlds.[9] Rather than representing the majority of humankind in terms of what they lack, Alam suggested that we replace the terms "third world" and "LDCs" with the less judgmental, more descriptive term "majority world." In this categorization, "minority world" refers to that fraction of humankind that is relatively well off. This reframing is a ready reminder of the responsibility that comes with being part of the minority world—that one billion of the world's seven billion people who live in countries where per capita income is more than US$12,195 *per year*.[10]

When it comes to "the economy," reframing has been an important strategy used by working people since the Industrial Revolution. Rather than going along with the image of an efficient but soulless machine, many political movements have framed the economy as a vast arena of combat among workers, employers, and the state. In this framing the economy becomes a battleground in which competing forces wrestle for their piece of the economic pie, making alliances and compromises along the way to achieve their goals or engaging in outright warfare in an effort to command the heights of the economic landscape.

The economic actor in this economy is a member of either the working class or the capitalist class, or some fraction of either, and his or her actions are channeled into class struggle. This framing of the economy, though no longer enjoying the currency it once had, has undoubtedly been influential over the course of the past two hundred years. It has inspired socialist revolutions and union movements (and, more recently, the Occupy Wall Street movement) that have also aimed to take back the economy for people and the planet.

The reframing we offer in this book takes its inspiration from this history of economic reframing but offers a very different picture. Our interest is in creating community economies by opening up the economy to the wide diversity of practices that contribute to social, material, and environmental well-being. If we want to take back the economy as a space of ethical decision making not only at the shop counter or at the barricades, we need to draw on a different framing device.

THE ECONOMY AS AN ICEBERG

Our first step toward reframing represents the economy as an iceberg. Above the waterline are the economic activities that are visible in mainstream economic accounts. These are the sorts of activities that are regularly reported on the evening news and that are seen as making up a "capitalist" economy. Below the waterline is a range of people, places, and activities that contribute to our well-being. If we do hear about them on the evening news or read about them in the newspaper, they're likely to be portrayed in novelty or human-interest items, not in pieces on core economic activities.

The iceberg can be used to make an inventory of all the economic practices an individual is involved in, or it can be used to record the economic activities taking place in a community, region, or nation. The iceberg presents a different understanding of what constitutes the economy. Some people think of capitalism as interchangeable with the notion of economy. We don't. We use the idea of an iceberg economy to acknowledge the economic diversity that abounds in this world. The

iceberg also allows us to explore interrelationships that cannot be captured by mechanical market feedback loops or the victories and defeats of class struggle. Once we include what is hidden below the waterline—and possibly keeping us afloat as a society—we expand our prospects for taking back the economy. We potentially multiply the opportunities for ethical actions.

Embroidering in Northern Gujarat was an unpaid activity that women did in their households until SEWA recognized its potential to help secure livelihoods for the embroiderers and their families. SEWA and the embroiderers are now engaged in a whole new array of ethically driven economic decisions. Without forsaking its commitment to maximizing members' participation and benefits, SEWA has established an internationally competitive company (STFC). The artisan embroiderers assist others in their area to join SEWA and become shareholders in STFC. In so doing, they learn about making commercial decisions in a cooperative context with other shareholders. Artisan embroidery, once hidden beneath the waterline of the economic iceberg, has become an activity that has introduced new economic arenas and new economic practices into women's daily lives.

We had no value for our work and never thought of getting income by selling [our embroidery]. But with the help of SEWA and our company STFC it has now become possible.

Rudiben Jivabhai Rava, embroidery artisan, Babra Village, Gujarat

Sheena's daily routine, on the other hand, is drawing on economic arenas and practices not usually associated with the world of fashion. She is engaging with activities that largely occur below the waterline, such as reusing, recycling, donating, buying from thrift stores, and making things by hand. Sheena is showing how these activities can help create a fashion world that takes into account environmental and social consequences.

Reframing the economy through the iceberg is a first, somewhat chaotic step toward sorting out in a more systematic way the diverse economic practices we have to work with. If we are going to take back the economy "any time, any place," we need to know what we are starting with. The diverse economy offers a template for a more comprehensive inventory.

Each column in the diverse economy figure represents a different aspect of the economy—labor practices, business enterprises, transactions of goods and services, property ownership, and finance. Each column is divided into cells that relate to the iceberg economy. The top cells refer to those economic activities that are usually above the waterline (and recognized in the mainstream framing of the economy as a machine). The bottom cells refer to those economic activities that are usually under the waterline, hidden and generally unrecognized as making an economic contribution. In the middle cells are activities that are like the mainstream activities but involve an alternative element. For example, alternative paid labor includes arrangements in which workers are paid not in cash but in kind, with goods or services. Alternative capitalist enterprises include businesses driven not by the goal of turning a profit but by a commitment to producing social or environmental well-being.

THE DIVERSE ECONOMY				
LABOR	ENTERPRISE	TRANSACTIONS	PROPERTY	FINANCE
Wage	Capitalist	Market	Private	Mainstream Market
Alternative Paid	Alternative Capitalist	Alternative Market	Alternative Private	Alternative Market
Unpaid	Noncapitalist	Nonmarket	Open Access	Nonmarket

Unlike the machine economy, this diverse economy makes no presumptions about predictable relationships between economic activities. Nor does it categorize people into classes according to their economic involvements. It is a reframing that highlights diversity and multiplicity. People participate in many different activities across the diverse economy. They are economic actors on many fronts.

Similarly, sectors of industry are comprised of a range of diverse economic activities. For example, in the diverse economy of fashion shown in the nearby figure, there are a host of economic activities (including Sheena's open-access online blogging about the Uniform Project™) and economic entities (including STFC, an alternative not-for-profit company in which the embroiderers are shareholders).

The diversity that already exists, and that we are all part of, is the basis for building community economies. The diverse economy helps reveal the economic activities that might be strengthened and developed in order to take back the economy for people and the planet.

THE DIFFERENCE REFRAMING MAKES

Each chapter of this book takes one column from the diverse economy figure and explores it from the perspective of *community economies*—economies in which ethical negotiations around our interdependence with each other and the environment are put center stage.

There are no simple answers to the dilemmas that we overviewed in the Introduction—dilemmas as to how to survive well, how to distribute surplus, how to encounter others as we seek to survive well, what and how to consume, how to care for our commons now and into the

ACTORS AND ACTIONS IN A DIVERSE ECONOMY OF FASHION				
LABOR	**ENTERPRISE**	**TRANSACTIONS**	**PROPERTY**	**FINANCE**
Wage • Low-wage workers in a clothing factory in Costa Rica • Salaried sales manager in a clothing retailer in Hong Kong	**Capitalist** • Large clothing manufacturer operating across Southeast Asia • Small clothing retailer in London that employs ten staff	**Market** • Retail outlets in shopping malls, airports, and main streets across the United States • International mail-order and online sales by prêt-à-porter labels based in the United States	**Private** • Trademarked labels and designs of fashion houses in Paris	**Mainstream Market** • Bank finance for expansion of Canadian retail chain into the United States
Alternative Paid • Self-employed fashion designer in New Zealand • Home-based piece worker in Honduras	**Alternative Capitalist** • Organic cotton company that uses no herbicides or pesticides • STFC not-for-profit company in which the embroiderers are shareholders	**Alternative Market** • Thrift shops run by charities • Online sales by individuals • Mitumba (second-hand clothing) markets in Tanzania	**Alternative Private** • Clothing shared between siblings in a household	**Alternative Market** • Microfinance loan to a woman in Bangladesh to buy a sewing machine
Unpaid • Householder sewing clothes for self and family members • Friends helping each other sort out their clothing wardrobes	**Noncapitalist** • Cooperative of machinists in Argentina	**Nonmarket** • Parents giving baby clothes for best friend's new baby • Family donating winter clothes to an international charity working in an earthquake-affected area	**Open Access** • Sheena's online blog that describes how different fashion looks have been put together	**Nonmarket** • Loan from family members to help start a small fashion business

future, and how to store and use savings and surplus so that we and all other species continue to have a life on this planet.

In the chapters of this book we foreground people who are negotiating the challenges of living well together. Like Sheena and SEWA, they want to make a difference. The decisions they make and the actions they take may not always be to our liking; we may think the trade-offs involved are insufficient for the task at hand. But these are our fellow travelers. They are also resisting the idea that there is a machine economy that dictates our actions and positions us as self-contained economic units. Instead, they are reaching out and connecting with people from different economic and geographic locations; they are taking seriously the economic work that needs to be done to redress environmental harms. Like hundreds of thousands across the globe, these are the people who can teach us by opening up new worlds of possibility.

2.
Take Back Work
Surviving Well

WHAT *IS* WORK?

Work is what we do for a living—it's what we do to survive. Work gives us an identity. It's a way of defining who we are. When we meet people for the first time, we usually want to know what they do for a living. We're interested in how much they are paid and what status is attached to their position.

Work has the potential to be a source of great pleasure and meaning—it can be where intellectual and practical challenges are posed and met, where we can create new things, use our ingenuity, interact with others, and accomplish things. Whether it is raising a child, running a farm, caring for the sick, making airplanes, managing personnel, defending criminals, or programming computers—all kinds of work can be fulfilling.

But work can also be a drudge. It can be repetitive, physically demanding, unsafe, isolated, and so low paid that it barely covers living costs. It can take over people's lives.

In some low-wage sectors people are working longer and longer simply to get by. Those with well-paying jobs are also working longer and longer, perhaps because this is what the job demands or perhaps to buy the things that they think they need. And in countries where the majority of working people do unpaid subsistence and caring work, they are increasingly forced to find ways of paying for basic needs like schooling and medical care. They must find ways of making money to supplement whatever else they do to survive.

All over the world, it seems, quality of life and health are being jeopardized by long workdays and workweeks. And there is no evidence that working longer or for more money increases our happiness. Indeed, national-level data show that despite increasing incomes since the 1950s, levels of happiness have not increased, and in some countries they have decreased.[1] In many households across the globe, the balance is skewed; too much time is being spent working for money and, as a consequence, there's not enough time for life.

Now we have discovered that increased income is an addiction—the more money and possessions we have, the more we need to acquire to feel happy.[2] And there is mounting evidence that there are social and psychological costs associated with material- and consumption-focused lifestyles. When incomes increase and when the gap between the highest- and lowest-paid workers widens, a host of modern-day health problems follow—rising levels of social isolation, depression, and alcohol and drug abuse.[3]

The usual story of progress is that as majority world countries are integrated into the "global economy," waged work will displace unpaid work and become *the* work that people do. Certainly this is happening in countries like China and India and in Southeast Asia as tens of millions of people are becoming wage earners.

This could all be well and good but for the fact that, with the doubling of the global paid labor force in the 1980s and 1990s, more and more of us are spending our hard-earned money on more and more "stuff."[4] In the constant drive for satisfaction we are eating into our planet's resources at an unsustainable rate and polluting our environment at unprecedented levels.

There is never any point at which we will be able to claim that enough is enough.

Tim Jackson, *Prosperity without Growth: Economics for a Finite Planet*

Across the globe, work as we know it is not achieving the goal of surviving well. We are working more but surviving poorly. We are overconsuming the earth's resources, undermining our health, and not improving our levels of happiness. Can we rebalance the scales? We think we can, but we might need to step back from the work treadmill and think about what we really need to survive well.

This is not going to be easy. When we've become so heavily invested in the things that money can buy, there's a lot at stake. But if we are to take back the economy, we need to reconsider our working lives in the context of our own well-being and the well-being of other humans and the planet. Let's look at how two different groups are dealing with this very real dilemma.

LIVING TO WORK OR WORKING TO LIVE?

Downshifters are workers who have thought carefully about the work–life balance and made the decision to overhaul their lives. These individuals make a conscious choice to reduce their income but improve their quality of life. They cut back on their paid work, take up lower-paying jobs, move to less expensive houses or regions, change careers, or stop paid work completely. Studies show that between one-fifth and one-fourth of the U.S., Australian, and British populations in their thirties, forties, and fifties voluntarily downshifted during the 1990s.[5]

While their incomes may have shifted down, everything else has shifted up.

Christie Breakspear and Clive Hamilton, *Getting a Life: Understanding the Downshifting Phenomenon in Australia*

Downshifters make the change because they want to spend more time with their family, live healthier lives, find more fulfillment and happiness, live in a less material way, or reduce their impact on the environment. Importantly, downshifters come from across the range of income groups and social grades. In Britain, for example, 25 percent of semi-skilled manual workers and apprentices downshifted between 1993 and 2003, as did 27 percent of executives, managers, and professionals.[6]

And what do these downshifters do with their time? They stop and smell the roses! They don't necessarily work less; they do different kinds of work—spending time caring for their families and friends, volunteering informally or in organized community groups, studying things they had always wanted to learn about. They make, swap, and gift things instead of buying them. They take up hobbies, relax more, exercise more, sleep more. Overall, they take control of their lives and start to enjoy well-rounded and meaningful days and weeks at a calmer pace.

A BMW won't give you a hug or draw you a picture.

Christie Breakspear and Clive Hamilton, *Getting a Life*

At the other end of the work spectrum are many

of us who feel bound to the need for a well-paying job to secure our families' well-being. In the resources sector in Australia, workers are attracted to high incomes and the promise of material security. Coal miners, for example, earn on average around A$120,000 per annum, 33 percent more than the next-highest-paid group of workers.[7] This privileged position in the labor force comes courtesy of the great profits made by coal companies operating in a nation that is the world's largest black coal exporter.

The money might be great—but there's a cost. Miners work the longest hours of any employee group, and mines operate continuously. So miners work twelve-hour shifts excavating and crushing coal or loading it onto the huge ships that take it to the steel furnaces and power stations of Japan, South Korea, Taiwan, China, and India. With coal miners working schedules such as four days on and four days off, often at a distance from their families, it's not surprising that employees in the industry score it as having the second-worst work–life balance (information, media, and telecommunications workers score theirs as having the worst balance).[8] Families run on one schedule, and miners run on another—life turns into different merry-go-rounds.[9]

This situation is a long way from that of the 1970s, when miners were the first in Australia to achieve a family-friendly seven-hour day and a thirty-five-hour workweek (with weekends off). But that was just at the beginning of the open-cut mining boom and before the exponential increase in international demand for Australian coal. As the industry has grown, so has the pace of work intensified and payment for work skyrocketed.[10]

Many coal miners enter the industry knowing that they are putting their work–life balance at risk. They start with a vow to stay only a few years, make good money, and then get out fast. Unfortunately, it's easy to say, less easy to do. There's even a name for their situation in the industry—the "golden handcuffs." Miners and their families get used to the hefty pay package, spend big, and often get caught up in the high levels of debt that can come with high incomes.

This is a familiar story of money speaking louder than anything else. And it's a story of a cycle that many of us are bound up in. Even when we know that long hours and harsh conditions are undermining our well-being, we can find ways of justifying what we're doing—"We'll only do it for a short time, and then we'll stop" and "It *will* pay off in the long run."

Perhaps we can even justify the environmental impact of our work—"I'm just one worker trying to do the best I can by my family; I'm not having *that* big an impact" or "My work contributes to a strong economy that everyone benefits from, and it will help secure the nation's future."

These are the kinds of refrains that are likely to circulate in our minds when we face up to the dilemmas of managing work and the well-being of ourselves, our families, our communities, and our planet. And the question remains—does well-being result? Are we surviving well?

The roster and the long shifts make you very old, very quick. Anybody that wants to get into it I recommend they do it early in their life, get in, be diligent, make your little fortune, and get out because you get really old, really quick.

Beryl, mine worker

SURVIVING WELL: A KEY CONCERN FOR A COMMUNITY ECONOMY

What does it mean to survive well? We know that the most common answer is that surviving well means getting a well-paying job that provides material security. But as we have seen, greater material security does not always add up to greater well-being. According to the latest global study, material security is only *one* of the elements essential for human happiness: "Well-being is about the combination of our love for what we do each day, the quality of our relationships, the security of our finances, the vibrancy of our physical health, and the pride we take in what we have contributed to our communities. Most importantly, it's about how these five elements *interact*."[11]

This research tells us that to survive well we need to achieve a mix of the five different types of well-being:

- *Material well-being,* which comes from having the resources to meet our basic needs and being satisfied with the resources we have.
- *Occupational well-being,* which comes from a sense of enjoyment of what we do each day, whether in a conventional job or as a student, a parent, a volunteer, or a retiree.

- *Social well-being,* which comes from having close personal relationships and a supportive social network.
- *Community well-being,* which comes from being involved in community activities.
- *Physical well-being,* which comes from good health and a safe living environment.[12]

We are interested in creating community economies in which we think and act ethically in relation to each other and the environment. One starting point is to think about the work that we do and the ways this work might be contributing to or undermining these five elements of well-being and thereby affecting both our own and others' abilities to survive well. In community economies we aim for a balance among these five contributors to surviving well. This means having the time and energy to combine different forms of work. But when so much of our labor time is put into making money, how can we allow for such a mix? How might we negotiate a better balance?

Limiting the time we spend in paid work so that there is time left for a dignified life has long been a goal of working people. We can learn a lot from looking at the struggles and successes that have been waged and won around this key concern of a community economy.

To help us understand how negotiations have differentially affected the working lives of men and women, we can use the following tools:

1. A *Twenty-Four-Hour Clock* on which the total hours of different kinds of activity are recorded.
2. A *Well-being Scorecard* on which the five types of well-being are rated on a scale from 1 (poor) to 2 (sufficient) to 3 (excellent).
3. A *Balance Scale* on which we represent how labor time spent earning money is balanced with labor time spent on other sorts of well-being (social, community, and physical).

From the mid-nineteenth century on, a central demand of the workers' movement was to limit the workday to eight hours so that wage workers could have a balanced life that would include eight hours of

WORKINGMAN'S 24-HOUR CLOCK

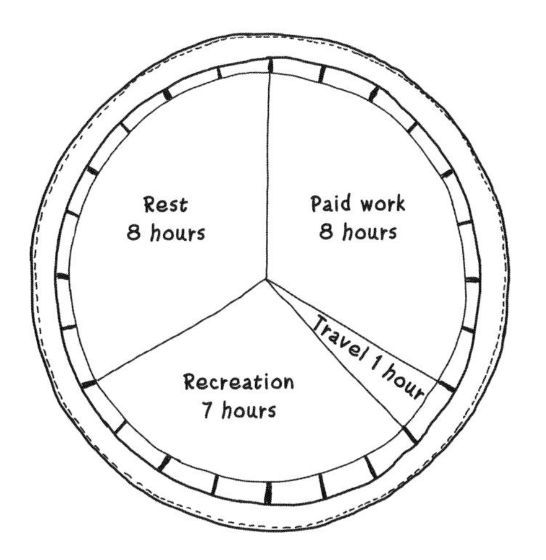

WELL-BEING SCORECARD

WORKER'S WELL-BEING	1	2	3
Material		X	
Occupational		X	
Social			X
Community			X
Physical			X

recreation and eight of rest (with two days off at the end of the workweek).[13] In eight hours of labor, the workingman was supposed to be able to earn enough to support a family at a decent standard of living. He was not to be too physically run down to play tennis or baseball as recreation or to have the energy to tend a vegetable patch or volunteer for community projects on the weekend.

The workingman's Twenty-Four-Hour Clock shown here reflects hours and conditions of work that are well regulated. The Well-being Scorecard shows ratings sufficient for material security and occupational satisfaction. Because the workday reflected by the Twenty-Four-Hour Clock still leaves plenty of time for other activities, the scorecard shows social, community, and physical well-being all rated as excellent. So the Balance Scale for this workingman shows that his work–life balance appears to be pretty even.

Unionization was a key collective action that achieved this ideal for workers in certain industrial sectors in some countries over the twentieth century. Unfortunately, at the start of the twenty-first century this ideal is still far from the norm for the bulk of wage workers the world over.

When we look more closely at this ideal in its original historical

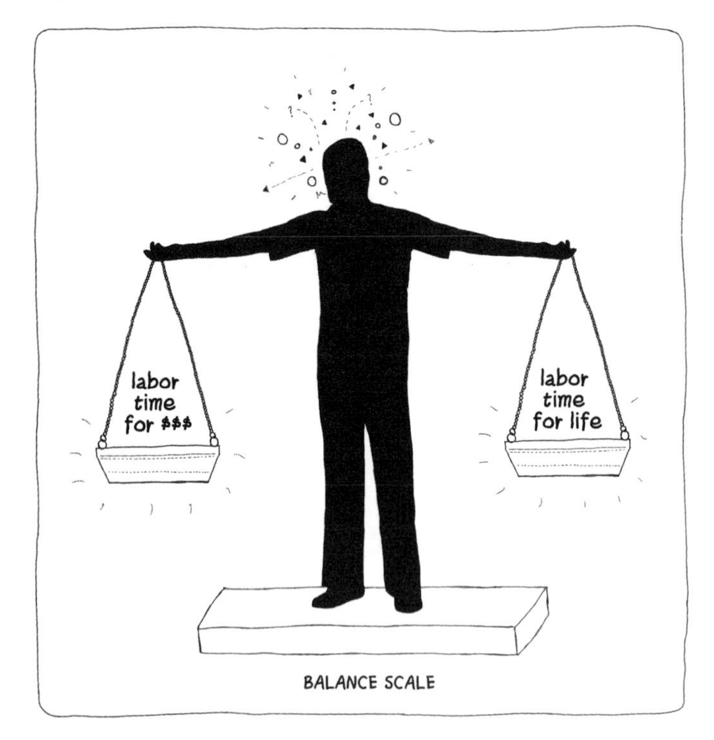

context, we see that the balance it sought for workers was predicated on the hidden labor of women. The well-being of the male worker and his offspring depended on women's unpaid housework, child care, parental care, community work, and social networking. A balanced workday for men did not always mean a balanced workday for women. As the Twenty-Four-Hour Clock of activities of the worker's wife shows, women's unpaid labor time could swing the balance significantly.

Some women found unpaid labor in the household and the community a source of pleasure and satisfaction. But for other women, the labor time they put into producing material, social, community, and physical well-being for others was at the expense of their own well-being on all five counts. We show two different Well-being Scorecards to illustrate this difference. The size of the wage coming into the household was often, but not always, a determinant of how a woman experienced her workday. For middle-class wives of salaried workers who could afford labor-saving devices and even paid household help, the work of running households was perhaps less onerous and the boundary between "work" and "recreation" more blurred. And yet many in the same social class experienced unhappiness and lack of fullfilment despite their well-to-do suburban lifestyle.

Meanwhile, in households where women took paid employment to make ends meet or where there was no "breadwinner" but a single working mother, the double day was the norm, as shown in the single mother's Twenty-Four-Hour Clock. Some women in this situation may have been supported by strong networks of extended family, but low-paying jobs and long working hours (in and out of the home) often meant there was little opportunity for these women to achieve well-being on any front, as the scorecard shows. Of course, for some women low material and

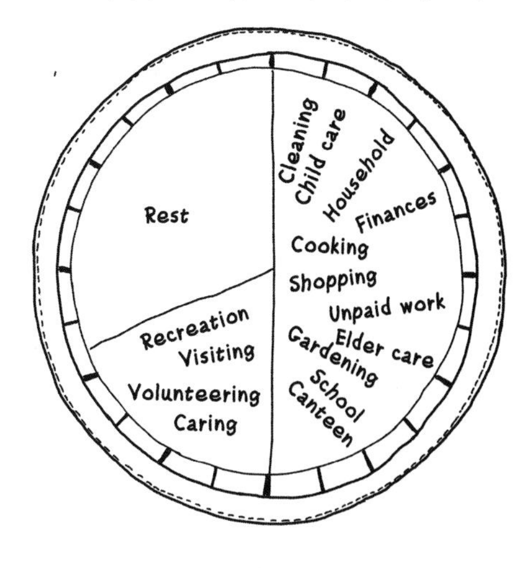

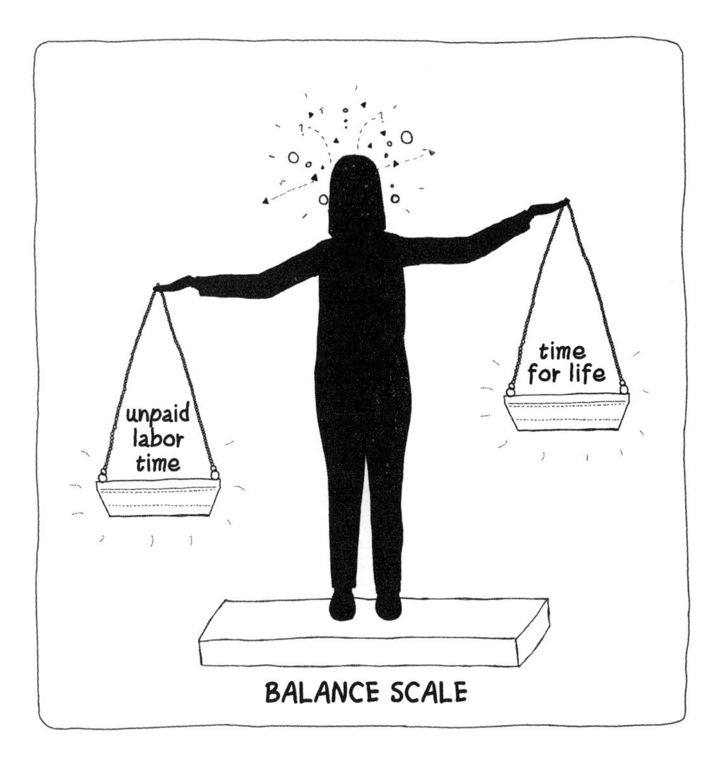

BALANCE SCALE

occupational well-being may have more than made up for freedom from abusive relationships.

The feminist movement drew attention to women's unpaid housework and caring and emotional work, broadening the conception of what work is necessary for human survival. In the twentieth century the minority-world women's liberation movement began to question how much occupational well-being women obtained from their unpaid work in families. The movement demanded more opportunities for women to achieve occupational fulfillment outside of the home. Feminist activism and wartime experiences paved the way for increased entry into the paid workforce by married women and mothers. And other factors such as rising housing costs and increased levels of household debt accelerated the move. By the end of the twentieth century, the double day was no longer confined to working-class women in the minority and majority worlds but was embraced by a greater percentage of the female population. The call for greater sharing of domestic labor by men accompanied this move, just as the regulatory controls on paid working hours seemed to loosen.

The problem that has no name.

Betty Friedan, *The Feminine Mystique*

The successes of the movement for a workingman's eight-hour day and the successes of the feminist movement have interacted in complex and contradictory ways over time. Today it seems that women and men are working longer than ever before. The balance of eight hours paid work, eight hours rest, and eight hours to do what we will is no longer

TWO EXTREMES OF WELL-BEING FOR "STAY-AT-HOME" WOMEN

WELL-BEING	1	2	3
Material	X		
Occupational	X		
Social	X		
Community	X		
Physical	X		

WELL-BEING	1	2	3
Material			X
Occupational			X
Social			X
Community			X
Physical			X

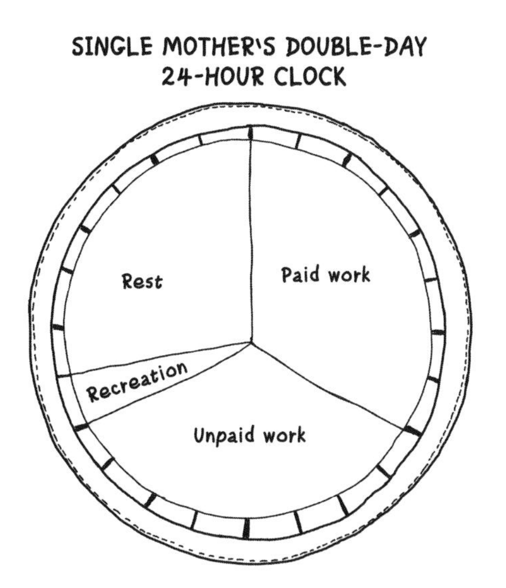

WELL-BEING SCORECARD

SINGLE MOTHER'S WELL-BEING	1	2	3
Material	X		
Occupational	X		
Social	X		
Community	X		
Physical	X		

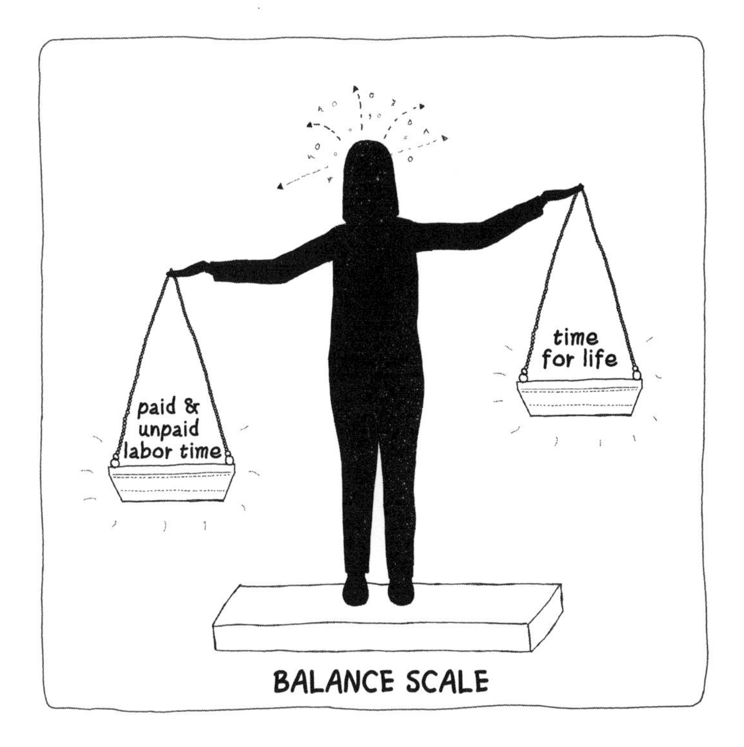

a common mantra, nor is it a common experience. Today we find a significant polarization in work lives.

Let's examine two lives that are based on real people in order to explore the challenges that confront us as we strategize how to take back work. Maya is a young professional woman who is benefiting from the successes feminism has wrought. Josef is an older man whose life has also been affected by the gender reframing achieved thorough feminism. We can use the Twenty-Four-Hour Clock, the Well-being Scorecard, and

MAYA'S DAY

Maya is a thirty-eight-year-old junior partner at a U.S. law firm for whom "success" is defined primarily in material terms. Occupational and physical well-being receive some attention, but social and community well-being are just about absent from Maya's life.

Maya starts her working day bleary-eyed at 4:30 a.m. with a thirty-minute commute to her gym and a sixty-minute workout with her personal trainer. She catches the train to work at 6:00 a.m., arriving at 6:30 a.m. While she travels, Maya answers a few e-mails and bills for her services in fifteen-minute increments. Maya's boss arrives later than she does, so she always leaves her office door open to let her boss know that she is in early and already hard at work. The morning goes by in a flurry of meetings and depositions for cases in which she is lead defense. She works during lunch and then continues the intense pace of work throughout the day until 7.30 p.m. She stops for Chinese takeout and continues to work until 9:00 p.m. It's then a one-hour commute home to her apartment, a thirty-minute break in front of the TV, and then to bed for six hours of sleep.

Maya is working long hours and is extremely well paid for her efforts. She lives in a luxury apartment with cleaning and maintenance services. She goes on a three-week overseas vacation each year, and her wardrobe is full of designer black suits and imported high heels. She enjoys a high-status position, but is she surviving well?

Maya lets off steam on Friday nights getting drunk with her colleagues, and then spends most of the weekend working on cases. There's little time for restorative activities, rest, or self-care, and certainly none for connection to a community outside of work. Sociologists would describe Maya as living in a world of "imploded sociality." While she may find some sociability, connection, and purpose through her work, we could just as easily imagine that a broader sense of connection and purpose might be missing from her life. Sometimes she wonders, is this liberation?

MAYA'S 24-HOUR CLOCK

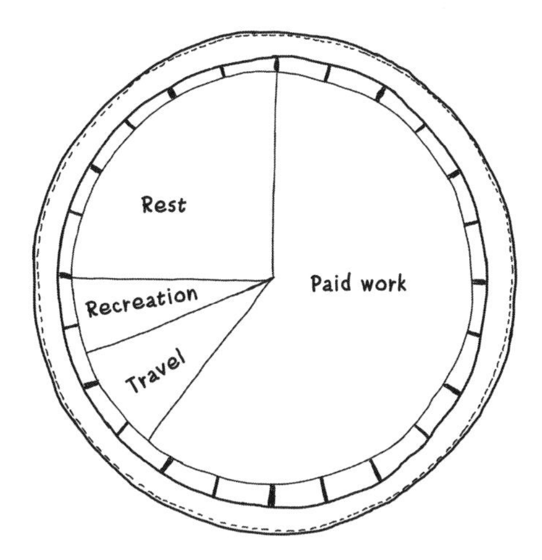

WELL-BEING SCORECARD

MAYA'S WELL-BEING	1	2	3
Material			X
Occupational		X	
Social	X		
Community	X		
Physical		X	

BALANCE SCALE

the work–life Balance Scale to highlight the ethical choices and trade-offs each makes as they aim to survive well.

The working lives of Maya and Josef are clearly two extremes. One is oriented toward outward success and material reward. The other is oriented around service to others and internal satisfaction. Most of us probably live some mix of these two. What's interesting from a community economy perspective is what different kinds of work enable. Maya's day is dominated by one kind of labor—paid professional work that allows her little time for friends, family, and community. Josef's life of multiactivity—of multiple forms of work—is geared toward achieving the multiple dimensions of well-being that are fundamental to human flourishing.[14]

Let's review the different kinds of work that Josef performs. Not only does he perform physical labor and emotional labor; he uses his intellect, organizational skills, and creative talents. His is a working life in which working for monetary income has been substituted with other kinds of work and remuneration. His labor is performed in return for alternative nonmonetary payments, such as *in-kind payments* (lunch in return for yard labor) and *reciprocal labor* (swapping work arrangements with other people, such as carpentry lessons for computer lessons). He also performs labor that is unpaid in a material sense but is rewarded emotionally. Josef engages in *unpaid housework* and *family care* for which he receives the appreciation of his children and separated wife, he does *self-provisioning labor* when he works in the community garden to grow produce or does his own housing repairs, and he gifts his *volunteer labor* alongside the schoolteachers and PLAY members.

The diversity of Josef's working life stands in stark contrast to the homogeneity of Maya's. Both are making a contribution to society, but his monetary income is a fraction of hers. In a community economy we can turn our creative thoughts to how the Mayas of the world might achieve more of a work–life balance and a wider range of well-being and how the Josefs of our community might access more money.

The tools introduced thus far help us to identify how we are balancing surviving well personally and in our households with allocating labor time to various ends. We have seen that collective actions to change

JOSEF'S DAY

Josef is a forty-two-year-old who lives outside the mainstream in Australia. As a younger man he dabbled in carpentry but then faced some major health challenges. He married and had a few children. With a mental illness that meant he could no longer find paying jobs, in his mid-thirties he went on a disability pension. He put time into bringing up his kids and getting his life back on track. The family moved to a smaller town where living is cheap. They moved into a rental property that Josef, after negotiation with the owner, was able to renovate using cast-off materials. Through connections at his local church, he started to volunteer his carpentry and other skilled services to families in need in his local community.

These days Josef rises at 7:00 a.m. to make breakfast for his two school-age children. The younger two live with his now separated wife, and he sees them only on weekends. After feeding the kids and animals around the house, it's off to school. During the school year he spends two hours working on the chicken pens and compost system he has constructed at the primary school. Working alongside one of the teachers, he helps instruct the class of students who have been allocated chicken care for that week.

At 11:00 a.m. he meets up with a crew of six other unemployed men in the neighborhood whom he has enrolled into a small volunteer social enterprise called PLAY, which stands for Play, Learning, Activity, Yakka (an Aboriginal term for hard work that is now part of Australian English). The PLAY group head to the house of a single parent with small children where they are constructing a shade arbor over a sand pit in the backyard. On the way they collect shade cloth donated by the local hardware store, timber from a building site whose materials they have permission to recycle, and some salad vegetables from the community garden where some of the members have garden beds. After two hours of work, the group stops for lunch and a rest. Lunch is the salad they have brought and a cake made by the young mother whose yard they are improving. Over lunch Josef counsels some of the younger men about recent upheavals in their lives. Another hour of work and cleanup from 2:00 to 3:00 p.m., and then it's back to the school for Josef.

He picks up his kids and some of their friends and takes them to the local swimming pool for a couple of hours. At 5:00 p.m. he's back home to supervise homework and prepare dinner. By 7:30 p.m. the chores are done, and Josef settles down with his children for an hour of music, reading aloud, and scrapbook making. After they are in bed at 8:30, he puts in two hours of work on the computer, writing a manual for other schools that want to set up integrated systems of chicken raising, compost collection, and water and waste management. From 10:30 p.m. to 11:00 p.m. he meditates, and then it's bedtime.

JOSEF'S 24-HOUR CLOCK

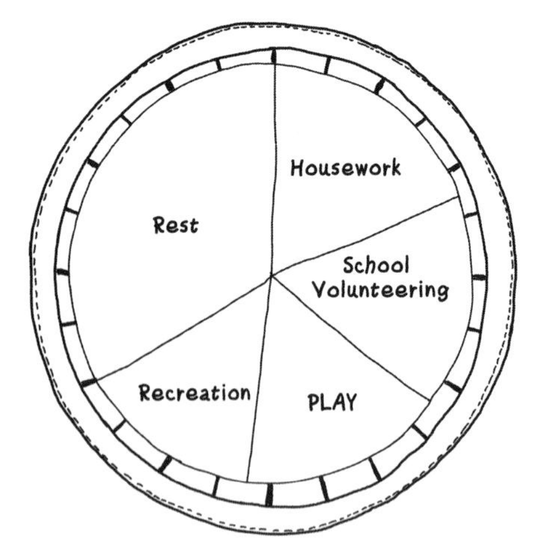

WELL-BEING SCORECARD

JOSEF'S WELL-BEING	1	2	3
Material		X	
Occupational			X
Social			X
Community			X
Physical			X

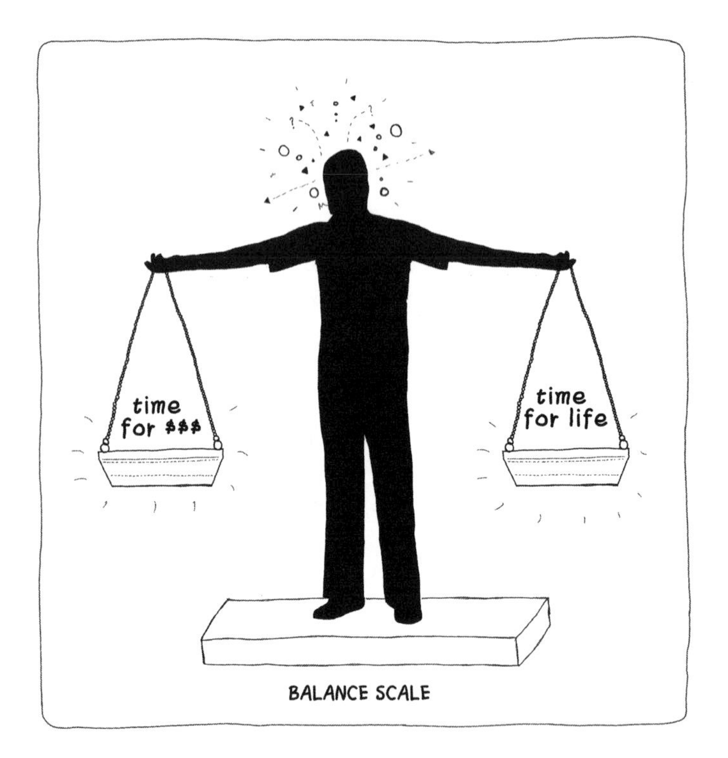

the way we work have reshaped working lives in both desired and unintended ways. Today gender equality and work–life balance seem to be at odds in an economy that privileges and prioritizes paid work.

How might we work to survive well in a community economy? What guiding principles might regulate our approach to work? Rather than answering these questions head on, we now turn to a consideration of the even bigger question of how we are balancing what we put our labors into and how the planet as a whole is surviving. Perhaps this perspective might help to clarify our ethical choices.

SURVIVING WELL COLLECTIVELY: ANOTHER KEY CONCERN FOR A COMMUNITY ECONOMY

What does it mean to survive well on this planet? Surely it must mean not destroying the very environment that sustains us with gifts of sunshine, air, water, soil, minerals, plants, and animals.

When we work harder and harder to consume more and more, we are doing just the opposite—destroying the possibility for all species, including humans, to survive well. But when we work hard to reduce our consumption of the earth's bounty, we contribute in small ways to redressing the imbalance that has arisen. This imbalance is not just between human consumption and planetary survival; it is also between the survival chances of different human communities.

One tool we can use to identify how our labor allocations contribute to collectively surviving well is by assessing the ecological footprint of our lifestyles. An *Ecological Footprint* is a measure of human demand on earth's biologically productive land and sea area. According to average consumption habits and the number of global hectares needed to support them, each country makes a different demand. In 2008, humanity's total ecological footprint was estimated at global hectares equal to 1.5 planet earths.[15] This means that we were using up the earth's life-giving resources faster than they could be regenerated. Of course, there is huge variation around this average for different nations, as shown in the table. Although it would take four planet earths to support global humanity if everyone were to adopt the consumption profile (as measured in terms of global hectares per capita) of the average North American, if we were to adopt that of a Cuban we would be living within our ecological means.

Just as there is marked variation around total humanity's ecological footprint, there is huge variation within each nation. Using any number of a range of calculators, we can estimate our individual or household ecological footprints. The outcome varies depending on how much labor we put into acquiring material possessions such as newer cars, bigger houses, and more international flights compared to how much we put into self-provisioning, collective transport, or green housing.

In Australia, for example, the average ecological footprint is 3.7, but when we calculate Josef's footprint we find that his pared-down lifestyle can be sustained with only 1.5 planets.[16] In a number of ways, Josef's working life is similar to that of Danilo, a poor tenant farmer and father of four in a village in one of the provinces of the Philippines, where the national average footprint is only 0.7 planets. Let's look at Danilo's workday to see how it is spent and then look at his Twenty-Four-Hour Clock and Well-being Scorecard.

In communities like Danilo's, families have found one way to increase their material well-being. Mothers and daughters are moving overseas to work as domestic servants, and they send a portion of what they earn back home to their families. But there is a tradeoff. In some families, social and even physical well-being has deteriorated as close familial relationships have been sacrificed in order to take up new employment opportunities.

The ecological footprint of Danilo's household would probably be lower than the national average for the Philippines, because he is in the poorest fraction of Filipino society. He has a high degree of local food security but very little purchasing power, unlike his fellow urban citizens, who rely heavily on imported food and are increasingly caught up in high-consumption lifestyles.

NATIONAL ECOLOGICAL FOOTPRINTS 2008

COUNTRY	PLANETS
USA	4.0
Australia	3.7
Canada	3.6
UK	2.6
Mexico	1.8
China	1.1
Cuba	1.0
Philippines	0.7
India	0.5
Timor Leste	0.3

Source: Global Footprint Network, "Ecological Footprint and Biocapacity in 2008," *National Footprint Accounts, 2011 edition*, http://www.footprintnetwork.org, accessed 31 May 2012; Global Footprint Network, *The National Footprint Accounts, 2011 Edition* (Oakland, Calif.: Global Footprint Network, 2012).

The amount of biologically productive land on the planet in 2008 was estimated at 12 billion global hectares (GHA). The figures above show the number of planets that would have been needed in 2008 if each of the world's 6.7 billion people used up the average per capita GHA needed to support the consumption habits of that country.

DANILO'S DAY

Danilo, a Filipino, wakes at the first sign of light. After a bowl of plain rice that his wife, Honorata, prepares for him, he starts work in the rice fields at 6:00 a.m. Depending on the season, he'll be planting, weeding, or harvesting the rice. He doesn't own the land; he works on someone else's land and receives an in-kind annual payment of 10 percent of the rice harvest. This provides the bulk of the family's food for the year.

He works for six hours and then stops at noon for lunch, usually a bowl of rice with a few green vegetables. After lunch and a short rest, he does unpaid work for four hours around his home garden, growing vegetables and fruit and raising pigs and chickens. Around 5:00 p.m. he goes down to the wharves, and if he's lucky he'll pick up some paid work helping to unload boats. Sometimes he works until 9:00 p.m., and then he and his fellow workers use their cash-in-hand payments to buy some noodles from a street vendor and have a few drinks and a few laughs together. He'll be home and in bed by midnight.

Not all the money Danilo earns will be spent after work, and he will use what's left to buy more permanent building materials for the family's house. When it comes time to do the work on the house, Danilo will draw on reciprocal labor arrangements, whereby neighbors and extended family members help him with building and maintenance and in return he'll help these people with their building projects. These self-help practices merge with social and community recreational activities as they are usually accompanied by communal meals, drinking, music, and dancing.

We can compare Danilo's ecological footprint with that of other people in different situations around the world. For example, let's just say that Danilo has an average footprint for the Philippines of 0.7, and let's compare this to the footprint of one of the Australian coal miners introduced earlier in the chapter. Let's assume that this coal miner has an average Australian footprint of 3.7 (though in all likelihood the coal miner will have an above-average ecological footprint). Danilo's footprint is five times smaller than that of the coal miner. By proportionally scaling their Twenty-Four-Hour Clocks so that Danilo's is five times smaller than the miner's, we can start to see the different planetary impacts of different ways of working. And by weighing their work–life balances against one another, we can see the effects on their lives.

When we put our differently sized Twenty-Four-Hour Clocks next

DANILO'S 24-HOUR CLOCK

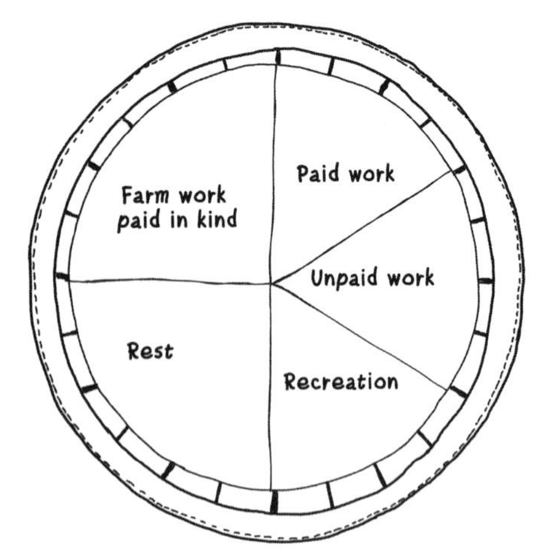

WELL-BEING SCORECARD

DANILO'S WELL-BEING	1	2	3
Material	X		
Occupational		X	
Social			X
Community			X
Physical		X	

AUSTRALIAN COAL MINER

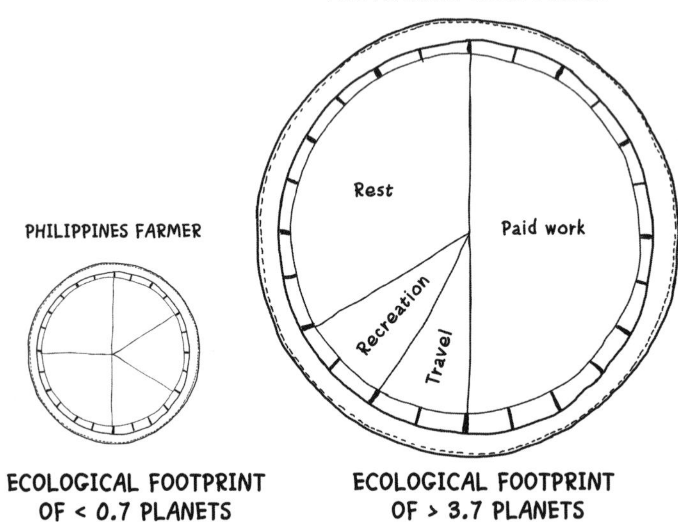

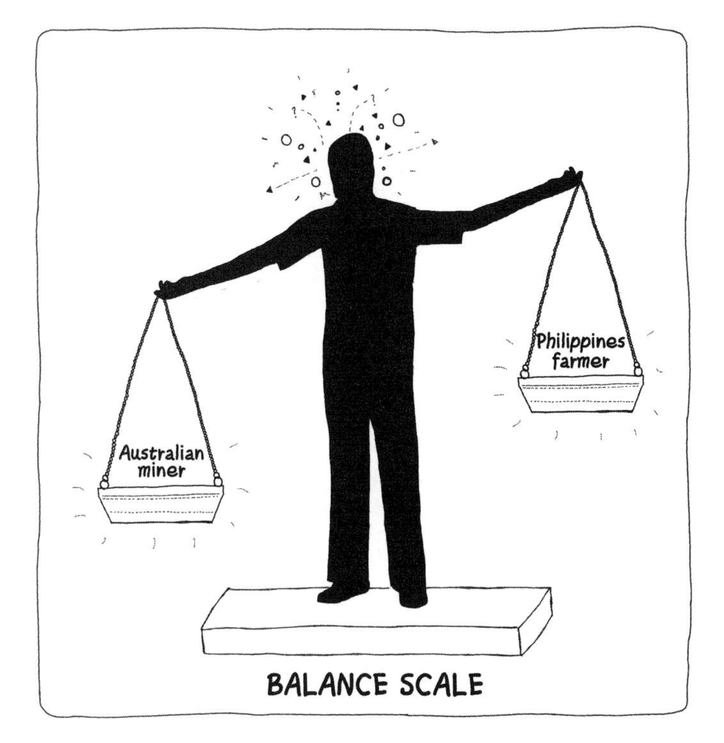

to each other, we can interrogate the similarities and differences and start to think about what it would take for us personally and collectively to reduce our ecological footprint. As part of a community economy, we can start to take responsibility for the impact of our methods of surviving well on the other human and nonhuman inhabitants of our planet.

TOOLS FOR SURVIVING WELL

Taking back work for people and the planet means looking at the mix of activities that people are engaging in to survive well. It means celebrating and supporting those forms of labor that are directly contributing to all aspects of individual and household well-being. There is a dominant conception that paid work is the best means of securing well-being because it provides an income for purchasing what we need. Certainly material well-being is critical, but that is not all there is. Overall well-being is achieved by the interactions among material, occupational, social, community, and physical well-being. Paid labor plays a role, but so do other forms of labor.

In this chapter we have touched on some of the diverse labor activities that people are participating in to secure their overall well-being—alternatively paid work such as reciprocal labor or work that is paid in kind, as well as unpaid labor such as housework, family care, neighborhood work, volunteering, and self-provisioning. The Diverse Labor Identifier can be used to distinguish these different kinds of work. The identifier also includes a wider range of labor than we have discussed, including indentured and slave labor and work for welfare. Not all of these work practices are desirable; indeed, we would want to see some stamped out because they do not help people to survive well at all (in the next section we look at some examples of organizations and campaigns that are taking action on these types of practices).

In a community economy we need to keep our eyes on the interdependencies between the different kinds of work we do. We need to be aware of how one kind of well-being interacts with other kinds and how the labor we are doing to survive well individually affects other people and the planet. We can do this with the help of a Twenty-Four-Hour Clock to look at all the activities we engage in. We can then assess how each contributes to our personal, household, and planetary well-being. Using the Well-being Scorecard, we can pinpoint the trade-offs we might be making between different kinds of well-being and reflect on whether these are contributing to a work–life balance that is healthy and sustainable. Then there's our ecological footprint to consider. By using

DIVERSE LABOR IDENTIFIER

PAID LABOR	ALTERNATIVE PAID LABOR	UNPAID LABOR
	Self-employed	Housework
	Cooperative	Family care
	Indentured	Neighborhood work
	Reciprocal labor	Volunteering
	In-kind	Self-provisioning
	Work for welfare	Slave labor

any of the readily available ecological footprint calculators that are available online we can assess the contribution our working life is making to the planet's well-being or destruction. Are we making a larger impact than our planet can bear? Are we making an impact that our planet can sustain? Or are we making a smaller impact, one that is well within our planet's ability to regenerate? Acting together, we can balance the scale, developing new habits of working differently to reduce our impact.

WELL-BEING SCORECARD

INDIVIDUAL	1 poor	2 sufficient	3 excellent
Material			
Occupational			
Social			
Community			
Physical			

PLANETARY	1 larger	2 same	3 smaller
Ecological Footprint			

COLLECTIVE ACTIONS FOR SURVIVING WELL

In a community economy we take ethical action by acknowledging how our survival is connected with that of others.

In this section we look at the actions by which people are taking back work so that it produces well-being for people and the planet.

Questions to consider as you read about these collective actions

- What aspects of material, occupational, social, community, and physical well-being are being addressed, and how are they being changed?
- What types of work are being combined to achieve the different types of well-being? What kind of work is increasing, and what kind is decreasing?
- Are trade-offs being made between the different types of well-being and different types of work? What are these trade-offs?
- What impact will these actions have on other people's well-being?
- What impact will these actions have on planetary well-being?

Fair Work and Wages

For too many people on this planet, work is precarious. It can be so poorly paid that even long hours or multiple jobs barely guarantee survival. Working conditions can be unsafe and abusive. In these circumstances, material well-being is difficult to achieve, let alone the other types of well-being. Building on the long history of workers' struggles, organizations across the globe are fighting for fair wages and working conditions.

ETHICAL ACTION: *Making sure people work in safety and have enough to meet their needs*

In the United States, the Universal Living Wage (ULW) campaign aims to reform national legislation so that payments for wage work are sufficient for people to meet their housing costs.[17] The campaign is driven by the fact that 42 percent of the nation's 3.5 million people that experience homelessness in the course of the year are working. The current federal minimum wage is $7.25 per hour; it does not match housing costs in most U.S. housing markets. Adopting the formula of the Department of Housing and Urban Development that no one should spend more than 30 percent of their income on housing, the ULW calculates the minimum wage required for a person working full time to be able to afford housing in different regions. If the minimum wage matched regional housing markets, the ongoing costs of homelessness to individuals and the nation would be minimized and workers could start to achieve material well-being.

In the United Kingdom, the Living Wage Campaign was launched by Citizens UK in 2001 to advocate for a minimum wage that allows workers to meet their costs of living and provide for their families. Over one hundred employers are now accredited as Living Wage Employers, including KPMG, Barclays, and the Olympic Delivery Authority. One of the most influential is the Greater London Authority (GLA). Each year the Living Wage Unit of GLA calculates how much the living wage should be. In 2011 a living wage for full-time work in London was £8.30 per hour; outside of London, it was £7.20 per hour. Like the Universal Living Wage campaign in the United States, the British Living Wage Campaign is trying to make sure that material well-being is achieved and that people do not need to work additional jobs or additional hours and thereby compromise other aspects of their well-being.

Antisweatshop campaigns address not just the wages that workers are paid but also the conditions in which people work. Established in 1989, the Clean Clothes Campaign (CCC) is an alliance of trade unions and nongovernment organizations (NGOs) from fifteen European countries.[18] CCC works with over two hundred unions and NGOs in the places where clothing is being produced in sweatshop conditions. When problems are identified, it lobbies the companies involved, works with the workers, and informs consumers. CCC has been successful in resolving 250 cases in which workers were being treated unfairly, and some companies have now adopted codes of conduct. Other organizations working on similar programs include the Fair Labor Association (U.S.), the No Sweat Campaign (U.K.), and Workers' Rights (Oxfam Australia). All are trying to make sure that workers' material and occupational well-being needs are met and that workers can start to achieve other aspects of well-being.

Government Inputs for Everyone's Survival

In many parts of the majority world, people like Danilo lead subsistence lives. They grow what they need and secure extra items through exchange relationships with their neighbors. There are often strong village-level supports that are embedded in rich social and community traditions. However, too often people in these circumstances have to pay for basic social services, particularly education, health care, and transportation. This puts pressure on families to find paid work, and this is partly why the mothers and the daughters of Danilo's neighbors are moving overseas as domestic workers.

Providing social services like education, health care, and transportation helps people to survive well. They can continue to lead low-impact subsistence lives, knowing that health care is available when they need it, that their children will have educational opportunities, and that transportation is available to help them get around.

These types of basic services are also critical in the minority world. When governments provide these services, people do not need to overwork to achieve material well-being; they are freed up to address all aspects of their well-being. The costs of providing these basic services are more than offset by not having to cover the costs of the mental and physical health effects of overwork, too much stress, and low levels of social and community well-being.

ETHICAL ACTION: *Making sure governments provide the basic supports that everyone benefits from*

Health is a key concern for many people across the globe. According to the World Health Organization, in most countries people rate health as "one of their highest priorities . . . behind only economic concerns, such as unemployment, low wages and a high cost of living."[19] Governments can help address this concern by providing universal health care—in other words, free (or almost free) health care for all their citizens. Although many minority-world countries like Germany and the United Kingdom have long-standing public health systems, countries in the majority world have only relatively recently developed universal health-care systems. In Venezuela, in 2003 the Misión Barrio Adentro (or Inside the Neighborhood program) was initiated to focus on the health of people living in the barrios (or slums). In the first year of the program there were over nine million patient visits.[20] The program was so successful that it was quickly extended to cover the entire country, and by 2006 some 73 percent of the population was covered with medical care and 71 percent with dental care. As a result, there has been a decline in infant mortality and childhood diseases such as meningitis and malnutrition, and in adults there has been improved diagnoses and follow-up treatments for illnesses such as diabetes and cardiovascular disease. Along with these types of outcomes, universal health care takes the pressure off families to have to work for cash to pay for health care (or to make the decision to go without health care and suffer through pain and illness).

Transport can be another key concern of households. The city of Curitiba in Southern Brazil has a celebrated example of mass transit: Bus Rapid Transit. Like many Brazilian cities, Curitiba saw explosive urban growth in the latter half of the twentieth century, particularly with the formation of favelas (or shantytowns) in outlying areas. Curitiba redesigned the existing road system to make room for dedicated bus lanes.[21] It reformed the zoning laws so that new enterprises and housing, offices and housing complexes must be built along the bus routes. In 2010 the fare was the U.S. equivalent of $1.10, $0.50 on Sundays. Some groups can travel for free, including people over age sixty-five and children under age five. Bus Rapid Transit is so popular that it does not have to be subsidized. The bus companies are paid by the government for every kilometer driven—which gives them an incentive to expand their services. The cheap fares and expansion of the bus system make public transport accessible to everyone—including the poor in outlying areas. Most citizens in Curitiba spend less than 10 percent of their income on transit, reducing what is required to survive well. The system has also reduced pollution from private motor vehicles, addressing not just planetary heath but the health effects of air pollution. An estimated one hundred similar bus ways have been completed in other countries, and another hundred are in various stages of completion. Importantly, the model has been taken up not just in the minority world but in rapidly urbanizing African countries like Nigeria and South Africa, as well as in India and China.

In the minority world, governments have developed a range of programs to help their citizens balance paid work with other working responsibilities. When it comes to caring for the newborn, countries in the Organisation for Economic Co-operation and Development provide paid parental leave for one parent for an average of around twenty weeks after the birth of a child.[22] In some countries, there is a carer's allowance for people who look after an adult with long-term care needs or a child with a severe disability.[23] In the United Kingdom, caregivers receive a direct payment to help them maintain their own physical, social, and community well-being. Carers are even encouraged to do things like take a holiday!

With just 24 hours in the day, caring time can simply crowd out paid employment. The emotional stress of caring work can make it difficult for carers to effectively hold down a paid job.

Andrew Leigh, *Informal Care and Labor Market Participation*

Redefining Work

In this chapter we have talked about downshifters who are cutting back on paid work in order to make time for more things in life. One of the things that downshifters often make time for is securing what they need without having to buy it. They might produce it themselves or acquire it by working with others. Efforts like this help to reduce the planetary impact of consumption.

ETHICAL ACTION: *Minimizing our use of resources and directly providing for ourselves and others*

To help people downshift and prioritize a different pace of life, there are Web sites such as A Homemade Life and Stepping Off. Many people downshift out of choice, but for some it is a matter of necessity. Cath Armstrong, the founder of Cheapskate, was in the middle of home renovations when she was laid off, her husband was laid off, and she discovered that she was pregnant with their third child.[24] She began by stretching her family's food budget as far as it could go and then discovered she had a real talent for self-provisioning—from home baking and preserving to home gardening and sewing. She even came up with ways to make her own washing powder (for a fifth of the price of ready-made products from the supermarket). Cath has now turned her passion for being a cheapskate into a Web site and a commercial newsletter that gathers and shares tips on how to live with less.

I don't believe that being frugal means that you have to be miserable. Being frugal is not spending my hard-earned money on the stuff that's not important.

Cath Armstrong, Cheapskate

Dawn, founder of the blog Frugal for Life, was living to excess. Her overspending and overconsuming had brought her to the point at which she filed for bankruptcy. As she cut back, something happened. Dawn took more and more pleasure in things; she discovered that her self-worth wasn't based on the things she had around her. So Dawn has committed herself to a lifelong project of living frugally—of finding ways to consume less while taking pleasure in doing more for herself. Through her blog Dawn shares her experiences with others.

Less is more in my world: less to worry about, less to find space for, less to keep up.

Dawn, Frugal for Life

Like other downshifters and frugalists, Dawn and Cath have reevaluated what is necessary to survive well. They have made the transition from being spenders to being savers, and they have done this by consuming less and self-provisioning more. They now deliberate on what really matters and what really contributes to their happiness and to surviving well.

Some workplaces are finding ways to impose a kind of downshifting on their employees—without hitting their employees' back pockets. In the United States, a few companies have introduced the 30/40 workweek—employees work for thirty hours but are paid for forty hours. The founder of the 30/40 workweek, Ron Healey, argues that the productivity of these workers increases because they are more focused and energized when on the job—and happier all around.[25]

The New Economics Foundation in Britain argues for a twenty-one-hour workweek in order to help address the work–life and the work–planetary survival imbalance (as well as other problems such as the growing divides between the rich and the poor and between the overworked and the underworked).[26]

This type of cutback has been tried before. In the 1930s (during the Great Depression), the Kellogg's factory in Battle Creek, Michigan, introduced a six-hour workday as a way to employ three hundred more workers (who shared the available work).[27] The hourly rate was increased slightly so that workers were only minimally affected. Productivity increased, and within five years workers were being paid for a six-hour day what they would have been paid for an eight-hour day. After the Second World War and as consumerist values spread, workers began to prioritize higher wages over shorter workdays. However, the six-hour day was popular with many women workers, who continued to work shorter hours until 1985, when the practice was finally discontinued.

Sharing What We Need to Survive Well

Another approach is to try to minimize what we need materially by sharing with other people. This can range from informal arrangements—say, one in which a group of neighbors share garden tools—to the development of whole communities to share just about everything, including their income.

ETHICAL ACTION: *Minimizing our use of resources by sharing with others*

Cohousing is an arrangement in which people have their own private residences but share some living areas—say, kitchens, laundries, workshops, and outdoor areas.[28] Cohousing is a means of reducing what people need materially. Instead of having a washing machine in everyone's house, there might be one or two washing machines that everyone shares. The shared spaces also mean that there is a strong social connection between neighbors—cohousers have to develop ways of living alongside their fellow cohousers. Cohousing is of particular interest to some groups. For people with young children, shared outdoor spaces can be designed so children can play safely together. For older people, there's the benefit of having both the privacy of their own homes and close connections with their neighbors. For low-income groups, cohousing can be a means of reducing not just the cost of housing but the cost of fitting out homes.

Living together on one's own.

National Association of Housing Communities for Elderly People in the Netherlands

Directly Contributing to the Well-being of Others

Governments can provide basic services that can help to improve people's well-being by reducing the costs associated with things like health care and transportation. Likewise, community organizations can also use existing resources, including labor, in order to increase people's well-being directly or reduce the cash they need to secure services such as education or goods such as housing.

ETHICAL ACTION: *Volunteering to help meet the needs of others*

In the previous chapter we introduced Akanksha, an educational organization that provides high-quality educational services to young people in the slums of Mumbai and Pune, India. It was started in 1990 by eighteen-year-old Shaheen Mistri and by 2011 was working with four thousand children through forty-seven after-school centers and nine schools.[29] Akanksha uses donations from individuals and corporations to run its educational services. It also relies on volunteer labor, and more than one thousand people have volunteered. This direct contribution of labor does not just help Akanksha to provide the educational services that help young people born into poverty to "break the cycle"; it also provides an opportunity for those who give their time to enrich their own social, community, and even occupational well-being.

Akanksha has been a turning point in my life. While I am trying to make a difference in children's lives, the children and the experience are making a difference in my life.

Poorvi Didi, volunteer, Akanksha Foundation

Millard Fuller, a self-made U.S. millionaire, wanted something more from his life. In 1965 he joined Koinonia Farm, an interracial Christian community in the American Deep South. Inspired by this group, he founded Habitat for Humanity.[30] Initially he provided housing materials at cost to low-income residents who could afford to pay for materials but were not in a position to get a loan from a bank to build a house. Since then, Habitat has evolved to use volunteer labor to help reduce the cost of building homes for people who need them—allowing poor residents to survive well by securing shelter for themselves with the help of others. Habitat has spread to ninety different countries, has built or repaired more than 500,000 houses, and has provided shelter for more than two million people worldwide.

WHERE TO FROM HERE?

In this chapter we have seen examples of the different types of actions that are being taken to help people survive well. There are efforts to improve people's material well-being when material survival is difficult to achieve. There are also efforts to cut back on material well-being, especially when overwork is undermining other aspects of well-being and overconsumption is undermining the planet's ability to survive. We have also seen how volunteering can directly benefit the recipient's material well-being while also benefiting that of the volunteer.

What would it take for you to survive well or to contribute to other people's or the planet's ability to survive well? To get started toward this goal, you might consider the following:

1. Are your wages fair and your working conditions safe? If not, are there groups or networks, such as the Clean Clothes

Campaign or the Universal Living Wage campaign, that you could connect with? Are you concerned about people whose wages are unfair and their working conditions unsafe? What could you do to improve their material and occupational well-being and help them survive well?

2. Do you have all the basic inputs and supports you need for your survival? Are there campaigns and initiatives you could contribute to that would help encourage governments to provide these services for their citizens?

3. Are there things you could do to directly help people with these types of services? Could you volunteer your labor to initiatives such as Akanksha or Habitat for Humanity? What effect might that have on your well-being?

4. What about the other aspects of your well-being? Do you work in such a way that you are compromising your social, community, and physical well-being for material well-being? Could you cut back on labor for money and secure what you need by using your labor in a different way? Could you get your employer to consider other patterns of work? What impact might that have on you, others around you, and the planet? What could you share with neighbours or friends and family in order to cut back on what you need materially?

In this chapter we have focused on the type of work we do and how this work contributes to our own ability, and that of other people and the planet, to survive well. We've argued that in order to build community economies we need to consider the mix of paid work, alternatively paid work, and unpaid work that can help us all to attain balanced well-being. In the next chapter we turn to the places where paid work is undertaken and ask how businesses might be reshaped in community economies in order to take account of the interdependencies between people and between people and the environment.

3.

Take Back Business

Distributing Surplus

WHAT *IS* BUSINESS?

Businesses are organizations in which goods and services are produced and exchanged. They are where entrepreneurs and workers transform resources, technology, and labor into something new. The mainstream message is that business is the font of economic growth from which wealth and well-being flow.

Despite this rhetoric, most business is not primarily organized around producing for the greater good. To use a familiar phrase, "Business is about problem-solving at a profit." It is the desire for profits that fuels dedication—even obsession—especially on the part of business owners.

Although for some, business is a source of great individual reward, for others it is a site of hardship and oppression—a place where exploitation is rife. For yet others, business is just a place to work and earn a living, an environment that claims the best hours of their waking day.

The social responsibility of business is to increase profits.

Milton Friedman, *New York Times*

So what actually goes on in a business enterprise? One way to look at it is to follow the process whereby old wealth is transformed into new. For the moment, let's focus on firms where something—a good or a service—is produced and then sold rather than ones that buy and sell already existing commodities.

Businesses use stored-up wealth, usually referred to as finance, to purchase material inputs such as raw materials, land, buildings and machinery, and labor inputs. During the production process labor adds to the existing wealth of inputs to produce something whose expanded value is reflected in its sale price. Depending on the ownership and governance structure of a firm, this new wealth is shared with producers and nonproducers both within the enterprise and beyond.

Over the last two hundred years, one form of business enterprise, the capitalist firm, has been lauded as the best way of organizing wealth transformation and achieving the most efficient production. The plant and equipment in a capitalist business are privately owned, employees are paid wages to work for set periods, commodities are produced and sold in markets, and profits are privately accumulated by the business owner or shareholders. The argument goes that private profits provide the appropriate incentive for entrepreneurs to take risks, compete with others, and put in the effort to achieve better outcomes. And private reward has flow-on benefits for many in the form of cheaper goods.

A major flaw in this argument is that by problem-solving at a profit we have overstepped a sustainable level of resource use. The depletion of our environment has exponentially risen. The new wealth produced by capitalist business has gobbled up minerals, nonrenewable energy, soil fertility, and plant and animal species at a voracious rate. These uncosted "gifts" of nature have been transformed into private profits while ecologies and atmospheres have been degraded to such an extent that livelihoods are threatened. Only now are we realizing just how heavily two hundred years of industrialization has affected planetary health.

On top of this fundamental problem, the new wealth created by capitalist business has not raised living standards equitably across the board. It's true that in some places individual and societal consumption levels have risen quickly and many people are now leading lives that were unimaginable even a generation or two ago. But both within and between countries, the distribution of new wealth has produced greater inequalities than ever before. In 2000, 1 percent of world's population owned 40 percent of global wealth and 10 percent of the population owned 85 percent of the wealth, while 50 percent of the world's population owned barely 1 percent.[1] It is this type of inequity that has propelled Occupy Wall Street movements in cities across the globe and given rise to the rallying cry "We are the 99 percent" (as opposed to the 1 percent of top income earners with whom wealth is concentrated).

It seems that business is a major contributor to the problems we and our planet face. But can it also be a critical vehicle for change? Could business direct new wealth toward planetary well-being?

In many enterprises (though ones not often recognized as "business," such as households, farms, cooperatives, and community and state organizations), new goods and services are produced and allocated and wealth is held or shared in different ways. Ethical concerns about claims on wealth and the distribution of benefits are identified and debated. There is nothing to stop mainstream business from becoming an innovative site of negotiation between producers and nonproducers about the production and distribution of new wealth.

What goes on in business is of major importance to how we live our daily lives and inhabit our planet. To take business back so that it contributes to the well-being of people and the planet, we need to look more closely at who makes decisions about producing and distributing new wealth. In some businesses in Argentina, decision-making power has shifted with dramatic outcomes.

TAKING BACK ABANDONED FACTORIES IN ARGENTINA

In October 2001, workers at Latin America's largest ceramic tile manufacturer, Zanón, closed the factory's gates, locking themselves in and the bosses out.[2] After months without pay, the workers had taken matters into their own hands and taken over the factory. Five months later, in March 2002, the furnaces were relit, the machines restarted, and tiles once again rolled off the production line. The worker takeover was vindicated when, seven years later, in August 2009, the legislature of the Patagonian province of Neuquén voted to expropriate the factory from its private owners and hand it over to the workers. FaSinPat (from Fábrica Sin Patrón or Factory without a Boss) had legally come of age.

Zanón's story is not unique. Throughout the 2000s, workers across Argentina were prompted by extraordinary circumstances to occupy and take back almost two hundred capitalist businesses. At Zanón, workers could not understand why, despite profits of around $50 million each year, production was being wound down, workers were being laid off, and wages were unpaid even though Zanón had been loaned money from the provincial government for wage payments. In scenes that have been replayed in businesses across Argentina, workers hypothesized that the profits had been sent overseas or lost in financial market speculation. Owners and managers could not be trusted with workers' jobs and livelihoods.

In the period since the workers took control of the ceramics factory, FaSinPat has gone from strength to strength. The workforce has almost doubled, to 470 workers, and output has increased from 5,000 square meters of tiles a month to 400,000. This has been achieved through a cooperative and democratic business model. Decisions are discussed at weekly assemblies, and once a month work ceases for eight hours for longer discussions and decision making on matters such as what to do with profits and whether to hire new workers. All workers receive the same salary (except for those in key areas such as machinery maintenance, who receive an extra 10 percent). Positions of responsibility are rotated. There is no extra pay attached to these positions, so, as one worker comments, "Workers who take on job responsibility choose to do so to learn something new."[3]

We bring the schoolchildren to visit to find out for themselves what a factory in production looks like and so they know they can build another kind of society. The first question they ask is, "Why isn't there a boss?"

Omar VillaBlanca, FaSinPat worker

Many of the workers at FaSinPat have little or no formal education. The assembly has therefore voted to devote some of their cooperative surplus to starting a primary school and a high school for workers. An engineer at the factory, Jorge Bermudez, explains that for him "the most exciting thing would be for all the compañeros to have the opportunity to rotate in all of the job posts in the factory, get an education, and train themselves in a technical profession."[4]

Perhaps most remarkable is FaSinPat's attitude toward the people of Neuquén, an attitude captured in the words of Reinaldo Giménez, one of the young workers: "We always said the factory isn't ours. We are using it, but it belongs to the community." This commitment is echoed in the words of another worker, Carlos Acuña: "The profits shouldn't go to us . . . but to the community."[5] FaSinPat has followed through on this attitude. For example, for twenty years the poor neighborhood adjacent to the factory had been asking the provincial government for a health clinic. At a FaSinPat assembly plant, the workers voted to use some of their new wealth, their cooperative's surplus, to build a community health center in the neighborhood—and it was completed in three months.

FaSinPat has donated ceramics to hundreds of community centers, libraries, schools, and hospitals. It has built homes for working families, and it hosts cultural, educational, and recreational programs, many for children in the city of Neuquén. One standout event was in September 2006, when FaSinPat hosted a rock concert that featured the legendary Argentinean heavy metal band Rata Blanca. Over fifteen thousand people gathered in the grounds of the factory to attend the concert. The workers organized the event and were able to keep ticket prices low by doing all the work, including building the massive stage.

The struggle has been long and hard for FaSinPat. Workers and their families were physically attacked and, in scenes reminiscent of Argentina's military dictatorship, even abducted and tortured. But along the way, the workers have demonstrated just what can be achieved in a factory without a boss. They have taken charge of the new wealth (the surplus) they collectively produce and have negotiated more dignified standards of survival not only for their own families but for the wider community. FaSinPat has become a symbol for workers in other Argentinean factories and internationally.

Zanón is not an isolated experience or crazy idea; it is a concrete experience that a group of workers have put into action.

Alejandro Quiroga, FaSinPat worker

THE SURVIVAL–SURPLUS NEXUS: A KEY CONCERN FOR A COMMUNITY ECONOMY

What is surplus? And how does it relate to survival? Surplus is something extra, left over, or not immediately needed. It is something that can be creatively shared or selfishly seized. There are many different ways of thinking about surplus, each with important implications for action and world shaping.

In a community garden, as discussed in the Introduction, surplus takes the form of more vegetables than the gardeners and their households can eat. In the worker-owned cooperative FaSinPat, surplus is that portion of new wealth (or newly produced value) that is left over after the workers' wages and creditors have been paid.

As we can see from these two examples, economic surplus cannot be identified outside of a relationship with nonsurplus—what is necessary for survival. How the boundaries of the surplus–survival nexus are drawn is vitally important. Whose survival sets the line over which something can be seen as "extra" or surplus? And who decides what happens to that extra bit? In a community economy we're interested in how surplus is produced, who owns it, who decides how it can be used, and how it can be deployed to produce well-being for people and the planet.

If we zoom out for a moment and view our planet home from outer space, it is obvious that the only real surplus to planetary survival is the excess of sunlight that bathes our firmament, bringing gifts of life and photosynthesis. On spaceship earth the distinction between surplus and necessity is purely an accounting frame that carves up a finite whole.[6] Nevertheless, down on the ground, how we think about the surplus–survival nexus has significant implications for what kind of world we inhabit.

In a capitalist business, matters of surplus and survival are well hidden. Production is organized, workers are paid, profits are made (or not), and this is the end of the story, or so the economists tell us. Yet capitalist industrialization has generated historically unprecedented volumes of new wealth, much of which has not been distributed toward widespread social or environmental well-being but has been privately appropriated and accumulated.

From a community economy perspective, this new wealth is composed of two main forms of surplus, one produced by human labor, the other "given"—or, more accurately, stolen—from the earth's reserves. To each form of surplus is attached a community whose survival needs are variously met or ignored. In the case of surplus produced by labor, it is workers, their families, and wider communities whose survival needs are implicated. In the case of surplus generated from the exploitation of the earth's gifts, it is the complex web of planetary beings whose survival needs are affected.

In a community economy we need an accounting system that helps us keep our eye on survival–surplus relations. We can explore this relationship with the aid of

1. *a People's Account and*
2. *Decision Flashpoints.*

For guidance we turn to one accounting frame that has inspired movements to take back surplus labor (known as surplus value) from capitalist owners and redirect it toward the survival needs of working people.[7] Let's begin by doing a People's Account of a highly profitable (fictitious but realistic) capitalist enterprise.

Bayswater Basketry was started in the 1970s by Jerry, who was working out of his parents' garage weaving handmade baskets and wicker furniture. Within a couple of years, Jerry had moved into a small factory to keep up with the stream of orders from local retailers. Jerry's big break came when he decided to move into a much larger factory at the scenic entrance to a popular bayside tourist town. There was room for a retail area and a café and restaurant for hungry travelers. The business took off and became one of the biggest in the area, as well as a popular tourist destination. Soon Jerry's distinctive baskets and furniture had an international market.

Bayswater Basketry now has a workforce of two hundred, and Jerry is recognized as a good employer. Even though he pays his staff a relatively low wage, he provides good benefits (including health insurance, lunches from the café, on-site child care and a gym, and a friendly, even egalitarian, work atmosphere). Jerry's business is also extremely profitable, and he has donated millions of dollars to local sporting groups and charities. In the region, Jerry is highly respected and held up as an innovative entrepreneur working for both his own and his community's benefit.

Let's look at how Jerry's business works using a simple bar graph to help us visualize our People's Account. The gross revenue (or takings) of Bayswater Baskets is around $100 million each year. From this revenue Jerry pays out $60 million annually to cover

- production inputs (e.g., basket- and furniture-making supplies, depreciation of machinery and equipment),

- the cost of running the factory (e.g., power and water),
- transportation costs (e.g., packaging and shipping), and
- material inputs and costs of running the retail outlet, café, and restaurant.

This leaves $40 million annually, which, according to some accounts, is the new value that Jerry *and his workers* have added through the production process to the $60 million of inputs.

<table>
<tr><th colspan="10">A PEOPLE'S ACCOUNT OF BAYSWATER BASKETRY</th></tr>
<tr><td colspan="10">Total revenue (in millions of dollars)</td></tr>
<tr><td>10</td><td>20</td><td>30</td><td>40</td><td>50</td><td>60</td><td>70</td><td>80</td><td>90</td><td>100</td></tr>
<tr><td colspan="6">Nonlabor production inputs
$60 million</td><td colspan="4">Value added by Jerry and the workers' labor
$40 million</td></tr>
</table>

Workers at Bayswater Basketry receive an annual average wage of $20,000, and, when benefits are added in, the average total compensation is more like $25,000. So Jerry's bill for total wages (including benefits) comes to about $5 million each year. This $5 million amounts to the survival payment Jerry's workforce receives—enough remuneration to pay for the goods and services that ensure they turn up every day for their shift. In our People's Account this must be extracted from the $40 million of "value added" because it represents the cost of the labor input.

Once this amount is extracted from the $40 million, there is a remaining $35 million. This is the new wealth produced—what we designate as surplus value.

While the surplus value, or new wealth, that arises from production can be used for transformative ends, there are many claims on it that potentially reduce its power. Surplus value is by no means what we commonly understand as profit.

There are additional business payments that Jerry is obliged to make if he wants his business to survive. These he must make from

<table>
<tr><th colspan="10">A PEOPLE'S ACCOUNT OF BAYSWATER BASKETRY</th></tr>
<tr><td colspan="10">Total revenue (in millions of dollars)</td></tr>
<tr><td>10</td><td>20</td><td>30</td><td>40</td><td>50</td><td>60</td><td>70</td><td>80</td><td>90</td><td>100</td></tr>
<tr><td colspan="6">Nonlabor production inputs
$60 million</td><td>Labor
$5
million</td><td colspan="3">Surplus value
$35 million</td></tr>
</table>

distributions of surplus value. Some of these he rails against and tries to minimize, such as local, state, and federal taxes. Others he willingly purchases as a risk-averse individual, such as insurance, accounting, and advertising services.

There are also retained earnings to be put aside for investment in future expansion or to weather an economic downturn. Depending on how expansionist or lucky Jerry feels in any one year, the amount that he sets aside as retained earnings varies.

All together, this long list of business payments amounts to $15 million—a lot of bites out of Jerry's pie. But it turns out that there's always something left over. In fact, there's $20 million of new wealth each year for Jerry. Not bad for a boy who started out in his parents' garage.

<table>
<tr><th colspan="10">A PEOPLE'S ACCOUNT OF BAYSWATER BASKETRY</th></tr>
<tr><td colspan="10">Total revenue (in millions of dollars)</td></tr>
<tr><td>10</td><td>20</td><td>30</td><td>40</td><td>50</td><td>60</td><td>70</td><td>80</td><td>90</td><td>100</td></tr>
<tr><td colspan="6" rowspan="2">Nonlabor production inputs
$60 million</td><td rowspan="2">Labor
$5
million</td><td colspan="3">Surplus</td></tr>
<tr><td>Business
payments
$15
million</td><td colspan="2">Jerry's new
wealth
$20 million</td></tr>
</table>

The large amounts of earnings that flow to business owners like Jerry are usually justified as a reward for entrepreneurial accomplishments and the business risks that owners take. But how just is it that an owner receives $20 million each year while each worker is paid 1,000 times less ($20,000 per year without benefits)?

How has Jerry's success been created? Why does the bulk of the new wealth created flow into Jerry's pocket? Is it a just return on Jerry's entrepreneurial skill? Or is something else going on? Could this something else be important in taking back the economy for planetary and social health?

Let's unpack the mystery of Jerry's success by looking at the annual $40 million of "value added" through the lens of what happens in an average workday of eight hours. The total workforce's annual wage bill of $5 million represents 12.5 percent or one-eighth of the $40 million of value added in production. This means that the workers are making the value of what they are paid as a wage (their survival payment) in just one hour of their eight-hour workday.

A PEOPLE'S ACCOUNT OF BAYSWATER BASKETRY

Hours of the workday							
1	2	3	4	5	6	7	8
Survival payment	Surplus value						

In the remaining seven hours the workers produce value that amounts to seven times what they earn. The workers are paid enough to keep them going, but they have no claim on the rest of the new wealth that they helped to produce. In the same way, the natural environment has no claim on the new wealth—even though Jerry uses its resources in his production process. These resources include the various ecosystems that support the willows, sweetgrasses, and bulrushes that are woven into different types of baskets, as well as the habitats that are lost when mountaintops are removed to extract the coal that produces the power that Bayswater Basketry consumes.

Jerry owns the new wealth or surplus value by virtue of being a private business owner. And it is this new wealth fund that he, alone, has the power to distribute. Sure, government taxes, insurance companies, accounting and advertising firms, and the long-term survival needs of his business place certain demands on this surplus. But the rest is Jerry's for him to do with what he will. As we see below, Jerry has lots of ideas about how to enjoy his new wealth.

<table>
<tr><th colspan="8">A PEOPLE'S ACCOUNT OF BAYSWATER BASKETRY</th></tr>
<tr><td colspan="8">Decision flashpoints</td></tr>
<tr><td colspan="8">Hours of the workday</td></tr>
<tr><td>1</td><td>2</td><td>3</td><td>4</td><td>5</td><td>6</td><td>7</td><td>8</td></tr>
<tr><td>Survival payment</td><td colspan="7">Surplus value</td></tr>
<tr><td rowspan="2">In one hour, workers produce products equal to their wage

Wages are used for:
• food
• housing
• medical care
• schooling
• clothing
• savings</td><td colspan="7">The rest of the workday the workers produce surplus for Jerry</td></tr>
<tr><td colspan="3">Jerry's business payments

In three hours, workers produce products equal to the value of
• taxes
• interest
• rent
• insurance
• accounting
• advertising
• retained earnings</td><td colspan="4">Jerry's private wealth

The last four hours of the workday belong to Jerry alone. He spends this surplus on things such as
• a new house with a swimming pool and tennis court
• guest accommodations incorporating a movie theater for entertainment
• maintaining his luxury ocean-going cruiser and jet skis
• skiing holidays in Europe
• private school fees for his children
• investment in stocks and shares to increase his wealth
• donations to local sporting groups and charities</td></tr>
</table>

Bayswater Basketry is a capitalist enterprise—Jerry owns the business, and he owns the surplus value that "his" workers produce. At each of the "decision flashpoints" shown in the figure, it is Jerry who decides what happens—where the surplus–survival distinction is drawn and how to distribute his surplus. It is he who determines what is an adequate survival payment for his workforce and whether to spend money on more advertising for the business or on some consumption item for his own comfort.

The promise of personal gain is an intoxicating incentive that motivates even the smallest operator. Many would-be Jerrys are working hard as self-employed sole proprietors, hoping to make it big. In sole proprietorships, business owners are workers, financiers, managers, janitors, and marketers all in one. Owners must work incredibly long hours, often for little monetary reward above and beyond a survival payment. Holidays are rare and luxuries forgone. The challenge of self-reliance, the freedom of independence from a boss, and the potential for making it rich are rewards enough to keep going. For our fictitious Jerry, this potential was realized. But in reality 50 percent of new firms (the bulk of which are small businesses) fail in their first five years.[8] For many entrepreneurs the work–life imbalance becomes intolerable and the surplus side of the survival–surplus nexus remains a mirage.

Workers in Argentina took over the Zanón factory in 2001 because of what they saw as the owner's mismanagement of their survival payments and the surplus they had produced. Employees were not being paid, and the factory was being neglected. Even basic first aid equipment was not being maintained, a situation that was brought to a head in 2000 when a twenty-year-old worker died from a respiratory-related heart attack and his coworkers found that the oxygen tanks in the factory were empty—and useless.

After the takeover, FaSinPat workers prioritized paying themselves a minimum living wage. They agreed to share the same wage with the exception of those in key areas such as machinery maintenance, who were granted an extra 10 percent. This decision was not based on seniority or level of education but on how essential the work was to the day-to-day manufacturing operation. The workers also agreed to put on hold any pay raises.

In many business takeovers in Argentina in the 2000s, worker cooperatives initially decided to reduce their survival payment—their wage—in order to pay off old debts that the previous owners had accumulated. Some even went for weeks working without pay. They took this drastic action as a temporary measure in order to generate enough surplus to reinvest and get the businesses back on their feet and thereby ensure their own job stability. As we show in the People's Account of FaSinPat, as worker-owners it was *their* decision to negotiate the survival–surplus nexus, and, when their businesses were back in the black, it was *their* decision to raise their wages and distribute the surplus widely in the community. Ethical commitments to each other and to their families, their communities, and the future informed their decisions.

Now that we've increased production, improving quality and production output will become easier. Part of the profits are being put toward creating new jobs, improv[ing] machinery, and [buying] replacements for the machines. The other part of the profits generated is being put toward society.

Francisco Murillo, FaSinPat worker

The People's Account is a tool that highlights the survival–surplus nexus and the distribution of surplus within a business and beyond. It helps us to identify important Decision Flashpoints around new wealth creation and who is making these crucial decisions. Many of these flashpoints are the focus of considerable conflict, especially in capitalist enterprises where the drive to increase private wealth can override the dignified survival needs of workers, communities, and living ecosystems.

Since the development of capitalist enterprises in the eighteenth century, there has been continued struggle between business owners and workers around the survival–surplus nexus. Workers have organized into unions to push wages up to meet their own and their families' survival costs, and the owners of capitalist enterprises have used all sorts of means to drive down survival payments to workers so as to increase the amount of surplus value that they can appropriate. One classic strategy has been to resist wage increases, another to break up unions by force or by capital flight.

Although governments all over the world have increasingly regulated workplaces and working conditions, the geography of regulation

<table>
<tr><th colspan="8">A PEOPLE'S ACCOUNT OF FASINPAT</th></tr>
<tr><td colspan="8">Decision flashpoints</td></tr>
<tr><td colspan="8">Hours of the workday</td></tr>
<tr><td>1</td><td>2</td><td>3</td><td>4</td><td>5</td><td>6</td><td>7</td><td>8</td></tr>
<tr><td colspan="4">Cooperators' survival payment</td><td colspan="4">Cooperators' surplus</td></tr>
<tr><td colspan="4">Cooperators decide on survival payments (their wage), including
• 10% loading for essential workers
• initial wage freeze
• wage increases as factory becomes viable

Wages are used for
• food
• housing
• medical care
• schooling
• clothing
• savings</td><td colspan="3">Business payments

In two to three hours, cooperators produce products equal to the value of
• taxes
• interest
• rent
• insurance
• accounting
• advertising

Cooperators decide to increase retained earnings to finance factory upgrade and retooling.

Cooperators decide to expand production and take in new worker-owners.</td><td>Collective wealth

Cooperators decide how to distribute their collective wealth in
• scholarships for their children's education
• community health clinic
• cultural events</td></tr>
</table>

remains uneven. Some capitalist businesses have responded to workers' demands for higher wages by moving to areas of cheaper wages and unregulated working hours. Since the 1970s, business migration has increasingly been to low-wage countries around the globe, not just low-wage regions within a country. Take, for example, the real-world case of Pacific Brands, a well-known capitalist clothing manufacturer in Australia. The board of directors recently decided to relocate several manufacturing facilities to China, shedding nearly two thousand Australian jobs in the process.[9]

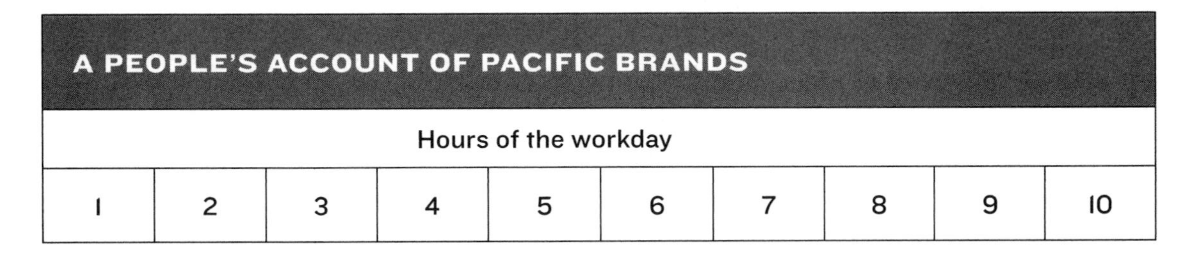

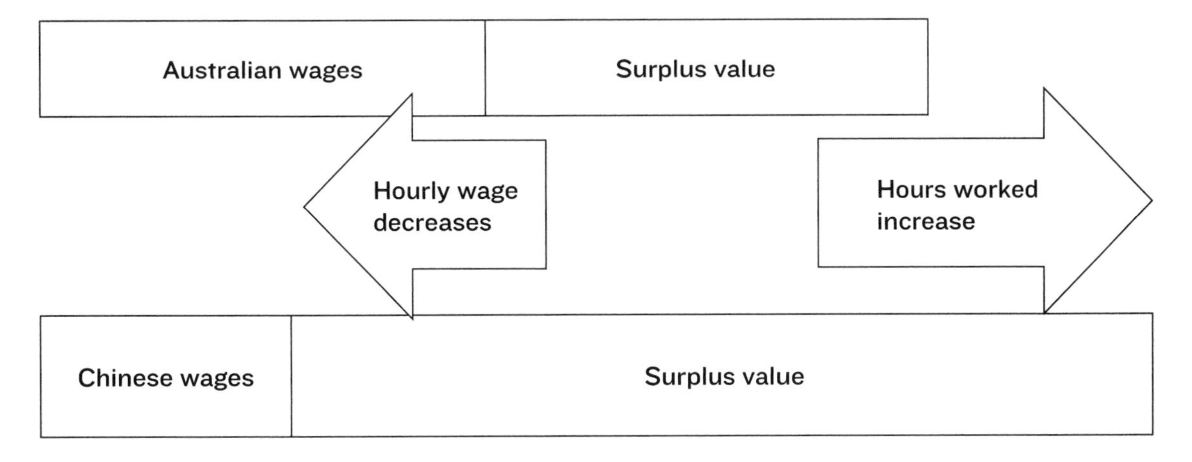

For Pacific Brands, maximizing surplus value means seeking a place where survival costs are lower than in Australia. Not only can hourly wage rates be reduced but the workday in China is much longer. The combination of low wage payments and long hours produces a much larger surplus, as indicated hypothetically in the People's Account of Pacific Brands.[10]

This relocation redraws the boundaries of an economic community, placing Chinese and Australian workers, with their very different survival needs (or average standards of living), alongside and in competition with each other. A clever entrepreneurial act undermines any ethic of care and concern held by minority-world workers with regard to workers in newly industrializing majority-world contexts. In a community economy we must take notice when our interdependence with others is manipulated in this way for private gain.

Mechanization also has an impact on the generation of new wealth and its distribution. Throughout history, the invention of machines and

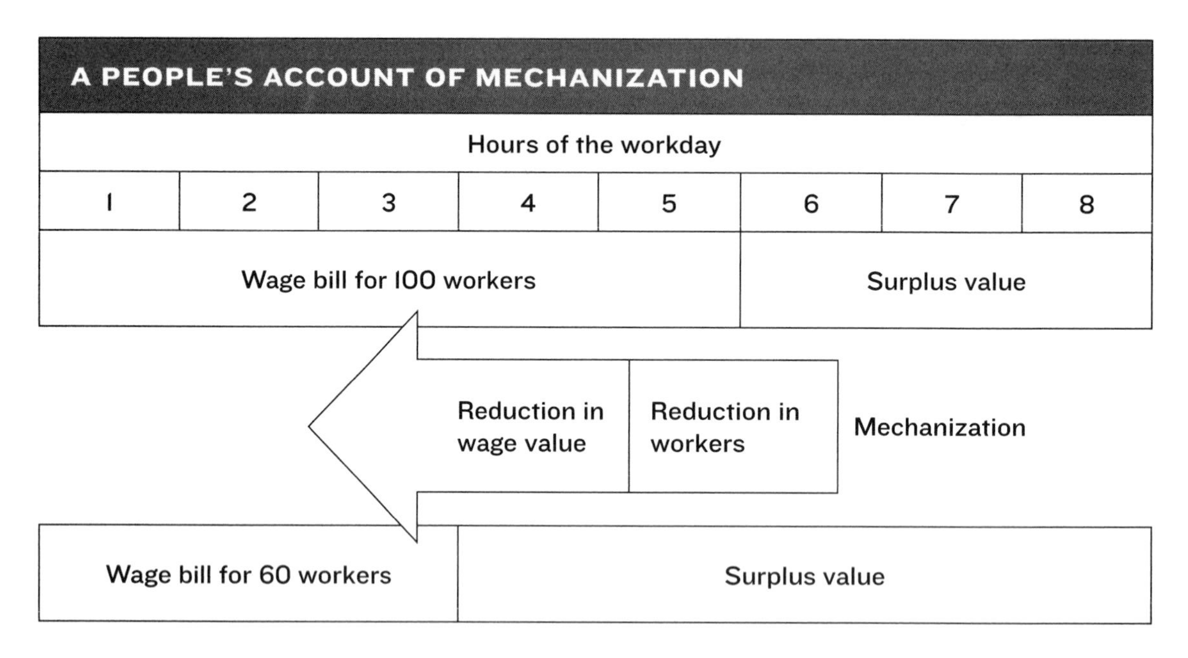

their widespread adoption have been welcomed for the physical labor-saving and safety benefits they afford. But paradoxically there has also been much opposition to something that lightens the burden of work. How machines are introduced into production and who benefits from them has important impacts.

Machines offer the capitalist entrepreneur the opportunity to replace labor, drive the wage bill down, and increase surplus value production. Machines also speed up and intensify production, and this means that workers can produce their survival payment in a shorter period of time and spend more of the workday producing surplus. Over time, as machines are widely adopted, goods become cheaper, the value of survival goods declines, and surplus value production is further increased.[11]

The history of antagonism to the introduction of machinery stems from fears of redundancy on the part of workers who have no other means of support than their survival wage payment. When threshing machines were introduced in England in the early part of the nineteenth century, thousands of agricultural laborers were made redundant and forced to migrate to cities in search of work. There they joined thousands of textile workers who had also lost their jobs because of the introduction of wide-frame looms. In both rural and urban settings, angry people broke machines in their frustration, and the Luddite movement (named after Ned Ludd, an early machine breaker) was born.

In exceptional cases, workers have been protected from job losses by philanthropic business owners and have been able to celebrate the benefits of labor-saving machines. The "Old Threshing Song," dating from the 1830s, makes one such case. It was collected by the Copper family in an area of England where Quaker estate owners maintained commitments to working families through the seasons of the year, in the face of changes in technology and over generations.[12]

It's all very well to have a machine
To thrash your wheat and barley clean,
To thrash it and wim it all fit for sale
Then go off to market so brisk and well
Singing rumble-dum-dairy flare up Mary
And make her old table shine.

Traditional, *Copper Family Song Book*

Preferable though capitalist philanthropy may be, it is only when the survival–surplus nexus becomes a focus of democratic deliberation by all involved that there is some guarantee of economic justice. In this context, mechanization can be a very different experience. When workers are the owners of their own cooperative business, as we saw in the case of FaSinPat, democratic deliberation is possible. And it is not only the survival–surplus nexus that becomes the focus of negotiation; it is also the distributions of surplus that can be democratically decided upon. To return to another guiding concern of a community economy, we look at how surplus can be deployed to produce well-being for people and the planet.

SURPLUS DISTRIBUTION: ANOTHER KEY CONCERN FOR A COMMUNITY ECONOMY

Surplus, that bit left over or extra, is one thing we have to work with to create new worlds. So far we have concentrated on the very different ways of negotiating the surplus–survival nexus within different kinds of enterprises and on moments when critical decisions are made about this nexus. We have produced a People's Account to track how surplus value is appropriated and deployed and by whom, as well as to identify decision flashpoints. In this section we look at the critical role business can play as a vehicle for directing how new wealth flows to people and the planet.

For a moment let's return to the issue of mechanization and see how, when democratically decided upon, surplus can be distributed so as to smooth out the jarring effects of labor displacement. Take, for example, the upgrading of white goods production in the worker-owned cooperatives of Mondragón in Spain.

The Mondragón Cooperative Corporation (MCC) is made up of a network of worker-owned cooperatives committed to democratic organization and maintaining employment in the Basque region of Spain.[13] The cooperators, keen to remain competitive in international markets, continue to upgrade their production processes through mechanization. When new state-of-the-art labor-saving machinery is introduced, displaced workers are deployed to other jobs or to other cooperatives in the regional network. Some are encouraged to go back to technical college to be trained in new production techniques. While doing so, they are supported by a maintenance wage.

The Mondragón Corporation is striking in that their annual strategic plan usually includes a job creation target. Most large corporations, in contrast, develop strategies to increase earnings through job reduction.

Greg MacLeod, *Harvard International Review*

During the recession of the 1980s, some cooperatives used up to 45 percent of their surplus to mechanize *and* to look after the worker-owners who were affected. Some of this surplus allocation came from what would usually flow to individual cooperators as a cooperative dividend. In this crisis, each cooperator was willing to forgo his or her individual share in order to keep their business viable and care for displaced workers.

Decisions around surplus distributions involve trade-offs between short- and long-term impacts. As we see in the example of Mondragón, to maintain their market share the worker-owners have to keep an eye on the future by upgrading technology and investing in research and development. But at the same time they have not lost sight of the short-term effects and have developed strategies to support workers who are affected by these changes.

In a commodity sector dominated by capitalist firms hell-bent on reducing production costs, maintaining market share is a major challenge for worker-owner cooperatives. Under such pressures, the core commitment to maintaining and increasing employment in worker-owned cooperatives in the Basque region of Spain has led to what some might judge an unwelcome codevelopment—the employment of noncooperator workers elsewhere. In recent years the MCC has shifted some components of production offshore and employed noncooperator workers in capitalist enterprises. Unlike the Pacific Brands move, however, this strategy is not one that pits one workforce against another but one that secures ongoing employment for worker-owner cooperators in one place and noncooperative employment in another. The MCC is committed to increasing workers' participation in the ownership and management of companies in its network. It is, however, realistic about the time it takes to build a truly cooperative culture of work, management, and ownership. Habits do not change overnight, and cooperativism cannot be imposed but must be continually reaffirmed and enabled. Thus a major investment for the MCC is cooperative education in the form of support for international cooperative education programs as well as its cooperative university and technical colleges.

If we want to take back the economy for people and the planet, we need transparency about who benefits from the business of business. We need to pinpoint what ethical commitments inform how businesses distribute surplus in various ways—to their investors, owners and shareholders, managers, workers, customers, and communities or to the planet *and* what trade-offs take place between these stakeholders and why.

Let's take a look at the two giant car manufacturers General Motors (GM) and Toyota to see how in recent times they have diverted private benefits to their shareholder-owners and chief executive officers (CEOs) at the expense of their workforces.[14]

In 1980 GM controlled over 45 percent of the U.S. auto market. From this dominant market position the company allocated a large portion of surplus value to fund its financial services division, GMAC. GM had found it could make more money from the interest on car loans than it could from making and selling cars. At the same time, as GMAC was expanding, GM was shutting factories, selling off productive assets, laying off workers—and paying exorbitant bonuses to senior managers to reward them for cutting back on costs.

GMAC gradually branched out from auto lending to other financial services, including the subprime mortgage market. But with the financial crisis of 2008, GMAC was hit hard. By 2010 it had pressured the U.S. government into three bailout injections of public money and the state had become the largest shareholder in the company (owning 56 percent of it).

GM shifted its operations from creating new wealth to lending and borrowing money. Toyota, by contrast, remained focused on car manufacturing. It directed its surplus value into a new niche product that is beginning to address the problem of carbon emissions. The company relocated plants to low-wage states in the United States, cut back on workers' benefits, and allocated surplus value to research and development that produced the first mass-market hybrid cars.

Both companies have pursued strategies that have devastated workforces in selected regions. But Toyota has taken heed of our planetary future and is turning its innovative energies toward product development that will help reduce greenhouse emissions. Might it be possible for business to reorient itself to different futures without the cost to its workers that Toyota has exacted?

The capitalist corporation Interface Carpets Inc. shows one way forward. This company is the world's largest producer of modular carpet and has over $1 billion in annual sales. In 1994 the CEO and founder, the late Ray Anderson, was preparing a speech detailing Interface's environmental policies. At the time he was reading Paul Hawken's book *The Ecology of Commerce*. This book prompted him to realize that his business was depleting the planet's natural environment and that he was a "plunderer." Anderson has gone on to say that this moment of self-recognition was like a spear that pierced his chest.[15]

I realized I was a plunderer and it was not a legacy I wanted to leave behind.

Ray Anderson, *LA Times*

From that moment, Ray Anderson committed the company to completely eliminating its negative environmental impacts by 2020. Interface Carpets has changed its products so that they can easily degrade or be recycled. It has minimized energy inputs and committed to a path of innovation that improves the environment while reducing waste and material input costs. By 2010, the company's greenhouse gas emissions were down by 35 percent from their level in 1996. The company has also "flattened" its corporate hierarchy in an attempt to encourage everyone at the firm to participate in the collaborative redesign of the products and the production process.

Interface Carpets has found a way to reduce its ecological footprint while maintaining good wage levels. It has embraced an ecologically responsible ethic of care for the planet and widened the boundaries of whose survival it supports. It now directs surplus to the well-being of our planet in recognition of the gifts it receives and, at the same time, accepts responsibility for its repair.

Plundering nature has traditionally been the basis of great riches. In the corporate capitalist mining sector, the unrecompensed gifts of nature provide massive new wealth, ensuring immense economic power. Surplus is generated by privately accessing minerals and fossiliferous fuels trapped in the earth's crust on land and under the sea. In many nations this "sovereign wealth" is privately exploited with little regard for the survival and well-being of earth's ecosystems and atmosphere. Workers in the highly mechanized mining and energy industries are often an elite that has managed to drive wages up, well above other people's survival standards (as we saw in the previous chapter). They have become beneficiaries, along with shareholders and CEOs, of the trade-offs being made by corporations between private gain and planetary degradation.

It is instructive to reflect on the end point of the progressive battles to increase survival payments for hardworking people fought by miners' unions since the beginning of the Industrial Revolution. Are workers entitled to keep upping their demands for higher and higher wages for themselves? When does consideration of the survival chances of nonminers or nonhuman beings get factored in? In a community economy we must take notice when our interdependence with others is denied or ignored for the benefit of a few.

In this section we have seen how ethical commitments govern the ways that cooperative enterprises distribute surplus and how even capitalist enterprises can draw on an ethic of care for people and the planet to help guide their decisions about surplus value. There is a new breed of enterprise that is specifically designed to shun private gain and work toward addressing societal and environmental concerns directly. Social enterprises, sometimes called community enterprises, produce goods and services with the main mission of serving a stated social or environmental purpose.[16] Their focus may be to train and employ groups who are usually excluded from the labor market (such as people with disabilities), or they may focus on environmental projects such as revegetation and environmental cleanup. There are many different forms of social enterprise; some are "nonprofits," whereas others see themselves as "more-than-profits." According to the Organisation for Economic Co-operation and Development, "They come in a variety of forms including employee owned businesses, credit unions, co-operatives, social cooperatives, development trusts, social firms, intermediate labour market (ILM) organisations, community businesses, or charities' trading arms."[17]

With commitment to an agreed mission as their core business, social enterprises variously aim for democratic decision making about governance and surplus distribution. A range of business stakeholders—employees, customers, suppliers, the wider community, and the environment, as well as investors, entrepreneurs, and managers—are recognized as having a say in how business is done and who benefits from it.

A social enterprise is not defined by its legal status but by its nature: its social aims and outcomes; the basis on which its social mission is embedded in its structure and governance; and the way it uses the profits it generates through trading activities.

New Economic Foundation / Shorebank Advisory Services, *Unlocking the Potential*

Homeboy Industries is a multifaceted social enterprise based in Los Angeles, whose core business is "gang rehab."[18] As their motto reads, "Nothing stops a bullet like a job." This organization offers counseling, education, tattoo removal, substance abuse and addiction assistance, job training, and job placements to young people who are former gang members, many of whom have spent time in jail. Homeboy Industries runs seven small businesses, including a bakery, a diner, Homegirl Cafe

A PEOPLE'S ACCOUNT OF ONE OF THE HOMEBOY INDUSTRIES							
Decision flashpoints							
Hours of the workday							
1	2	3	4	5	6	7	8
Young workers' survival payment				Surplus value and social surplus			
Ex-gang members paid a living wage and given free access to services (counseling, tattoo removal, legal services, education, training, clothes). Wages are used for • food • housing				Business payments • rent • insurance • accounting • retained earnings		Social wealth shared to • support services for young people • develop new businesses to expand the range of job-training possibilities	

and Catering, and a silkscreen and embroidery business. Young people get skills training and job experience in these businesses and are then assisted to find employment in other businesses. The social enterprise relies on grants from government and gifts from supporters as well as income from its Homeboy businesses to remain economically viable.

In the figure above we offer a hypothetical analysis of one of Homeboy's enterprises. The social enterprise makes decisions about how much to pay young people, as well as how to use the surplus value that is generated to keep the business operational and achieving its social purpose. What is different in this People's Account is that along with surplus value we include the government grants and philanthropic gifts that Homeboy receives, and we identify this as a form of social surplus. Together the surplus value and the social surplus constitute the social wealth that the enterprise uses to achieve its social mission.

Here we see business as a way of organizing the deployment of social wealth from large and small private donors and from government on behalf of all of us. In the context of a social enterprise run by committed social entrepreneurs, this wealth is put to a socially responsible end—meeting the needs of young people to restart their lives, gain self-respect, learn skills, and join together, even with former rival gang members, to build worthwhile lives.

Homeboy Industries is but one of a growing number of social enterprises in which people are taking back business and making it work not just for social purposes but also to address environmental concerns.

TOOLS FOR DISTRIBUTING SURPLUS

Taking back business for people and the planet involves encouraging a wide range of enterprise types. It means foregrounding and celebrating those that use their organizational capacities and ingenuity to improve and spread well-being, repair the planet, and create more sustainable ways of living. There is a dominant conception that private individual reward is the key to business success. But, as we have seen in this chapter, there are diverse rewards to be gained from business and a range of definitions and drivers of success.

In this chapter we have touched on only three types of businesses—capitalist enterprises, worker-owner cooperative enterprises, and social enterprises. In each, labor works with old wealth, transforming it into survival payments and new wealth that can be accounted for as surplus. In each type of enterprise this surplus is variously claimed as private, collective, or social wealth, and a different individual or group decides how this wealth will be distributed and to what ends.

The Diverse Enterprise Identifier can be used to distinguish a range of different kinds of enterprise, each with its own way of organizing surplus production, appropriation, and distribution. The Identifier includes a wider range of enterprises than we have discussed, including feudal and slave enterprises, self-employed businesses, and state-run enterprises. As we said earlier, not all of these enterprises are desirable; indeed, we would want to see some stamped out because their mo-

DIVERSE ENTERPRISE IDENTIFIER
CAPITALIST
ALTERNATIVE CAPITALIST Green capitalist firm Socially responsible firm State-run enterprise
NONCAPITALIST Cooperative Social enterprise Self-employed business Slave enterprise Feudal estate

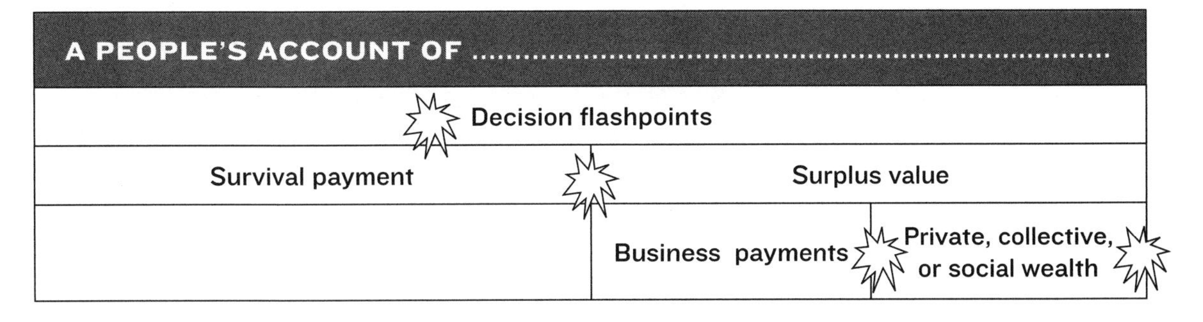

dus operandi is to minimize survival payments for workers and extract as much wealth as possible for owners.

In a community economy we must keep our collective eye on how new wealth is produced by enterprises and how this new wealth is used. We should remember that what is "surplus" and what is necessary for "survival" are interdependent. Various interdependencies also enter into the picture when decisions are made about distributions of surplus (including the ways in which surplus can be used to help sustain the very environment on which so many enterprises depend). The ways in which we distribute surplus will affect the survival chances not only of owners and producers but of nonowners, nonproducers, and environments. When we privilege one over the others, there are consequences that are often not visible in the short term. By exercising democratic and ethical deliberation over how we negotiate the surplus–survival nexus, we are more likely to manage this boundary and the distribution of surplus respectfully and to the widest possible benefit.

The People's Account and Decision Flashpoints are tools to help us to recognize enterprise diversity, surplus–survival interdependence, and surplus distributional outcomes. We can use these tools to develop reflective capacities that can lead to new habits and actions.

COLLECTIVE ACTIONS FOR DISTRIBUTING SURPLUS

In a community economy we negotiate how to spread the benefit bestowed by surplus to the well-being of people and the planet.

In this section we look at the ways people are taking back business and bringing the key concerns around surplus to the fore.

Questions to consider as you read about these collective actions

- What decisions are being made about the survival–surplus nexus?
- Who is making these decisions?
- Is the survival payment sufficient for the workers? Is it too much?
- Who is producing the surplus?
- Who owns the surplus that is being produced?
- How is the surplus being used? Is it being used to benefit individuals? Is it being used for broader societal and environmental benefit?
- What are the bounds of the economic community being produced by the accounting frame and benefit flow adopted?

Transition to More Participatory Forms of Enterprise

There are a variety of ways in which people are taking collective action to make enterprises into democratic spaces in order to involve more people in negotiations around the survival–surplus nexus and what's necessary for survival.

ETHICAL ACTION: *Democratizing ownership and negotiations around survival payments and surplus distributions*

Employee stock ownership plans (ESOPs) have become popular in minority-world countries. Private capitalist companies offer company stocks to workers as a way of democratizing ownership. In the United States, for example, there are over eleven thousand firms that are run as ESOP corporations. More than two-thirds of these became ESOPs on the retirement of the owner of a private firm.[19] The longer workers work for such a company, the more shares they acquire. When workers retire (or when they leave the company after working there for a set period of time, usually between three and five years), they sell their shares back to the company. ESOPs are therefore a form of retirement planning. King Arthur Flour, the oldest flour-making firm in the United States, became a 100 percent worker-owned ESOP firm in 1996, growing from 5 employees in 1990 to 160 in 2010. Employee-owners have a say in how the business is run—in how much they are paid and in what happens to the surplus that they generate. In 2008 King Arthur Flour was named by the WorldBlu List as one of the twenty-five most democratic workplaces in the world.[20]

To help businesses make the transition to ESOPs there are support organizations such as the ESOP Association in the United States, the ESOP Association Canada, the Australian Employee Ownership Association, the ESOP Centre in the United Kingdom, and the European Federation of Employee Share Ownership. ESOP worker-shareowners are directly involved in negotiating their survival–surplus nexus. They share the risks as well as the benefits of surplus value distribution.

In the very different context of Brazil, many agricultural laborers work in large feudal agricultural enterprises on estates where they live and work in conditions of slavery.[21] Laborers produce surplus for the estate owners, the fazendeiro. The workers have no say about their survival payment and what happens to the surplus they produce. Indeed, in many situations workers find that they owe money for the "privilege" of working as slaves, because the fazendeiro charges workers for the cost of the tools they use, their accommodation in cramped and unhygienic conditions, and even their food. These workers fall into debt, and their lives become completely controlled by the fazendeiro.

One organization struggling against this situation is the Landless Workers Movement (Movimento dos Trabalhadores Rurais Sem Terra, or MST, in Portuguese). When the Landless Workers Movement expropriates land, the settlers who take up residence and start to work the land include freed slaves. It is up to the settlers to decide how they want to organize their new agricultural enterprise. Some work as individual self-employed farmers on the land, while others elect to operate as cooperatives. One of these is Cooperdotchi, made up of five hundred families. In the transition from working in feudal and slave enterprises to working for themselves or for a collective, workers gain control over their survival payments and are able to benefit from privately or collectively owned new wealth.

Starting Worker-Owned Cooperative Enterprises

Some enterprises are taking what ESOPs do a step further by being completely bought out by the workers and becoming worker-owned cooperatives.

ETHICAL ACTION: *Democratizing ownership, management, wage setting, and surplus distribution*

Collective Copies was born in 1982 when the previously capitalist-owned business was bought out by four workers. Today there are thirteen worker-owners who manage the enterprise through weekly meetings, deciding on everything from the pay scale to the work rosters on a consensus basis.[22] The worker-owners have made two important decisions about their pay. First, the highest-paid worker-owners cannot be paid more than twice as much as the lowest-paid worker-owners (i.e., if the lowest-paid worker-owner receives $10 an hour, the highest-paid worker-owner can receive no more than $20 an hour). Second, worker-owners have to be paid enough to allow them to buy a home in the area. Eleven of the thirteen worker-owners are also homeowners. Another important decision that the worker-owners have to make is how to distribute the 10 percent of pretax profit that that they have determined should go to community groups in the area.

Collective Copies is one of over a dozen businesses in the Pioneer Valley of Western Massachusetts run as worker cooperatives. In 2005 these enterprises formed the Valley Alliance of Worker Cooperatives (VAWC), which is dedicated to promoting and supporting worker-owned cooperatives. Both Collective Copies and VAWC are guided by the belief that worker-ownership provides a unique opportunity for people to control their own economic destinies, for their benefit and the benefit of the community. They are negotiating the surplus–survival nexus and the question of how to distribute surplus through a deliberative ethical process.

Being a worker-owner you get to realize more of yourself. The thing that I get to do in my life is to try and put some of the principles that I really feel are important to work, at work.

Adam Trott, Collective Copies cooperator

In Thailand another group of workers have established their own cooperative.[23] In 2002 the Bed and Bath factory in Bangkok suddenly closed when its Thai owners left the country. Nine hundred workers were left without jobs (and 1,100 or so workers employed by smaller subcontractors in other parts of Thailand were affected). Workers protested for three months outside the Ministry of Labour Building until they received the compensation guaranteed to them under Thai law. After the protests ended, a small group of forty workers decided to start their own garment factory and label, Dignity Returns. They formed a cooperative factory, the Solidarity Group Cooperative, where all workers are owners and decisions are made by all worker-owners. Initially the worker-owners decided to pay themselves only a small survival payment so that they could repay the loans that had helped them start the cooperative. With the debt repaid, the survival payment has increased. The worker-owners have also decided that they want to work reasonable hours (e.g., to stop work at 5:00 p.m. on Saturdays and to not work on Sundays). This means that the worker-owners generate less surplus and receive less income than if they worked longer hours, but they have time for other activities. In the terms of what we discussed in chapter 2, they have established working conditions so that they can achieve all aspects of their well-being.

One of the challenges for the cooperative is that it relies on poorly compensated piecework that is subcontracted to it by larger factories. The company's goal is to produce entirely under its own label and sell directly to retailers and individual clients. To help it achieve this goal, the Solidarity Group joined with La Alameda cooperative from Argentina, and in June 2010 they launched their own international brand, No Chains. The two cooperatives work together on activities such as design and marketing.

Sometimes people outside say that we still have to work hard—it's no different from working in the old factory. But we know that it is different. In this place, there is no boss hanging over us or taking advantage of us. There are no threats or insults. And most important, in this place, we are in a factory of our very own.

Manop Kaewpaga,
Solidarity Group cooperator

Starting Social Enterprises

Social enterprises use business as a vehicle to produce a direct social or environmental good. Sometimes they emerge from a very local community need, but other times they are created in response to a withdrawal of government services. Whatever the origins, the numbers of social enterprises are rapidly growing in all countries.

ETHICAL ACTION: *Establishing businesses that meet social and environmental needs directly*

The Yackandandah Petrol Station in rural Victoria, Australia, was started in 2002 by residents when it was announced that the area's only petrol station was about to close.[24] The Yackandandah Community Development Company Pty Ltd (YCDCo) was formed to make sure the community continued to have access to what is, at the moment, an indispensable commodity. The enterprise was established as an unlisted public company—which meant that it could have shareholders without being listed on a stock exchange. The shareholders of YCDCo are local residents. This plays an important role in ensuring that the business is run with the interests of the community in mind. The business has run at a surplus since its inception. Fifty percent of its profits are returned to shareholders, and the other 50 percent goes to community projects.

The Laca Ginger Tea social enterprise was established by a small group of elderly women in the rural province of Bohol in the Philippines.[25] The group of women collectively process local ginger into a sweetened instant tea powder called *salabat* for sale in their region. The goal of the enterprise is to generate enough income to supplement mostly subsistence income. The women originally wanted to form a cooperative, but to register as a cooperative they needed twenty-five members. Instead they formed an informal association in order to develop their idea of running an enterprise that would produce small amounts of much-needed cash. As the demand for their tea increased, the women decided not to increase their own workload (which would increase their income but affect the other work they do to support their subsistence living). Instead they met demand by inviting other women to become part of the enterprise and enabling them to also have access to a small cash income.

As Laca Ginger Tea discovered, social enterprises can be an alternative to cooperatives when there are overly restrictive legal requirements for cooperative formation. In the United Kingdom there is so much interest in environmental and social-purpose businesses that a new legal structure has been developed—a community interest company (CIC). Directors of a CIC must convince the government regulator that the business produces a social good. CICs have a statutory "assets lock" that ensures that surplus is not privately distributed but flows to community purposes.[26]

Community Energy Solutions in the north of England became a community interest company in 2006.[27] It employs twenty people and works to improve home insulation and connect those in fuel poverty to natural gas mains and renewable energy technologies. The company works alongside the Department of Energy and Climate Change as well as local development authorities to improve the energy efficiency of social housing and private housing in poorer areas. Surpluses are reinvested in new projects, such as fitting solar photovoltaic panels in social housing projects to generate energy.

Hepburn Wind Cooperative in rural Victoria, Australia, is another social enterprise with an energy focus.[28] It was set up to work with nature to produce renewable energy. Work began in 2005 on an enterprise that would become Australia's first community-owned wind farm. Hepburn Wind Cooperative currently has 1,600 shareholders, more than half drawn from its local area, who contribute the minimum share value of $100. The annual surplus is used for the upkeep of two turbines, insurance, rent on the land, and contributions of $15,000 per wind turbine per year to a Community Sustainability Fund. The remainder is paid to shareholders as dividends.

Ethical Negotiations within Capitalism

Although some firms are becoming more participatory and transparent by adopting ESOP structures and others govern themselves and their surplus on a cooperative or community basis, there are firms in many countries that will continue to exist as capitalist firms. The conventional ownership structure, however, does not rule out the possibility of ethical transformations such as what we saw the late Ray Anderson accomplishing at Interface Carpets.

ETHICAL ACTION: *Distributing surplus to social and environmental ends*

Some attempts to make capitalist businesses behave in more socially and environmentally responsible ways have ambitious agendas. In 2011 the Relationship Foundation, a think tank based in the United Kingdom, launched an initiative called Transforming Capitalism from Within.[29] At the core of the plan developed by Jonathan Rushworth, a retired lawyer, and Dr. Michael Schulter, a former World Bank economist, is a ten-point charter. The charter is meant to encourage capitalist enterprises to respect all of the internal and external relationships that are part of corporate life. In the view of Rushworth and Schulter, the recent global financial crisis was the result of corporations' operating without considering these relationships and focusing solely on maximizing profits, to the ruin of society and the environment. The charter includes principles that govern corporate ownership and transparency, relations to workers and other stakeholders, and relations with suppliers, customers, and the community as a whole. Most noteworthy are principles to respect the dignity of all employees "by minimizing remuneration differentials within the business" (Principle 6) and to fulfill obligations to the wider society (Principle 10). If adopted, these principles would direct the attention of capitalist enterprises to the surplus–survival nexus as well as to distributions of surplus.

One firm that is experimenting with distributions of surplus is KereKere Coffee, which has been operating at the University of Melbourne, Australia, since 2007.[30] Customers decide how the profits from their purchases should be distributed—whether to the owner, to environmental or cultural projects, or to social charities. When customers buy a cup of coffee, they get a playing card that they can put in the box for their preferred distribution. So far around 40 percent of the profits have been distributed to the owner and the rest to projects and charities.

Collective Support for the Self-Employed

In both majority- and minority-world countries, tens of millions of people work for themselves in occupations ranging from tradesmen to creative consultants and from farmers to software designers. Although there is freedom in being one's own boss, there are still many ways in which business expenses are difficult to shoulder alone. There are collective actions that have allowed the self-employed to collectivize some of these expenses while retaining their autonomy.

ETHICAL ACTION: *Making self-employment viable*

Municipalities, states, and even federal governments can help defray start-up costs and other expenses for the self-employed. For example, the Franklin County Community Development Corporation (FCCDC) was started in Greenfield, Massachusetts, in 1979 with the express purpose of helping to start small businesses.[31] In addition to having a revolving loan fund and full-time consultancy staff, the FCCDC owns a business incubator that currently houses eight new ventures. More recently it added a commercial kitchen that is available to start-up ventures that want to produce value-added food products. Some of the companies started at the FCCDC, such as Real Pickles, have gone on to become quite successful small businesses that continue to make use of produce from local farmers. Support agencies like the one in Franklin County work to make small businesses, such as those run by the self-employed, more viable by reducing overhead expenses that would otherwise reduce their overall surplus generation.

There are also organizations that support self-employed professionals on a national scale. The Writers Guild of America (East and West) helps freelance writers in the United States. The East branch was born from the Author's League of America at the end of the twentieth century. Even though many screenwriters are self-employed, writers join together into the guilds in order to ensure that contract negotiations over royalties and other matters of concern are conducted with the best interests of the writers in mind. Collective organizations like the Writers Guild can play a critical role in helping self-employed people negotiate decent survival payments in their dealings with large and powerful corporations such as those in the media.

WHERE TO FROM HERE?

What would it take to ensure that new wealth is used to support society and our planet? To get started, you might consider the following questions:

1. What type of enterprise do you work for? If you are working for a small business, would an employee shared-ownership

scheme be an option, particularly as part of a succession plan for an owner who is nearing retirement? What organizations in your area might be able to advise you about employee shared ownership?

2. Would a complete worker buyout be an option, particularly to own and manage the business as a cooperative? Are you interested in starting a business? Would a cooperative venture be something that would suit you and a group of friends or colleagues? There are many organizations that can support new or emerging cooperatives. Is there one in your area that could help? Are there other cooperative businesses nearby that could advise you? If you're interested in supporting cooperatives, you could also make sure that you purchase goods and services produced through cooperatives (not just local ones, but ones in other parts of the world, such as The Solidarity Group).

3. Perhaps you might be interested in starting or working for a social enterprise where surplus is generated in order to fulfill social and environmental goals. Perhaps you have business skills that would be useful for social enterprises in your area. Increasingly, social enterprise support programs and funding are available through governments, community organizations, or philanthropic groups. Can you find out about what's offered in your area?

4. What capitalist enterprises do you encounter in your daily life? Are there ways you could transform how they operate? Even if they don't operate an explicit consumer program like that of KereKere Coffee, you could ask about their policies on ethical giving or ask if they use only recycled paper or fair-trade coffee, for example.

5. Perhaps you're self-employed. Are there support services in your area to help make self-employed businesses more viable? Are there other self-employed people with whom you could share some services (such as accounting or marketing)?

In this chapter we've shown how business can be taken back to produce people and planetary well-being. One thing that links various enterprises together are the relationships forged between suppliers and consumers in the marketplace. In the next chapter we explore how market transactions can also acknowledge and promote others' well-being. We also consider the full range of ways by which people connect with one another and acquire what they need to survive well.

4.

Take Back the Market

Encountering Others

WHAT *ARE* MARKETS?

In complex societies we rely on a vast number of other people for the goods and services we need to survive. We acquire many of these goods and services via "the market." In today's world, markets have assumed a peculiar power. They are heralded as the ideal system for coordinating complex transactions between producers and consumers. Price setting is the hallowed technique whereby supply is calibrated to meet demand. It's simple. If supply increases but demand is stable, prices go down and demand expands. If demand rises and supply can't keep up, prices rise and demand stabilizes—that is, until supplies increase and prices come down again.

These market dynamics are often portrayed as *naturally operating,* like tides or weather systems. Certainly they are seen as capable of *efficiently allocating* scarce resources. If left on their own to operate freely without barriers and handicaps, so the story goes, buyers and sellers meet each other as equals and prices are adjusted so that both get a fair deal. On the level playing field of the market, we are all members of a "democracy of consumers," free to exercise choice over what we want and free to achieve the highest possible standard of living we can buy.[1] In this democracy, price mediates our encounters with other people and environments that supply what we need to live well.

The efficiencies and freedoms of the market were especially praised in the eighteenth century as Europe cast off the obligations and tributes that structured relations between people under feudalism. Today they are praised in postsocialist countries that have abandoned the centralized inefficiencies of state allocation. The responsive, if anarchic, fluidity of markets is seen as preferable to the orchestration by autocrats and bureaucrats of the way our survival needs are met.

In our globally connected world, a large proportion of the products we consume comes from a great distance. But when we acquire what we need from distant others via the market, the nature of our encounters is masked.

Say we get a bargain by buying a supercheap T-shirt or pair of jogging shoes. We're probably thinking about the savings this will make to our personal or household budget. Perhaps our most immediate survival needs are being addressed, with the new items replacing our torn Ts or worn-out shoes. Or perhaps it is the psychological need to shop to feel good that drives us to add to an already overloaded wardrobe. Whatever the situation, the only thing we're thinking about is the price tag. It's hard to shift attention away from the pleasure of a good bargain to think about what lies behind its price.

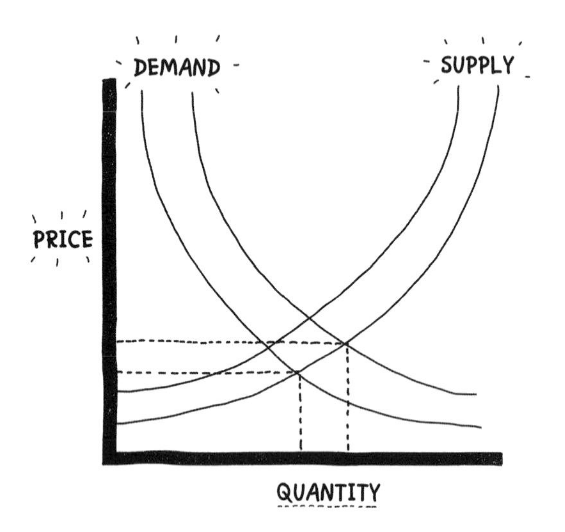

But what kind of encounter with others is represented by the price of a commodity? Does the price tell us about the working conditions of the young men and women who produced our bargain T-shirt or jogging shoes? Do we know if they were paid decent wages or whether their working environment was safe? And what about the environmental impacts of our bargains? Does the price indicate whether the cotton for our T-shirt was grown using genetically modified crops or pesticides that leave residual toxins in the soil?

As long as the price commands our attention, it's easy to discount these concerns. We can focus on our own consumption wants and seek satisfaction in consuming more. We can erase the ways our survival is interdependent with that of other human beings and natural environments. Ignorance is bargain-basement bliss.

But is that all there is? Beyond the thrill of the bargain is the reality of stuff—mountains of it that we buy only to throw it away barely used.[2] And masked by the price that appears to be fair are unknown people and distant environments whose situations may be far from fair.

Markets are one way we connect with others to obtain the things we need that we can't produce for ourselves. But what kinds of encounters do they really produce? Let's start by having a look at how one group of producers and consumers is devising ways of encountering each other.

MAKING TRADE WORK FOR PEOPLE

In the late 1980s, Japanese consumer cooperatives responded to the needs of starving sugarcane workers on the Philippines island of Negros when the international sugar market collapsed and farmers were left without a living.[3] Initially the cooperatives sent relief workers, food, and medical supplies across the sea to their southern neighbors. Concerned as to what the sugarcane farmers would do in the longer term, the consumer cooperatives established direct people-to-people trade of locally produced Mascobado brown sugar between Filipino farmers and Japanese consumers.

Japan and the Philippines have long been connected through trade, investment, and, not that long ago, military occupation. Japanese consumer cooperatives grew out of preindustrial mutual-assistance groups and have, since the 1960s, been ardent agitators for food safety and consumer rights. They have also been concerned about the plight of farmers in the rapidly disappearing Japanese countryside, and in the 1980s they extended this concern to the rural Philippines.

With the establishment of ethical trade between the Philippines and Japan, Alter Trade Japan Inc. was born. Its stated objectives are to support small farmers in growing products suited to their environment, to trade good food that is safe and nondestructive to the environment, and to foster encounters between people beyond borders.[4]

Today Alter Trade Japan arranges the trade of Balangon bananas from the Philippines; "eco-shrimps" from extensive shrimp farms in Indonesia; Nam Do Kimchi (pickles) from a Korean farmers' cooperative; organic coffee from Ecuador, Peru, Mexico, Tanzania, Haiti, Rwanda, and East Timor; natural sea salt from the once threatened salt pans of

France; organic green beans from Ecuador and Peru; and olive oil from Palestine. Through food trading, far-flung producers and consumers connect, recognizing each other as interdependent human beings.

Alter Trade Japan has reinstated trade as a mechanism for the type of people-to-people encounters that ensure that producers and consumers in very different circumstances can both survive well. This is a far cry from the way international trade often operates. Consider the other "Japanese story" that most of us know.

From the mid-1950s Japanese industrialization took off with strong protection and support from the government's Ministry of International Trade and Industry. Large corporations like Toyota, Toshiba, and Hitachi burst onto the world stage as exporters of cars, computers, and home appliances. Manufacturing countries around the globe were flooded with cheaper, high-quality goods, and consumers rejoiced. But in the industries threatened by imports, workers were laid off and plants closed. Increasing hostility was voiced about foreign products, the countries from which they came, and the trade agreements that allowed these products to "invade" established markets.

Some countries tried to block imports and protect their homegrown industries. Soon governments were locked in trade battles over who would benefit from "free trade." As global agreements were made and broken, large national companies internationalized their operations and ownership and adjusted to the presence of Japan as a new industrial power. Multinational firms abandoned communities and regions in their old industrial heartlands. They found new sites all over the world (often called "green-field" sites), leaving industrial plants at home to rust and working-age people to the mercy of unemployment lines.

The free movement of products is portrayed as a universal good. But without any ethical framing that specifies how we want to relate to one another, the most powerful nations or corporations get to set the conditions that define free trade. Invariably certain interest groups benefit at the expense of others. The need for people to survive well together is ignored, and national workforces are positioned in an antagonistic relationship. Throughout history, such situations have sparked war.

If goods don't cross borders, armies will.

Attributed to Frederic Bastiat, 1801–1850

Trade can pull people apart and set them in opposition or bring them together in networks of mutual support. Taking back markets means promoting economic encounters that help us to survive well together.

ENCOUNTERING DISTANT OTHERS: A KEY CONCERN OF A COMMUNITY ECONOMY

How do we survive well through our encounters with distant others? In a community economy, we are interested in stepping back from the hype about markets and thinking about how we encounter others in the process of surviving well together on this earth.

Markets may be portrayed as spaces in which the laws of supply and demand mean that people ultimately meet each other as equals. On this basis, markets need no more than to be left alone—and they certainly don't need the interference of those concerned about ethical encounters.

But ethics should not be erased from the market. When goods and services are traded we need to take into account not just the price we pay but the price distant others pay (whether fellow humans or other species). We can take back market transactions so that we honor the survival needs of those we share the planet with. And when we do that we might find that markets can provide satisfactions other than the short-lived pleasure of pure consumption.

We can explore our relationships with distant others with the aid of

1. a *Where From? Inventory,*
2. a *Distant Others Dandelion,*
3. a *Shopper's Checklist,* and
4. an *Ethical Shopper's Checklist.*

Most products that we buy have a "Made in . . . " label. This country-of-origin labeling allows us to begin to identify who the distant others are that we are connected to via trade. Many of the products we buy are produced in our own country, others in the minority world, and others in the majority world. Sometimes we can find out only the country of the wholesaler or the country where the product was packed, or we are

WHERE FROM? INVENTORY			
ITEM	DOMESTIC	MINORITY WORLD	MAJORITY WORLD
FOOD Fresh Canned Frozen Preserved or dried			
CLOTHING Outerwear Underwear FOOTWEAR			
ELECTRONICS Appliances Communication and entertainment equipment			

told only that the product was made from imported and local ingredients. In these cases we have to guess, or do more research, to find out more about the product's background.

One way to construct a picture of the distant others we are connected with might be to take a sample of the items in our household bought most recently and record their country of origin on a Where From? Inventory. To make this manageable, we could look at

- a selection of products from our last grocery shopping receipt,
- the outfit that we are wearing right at this moment, and
- the electronic appliances our household most recently purchased.

See the example of Katherine's Where From? Inventory.

On the basis of this inventory we can construct a Distant Others Dandelion of connection. Radiating out from the center (which represents the household where end consumption is happening) are lines representing all the products in the Where From? Inventory. The length of the line to

KATHERINE'S WHERE FROM? INVENTORY			
ITEM	**DOMESTIC**	**MINORITY WORLD**	**MAJORITY WORLD**
FOOD			
Fresh			
1. Cheese	Australia	....	....
2. Bread	Australia	....	....
3. Fish	....	....	Malaysia
Canned			
1. Coconut milk	....	....	Thailand
2. Tomatoes	....	Spain	....
3. Sardines	....	Italy	....
Frozen			
1. Ice cream	....	New Zealand	....
2. Pasta	Australia	....	....
3. Peas	Australia	....	....
Preserved or dried			
1. Rice	....	....	Pakistan
2. Tea	....	....	Indonesia
3. Mustard	....	France	....
CLOTHING			
Outerwear			
1. Blouse	Australia	....	....
2. Skirt	....	....	Asia
Underwear			
1. Panties	....	....	Asia
2. Bra	Australia	....	....
FOOTWEAR			
1. Sandals	....	Germany	....
ELECTRONICS			
Appliances			
1. Dishwasher	....	New Zealand	....
2. Cooktop	....	Italy	....
Communication and entertainment equipment			
1. TV	....	South Korea	....
2. Phone	....	....	China

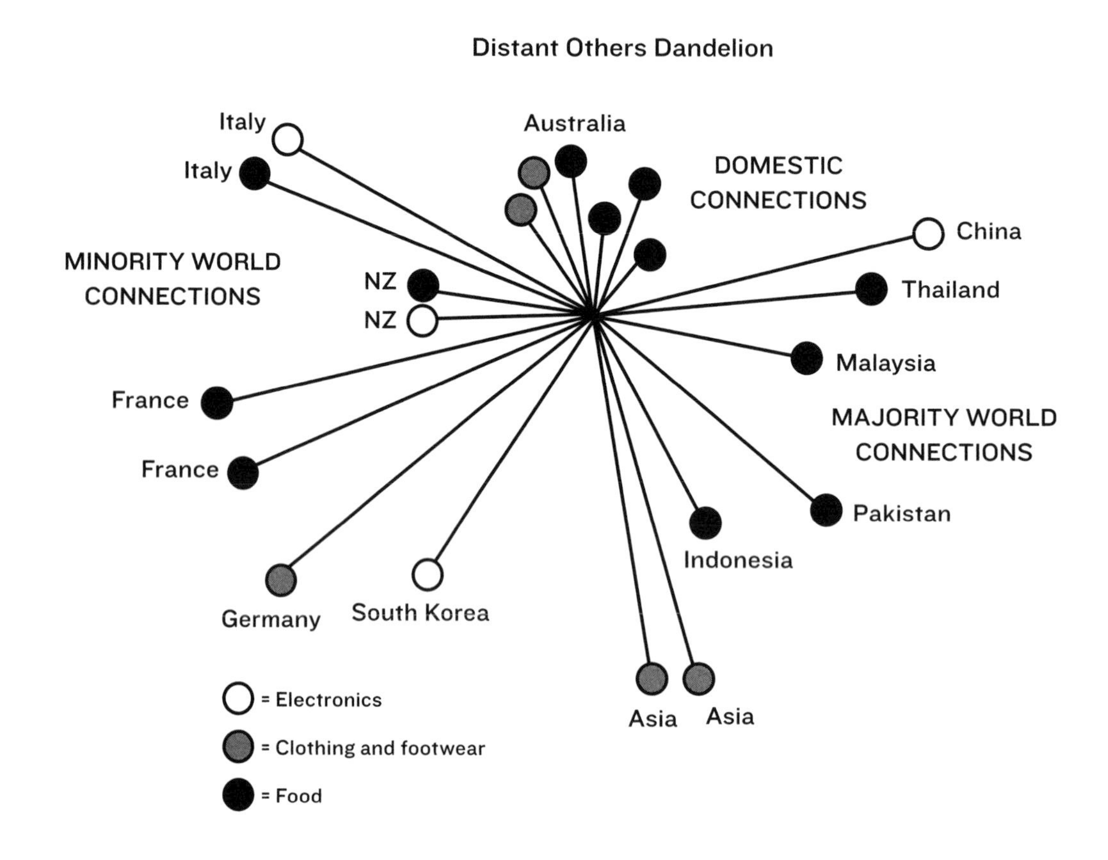

the dot representing the country of origin is meant to indicate its rough relative distance from the end consumption point. The shading of the dots indicates the different kinds of products.

This is a very different way of representing national and international trade relationships than the usual balance-of-trade statistical reports, which are much harder to relate to. Once we see ourselves and distant others in relation to each other like this, we can ask different questions of ourselves as we act in the celebrated "democracy of consumers" known as the market.

When we make a purchase, personal and immediate considerations are often uppermost in our minds. We think, Can I afford it at this price? Is it the best buy for what I need? Do I like it? The usual Shopper's Checklist focuses on the cost and utility of the product and our response to it.

But with the Distant Others Dandelion in mind we are prompted to ask different questions. Are the producers of the products I buy from my

SHOPPER'S CHECKLIST		
THE COST	**THE UTILITY**	**OUR SENSORY RESPONSE**
☐ Is it the right price?	☐ Is it functional? ☐ Will it last? ☐ Is it safe? ☐ Is it a reliable brand?	☐ Does it look good? ☐ Does it feel right? ☐ Does it taste nice? ☐ Does it sound right? ☐ Does it smell good?

own country or overseas getting a fair deal? Are there any harmful environmental effects of production? Are animals being treated humanely in this production process? In each context the labor, environmental, and humane conditions of production could vary dramatically.

To help us answer questions like these, groups in many countries now compile ethical consumer guides. For example, in Australia the Ethical Consumer Group (a community-based organization) regularly produces a guide that is designed for shoppers to use in supermarkets. The Ethical Consumer Guide lists the different brands of products commonly found on supermarket shelves, identifies the company that owns each brand and its country of ownership, and rates the company according to whether there has been praise for or criticism of the company's social and environmental performance.

The Ethical Consumer Group is just one such "ratings agency." In the United States, ethical ratings agencies include Green America (which runs an Ethical Shopper program) and Knowmore.org. In the United Kingdom, there is the Ethical Consumer Research Association (which runs Ethical Consumer and an Ethiscore program). Some ratings agencies address specific products. For example, Greenpeace has a *Guide to Greener Electronics* that rates electronics companies' policies on toxic chemicals, recycling, and climate change.

Among them, these ratings agencies provide information on the companies that offer goods and services from airlines and alcohol to tea and toys. And they consider a whole range of people and planet connections. For example, the Ethical Consumer Research Association in the United Kingdom rates companies and products according to five categories.

THE ETHICAL CONSUMER RESEARCH ASSOCIATION'S CATEGORIES FOR ETHICAL RATINGS	
Animals	Animal testing, factory farming, animal rights
Environment	Environmental reporting, nuclear power, climate change, pollutions and toxins, habitats and resources
People	Human rights, workers' rights, supply chain management, irresponsible marketing, arms and military supply
Politics	Antisocial finance, boycott calls, genetic engineering, political activities
Sustainability	Company ethos, product sustainability (including organic, fair trade, energy-efficient products)

Source: "Our Ethical Ratings," Ethical Consumer Research Association Web site, http://www.ethicalconsumer.org/.

ETHICAL SHOPPER'S CHECKLIST

THE COST	THE UTILITY	OUR SENSORY RESPONSE	THE PEOPLE AND PLANET CONNECTIONS
☐ Is it the right price?	☐ Is it functional? ☐ Will it last? ☐ Is it safe? ☐ Is it a reliable brand?	☐ Does it look good? ☐ Does it feel right? ☐ Does it taste nice? ☐ Does it sound right? ☐ Does it smell good?	**Animals** ☐ Are animals treated humanely? **Environment** ☐ Are the environmental impacts of production addressed? **People** ☐ Is well-being taken into account? **Politics** ☐ Are the politics just? **Sustainability** ☐ Does the product have a neutral or positive impact?

We can use the information from these ethical ratings agencies to expand the Shopper's Checklist and create an Ethical Shopper's Checklist.

These consumer guides and checklists are extremely useful in helping us to find out more about products and the companies that produce them—and we should certainly use them when we're deciding what or whether to buy. However, often we're considering technologically sophisticated products that have many inputs that can be difficult to trace. We need to think about all the interconnections that we are part of when, as consumers, we pull products through the "supply chain" to their end use.

The supply chain highlights the complexity involved in getting many products into the hands of consumers—from the initial sourcing and refining of raw materials to the assembling of a host of component parts into a single product to the multiple layers of wholesalers and retailers that play roles in passing the product along the chain.[5]

Supply Chain

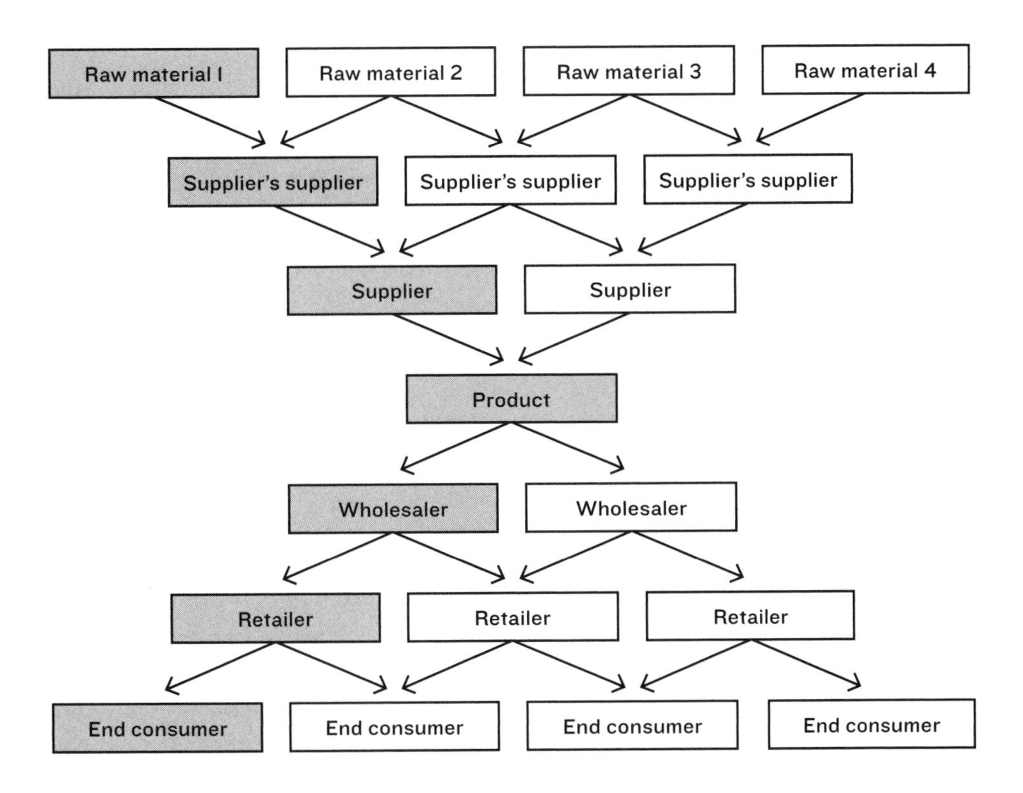

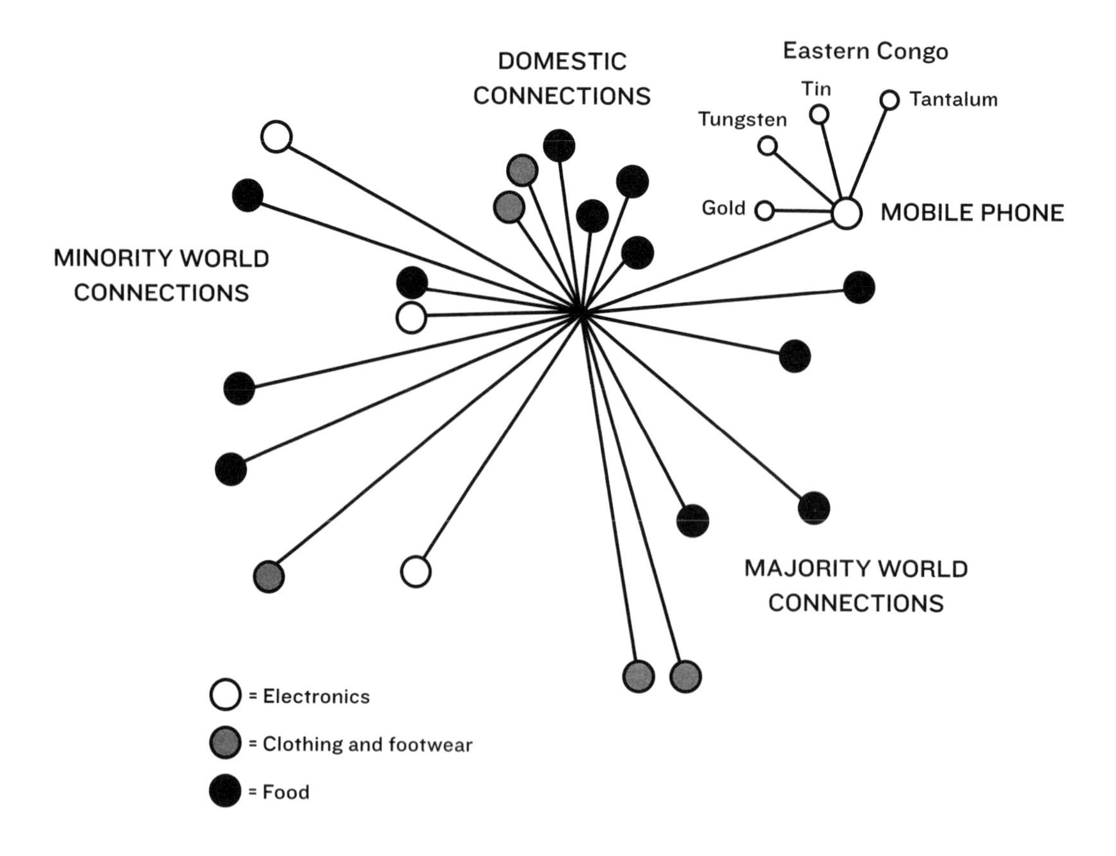

Demand does indeed stimulate supply. But what else does our demand stimulate? Let's take another look at one of the links on our Distant Others Dandelion and identify just a few of the raw materials that were used in the mobile phone that was assembled in China (and was one of the products in Katherine's Where From? Inventory).

When we buy a slick new mobile phone we may be indirectly funding ongoing warfare in Africa. Electronic gadgets like mobile phones require inputs of rare minerals—gold, as part of the wiring; tantalum, for electrical storage; tin, as a solder on circuit boards; and tungsten, for the vibration function on cell phones.[6] These minerals are called "conflict minerals." Why? Because they are often sourced from the eastern Congo, where most of the mines are operated by rebel and militia groups. These groups make millions of dollars by illegally exporting the minerals through eastern Africa to regions like East Asia for processing and entry into the global market.

The millions made in the eastern Congo largely go into funding armed forces and militia groups such as the Democratic Forces for the Liberation of Rwanda (FDLR), a Hutu militia that is intent on continuing to wage war against the Tutsi-led government in neighboring Rwanda. The almost two-decades-long conflict between extremist Hutu and Tutsi and between the Democratic Republic of Congo and Rwanda has led to the deaths of more than five million people—the greatest number of people who have died in war since World War II. And the violence and trauma continue in this region, which has been called "the rape capital of the world."[7] As long as it can make millions from the illegal sale of minerals, the militia will be well armed and able to operate with relative impunity.

When the FDLR come to a mine, the first thing they do is get the girls and abuse them. Then they force many people to work and kill those who don't want to work.

Jacques, former militia commander, Nyangezi, South Kivu, eastern Congo

In the figure of the Mobile Phone Supply Chain, we show the supply chain for a mobile phone for just the 3Ts (as they are called)—tantalum, tin, and tungsten.[8] From the mines in the eastern Congo the minerals are transported to trading houses close to the borders of Burundi and Rwanda. The minerals are then bought by exporters, who ship some of the minerals legally (with taxes paid to the Congolese government) but ship most illegally across the borders into neighboring countries. From there the minerals enter the global supply chain, where they are bought by foreign buyers from countries like Belgium and Malaysia. They are refined in different parts of the globe, and then they are sold to circuit board manufacturers and finally to the mobile phone manufacturers. The journey from the mine to the mobile is only one small part of the overall process of building a mobile phone—it's a complicated process that links us to people in unexpected places (and we haven't even considered what happens on the journey from the manufacturer to the end consumer).[9]

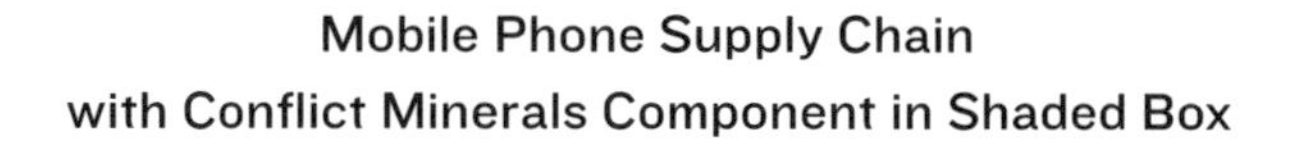
Mobile Phone Supply Chain
with Conflict Minerals Component in Shaded Box

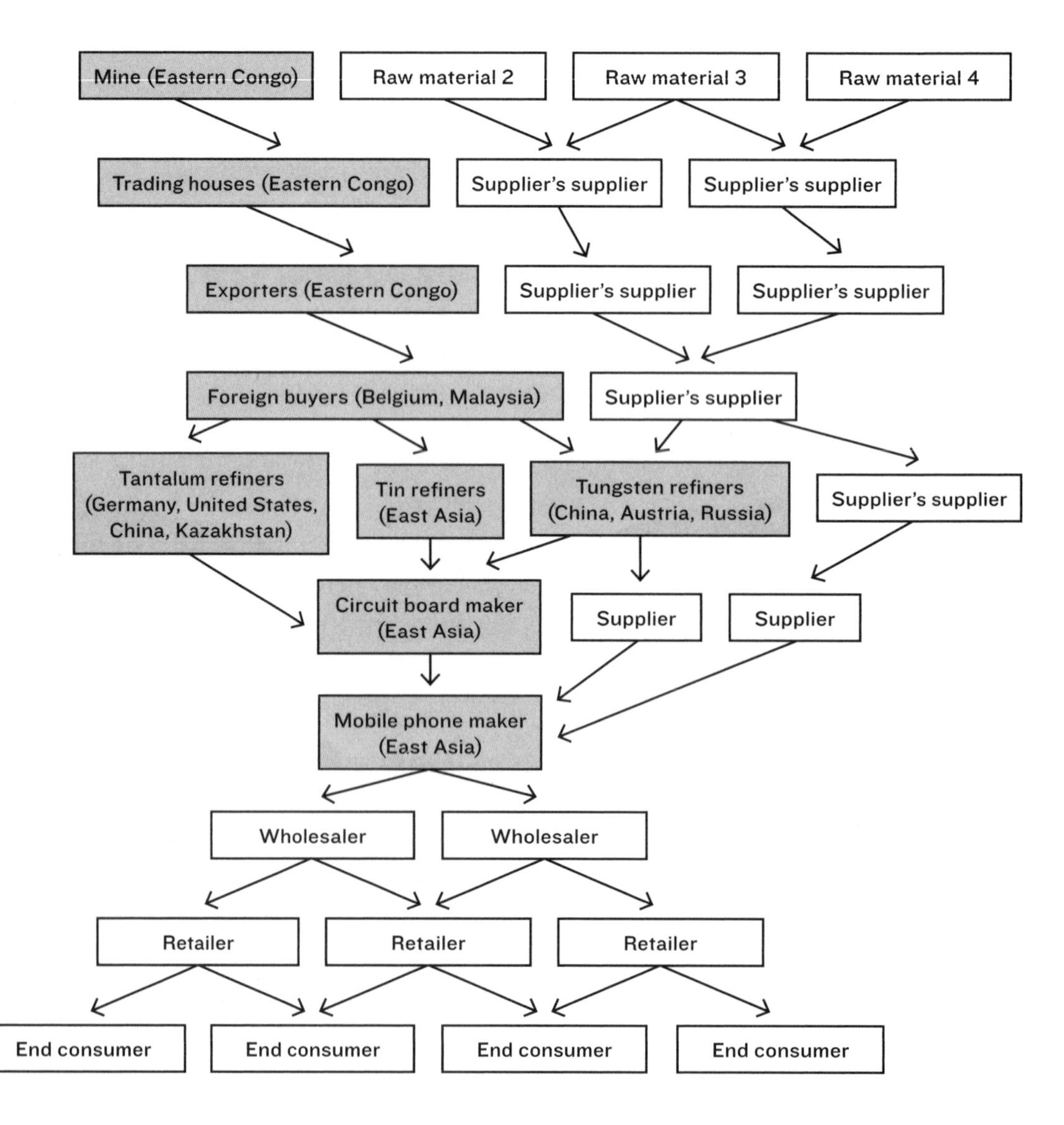
Mine (Eastern Congo)
Raw material 2
Raw material 3
Raw material 4
Trading houses (Eastern Congo)
Supplier's supplier
Supplier's supplier
Exporters (Eastern Congo)
Supplier's supplier
Supplier's supplier
Foreign buyers (Belgium, Malaysia)
Supplier's supplier
Tantalum refiners (Germany, United States, China, Kazakhstan)
Tin refiners (East Asia)
Tungsten refiners (China, Austria, Russia)
Supplier's supplier
Circuit board maker (East Asia)
Supplier
Supplier
Mobile phone maker (East Asia)
Wholesaler
Wholesaler
Retailer
Retailer
Retailer
End consumer
End consumer
End consumer
End consumer

This example shows how the market supply chain provides anonymity. With each stage we are one step removed from the acts of blood and violence that are all part of that shiny new mobile phone. Apart from not buying a new mobile phone, it might seem that there is little that we can do. But change is afoot, with a range of actors working on initiatives to stem the flow of conflict minerals into the electronics industry. Efforts include a UN resolution calling on industry and government to take steps to keep conflict minerals out of the supply chain and voluntary industry programs such as the joint Electronic Industry Citizenship Coalition® (EICC) and the Global e-Sustainability Initiative's (GeSI's) program to assess the sources of minerals that are being refined by the smelters in the supply chain. There is also the Enough Project's system of rating how well electronics companies are addressing the issue of conflict minerals—and of course we can use this information as consumers when we're deciding on an electronics product.[10] These initiatives to keep conflict minerals out of the supply chain have been motivated by the Kimberley Process, an international certification program launched in 2003 to keep "blood diamonds" or "conflict diamonds" from entering the global diamond supply chain. Like the initiatives on conflict minerals, the Kimberley Process came about through the combined efforts of government, industry, and nongovernmental organizations.[11]

We know that initiatives such as those on conflict minerals that might start with just a small group of concerned actors can be the basis for change in mainstream market practices. For example, as of 1 January 2012 the European Union banned the use of battery cages for egg-laying hens. This was the culmination of a long political struggle that was started in the 1960s by campaigners who were concerned with the inhumane nature of "factory farming." Over the years, what was once seen as an acceptable and efficient farming practice has been reframed as cruel and unwarranted. Ethical concerns about the interconnections between human and nonhuman species have come to the fore, and market practices have been reshaped through the use of regulation.

This example reminds us that the markets supplying goods and services so critical to our surviving well *can* be regulated to take account of our interconnections with distant others and those "shadow places" that support our lives.[12] Such regulation will help to realize the Ethical Shopper's Checklist we introduced earlier.

Many of the goods (and increasingly services such as accounting) that crisscross the planet are regulated by agreements that elected governments negotiate on our behalf through the World Trade Organization (WTO). The prevailing wisdom at this level of interaction is that the freer the trade, the better for all. Is this always the case, though?

Let's look at one example that illustrates the complex geopolitics that lies behind a simple transaction like buying a banana. In the 1970s, countries in the European Community acted on a sense of responsibility to their former colonies in Africa, the Caribbean, and the Pacific. They signed the Lomé Convention, an agreement that gave products from these former colonies free entry to European markets. Bananas were one product governed by the Convention.

Many people applauded our youthful idealism but told us that we had no hope of ever changing a major industry. They were wrong.

Peter Singer,
Europe's Ethical Eggs-ample

This would seem to be in line with the philosophy of the WTO, which promotes the removal of tariffs because government taxes on imported goods are seen as interfering with the operation of the free market and disadvantaging the consumer by adding an extra cost. But the WTO did not approve of what European countries were doing. Why? Because at the same time that bananas from the former colonies had free access to European markets, bananas from other parts of the world, chiefly Latin America, had a tariff, an extra cost, placed on them.

Why would European countries give preferential treatment to products from one part of the world and not another? Bananas from Latin America are cheap. They are grown on large-scale plantations that are owned by multinational corporations like Chiquita, Dole, and Del Monte. These plantations are highly mechanized, so the labor costs are relatively minimal. In contrast, bananas from the former colonies are more expensive because they are grown on small, family-based farms where production is labor intensive. Many of these farms are run by women who are the descendants of slaves. European countries wanted the bananas from these farms—from the people whose daily lives are bound up with the legacy of colonization—to be able to compete with the bananas from the Latin American plantations. So they placed a tariff on bananas from Latin America.

In 1996 the United States, backed by U.S.-based banana corporations and supported by Latin American countries such as Ecuador, complained to the WTO that Latin American bananas were being discriminated against.[13] In 2009, after a protracted "banana war" waged through the legal minutiae of the WTO, an agreement was reached. European countries were required to reduce the tariffs on Latin American bananas.

For the European consumer this was great news. Even cheaper bananas! For the major corporations that have plantations in Latin America, it was great news, too. Their cheap bananas now have unimpeded access to European markets. Without doubt the three largest banana corporations (Chiquita, Dole, and Del Monte) will increase their market share—currently at around 70 percent of the global trade in bananas.[14] Shareholders can expect the dividends to flow.

For the smallholder banana growers in the Caribbean (and those in African and Pacific countries who are also impacted), the WTO agreement was not such great news. A former trade negotiator for the Caribbean, Sir Ronald Sanders, predicts that the region's banana growers will be "wiped out of that market."[15]

The WTO agreement focuses on a narrow set of concerns—the marketplace relationships between sellers and buyers. The agreement discounts a wider set of concerns about the human impacts of different forms of production. It also erases the environmental costs that go with the high use of fertilizers, pesticides, and fungicides on large-scale plantations. The agreement erases the ways our economic transactions connect us with others and with our living environment.

This nonsense of "cheap" bananas. Someone has to pay up front. They have to pay in blood or in terms of poverty. Because the person who comes and works for you for less than a U.S. dollar a day, he is giving you his wealth. He is giving you the wealth of his children.

Lesley Grant, National Banana Growers Association in Saint Vincent and the Grenadines

Behind the price of any product can be a whole history and politics of international relations that is hard to fathom. If we are to take back

A PEOPLE'S TRADE POLICY

1. **A guaranteed minimum price**

   For products that are labeled as fair trade there's a guaranteed minimum price that is paid to farmers. The fair-trade minimum price is enough for farmers to make a living. Currently the guaranteed minimum price for fair-trade coffee is between US$1.01 and US$1.45 per pound, depending on the type of coffee. If the price of conventional coffee goes above the guaranteed minimum, the price for fair-trade coffee also goes up, but it never drops below the guaranteed minimum. The pricing arrangement for conventional coffee is very different. Over the past twenty years or so, the price of conventional coffee has yo-yoed between US$0.45 and $2.00 per pound. When the prices are low, farmers' survival is jeopardized; and when the prices bounce around, farmers cannot easily plan for future crops. Fair trade removes the uncertainty and guarantees farmers their livelihoods.

2. **A fair trade premium**

   Fair-trade farmers also receive an extra payment to help support their environment and communities. The fair-trade premium for coffee is currently US$0.10 per pound (or US$0.20 per pound for organic coffee). The premium is paid to the cooperatives of fair-trade farmers. The farmers who are members of the cooperatives decide how the premium will be spent, and it's usually spent on village projects such as health clinics, schools, and basic infrastructure such as roads and water supply systems. The cooperatives also deal directly with the importers of their produce, and this removes the layers of middlemen (also known as "coyotes"), who are merciless in their "negotiations" with individual farmers, particularly those who live in remote areas and have limited access to credit, transportation for their crops, and information.

Source: Ellen Pay, "The Market for Organic and Fair Trade Coffee," study prepared in the framework of FAO project GCP/RAF/404/GER (Food and Agricultural Organisation, Rome, 2009).

the economy for people and the planet, we must look into ways of making our encounters with distant others less indirect.

As the story at the beginning of this chapter shows, Japanese consumers have organized a way to encounter distant others by establishing people-to-people connections across national divides. The alternative trading network set up by Alter Trade Japan Inc. involves a more direct supply chain that allows for Philippines bananas to reach Japanese consumers at prices that sustain poor farmers. Consumers are no longer positioned in a "democracy" where they vote to drive the price down as low as it can go and where their freedom of choice is bought at the expense of producers who are slaves to the market. Alternative trade networks enroll consumers and producers in a new international community in which an ethic of care for distant others is built into the pricing mechanism.

Over recent years, there has been a rapid expansion of alternative trade networks in the form of fair trade. International certification bodies such as Fairtrade International (FLO) have developed fair pricing mechanisms that take into account the well-being of the producers. In place of the free-trade policies of entities like the WTO, fair-trade organizations offer a people's trade policy that has two pricing components—a guaranteed minimum price and a fair-trade premium (as we discuss in terms of coffee in the nearby figure).

For consumers in Europe who are concerned about the human impacts of the banana wars on the well-being of people in their former colonies and the environmental impacts of large-scale production, there is a fair-trade alternative. In some Caribbean, African, and Pacific Island nations affected by the banana wars, farmers have joined together to become fair-trade producers. And retailers and consumers in European countries like the United Kingdom are supporting these producers. Around one-fourth of all bananas purchased in the United Kingdom are fair-trade bananas (while in Switzerland over one-half of bananas are fair trade).[16]

A community economy is a space of decision making in which we negotiate our interdependence with other humans, other species, and our environment. These negotiations are never finalized. Building community economies is an ongoing project. We see this in the alter- and fair-trade arena. For example, one of the products that Alter Trade Japan trades is eco-shrimps, but some organizations are concerned about the social and environmental impacts of the extensive farming methods that are used.[17] Likewise there

Fairtrade has saved the Islands. Without it we would be in desperate trouble.

Cornelius Lynch, secretary of the Fairtrade Committee, St. Lucia are concerns about some aspects of fair and organic trade between the majority and minority worlds. For example, there are concerns that the certification process prioritizes the interests of minority-world consumers over the reality of production in majority-world contexts.[18] Of course this does not mean that we should avoid alter- and fair-trade products. Rather, it highlights that we need to be vigilant and continuously review what goes into our shopping baskets. Yes, this may cost us time (although this type of information is increasingly readily available via Internet searches). But perhaps we need to weigh this cost against the global cost of not doing so.

Our encounters with distant others via the market can enable livelihoods to flourish around the world if we attend to more than our own needs in our trade transactions. Markets *can* be a space of care as well as of consumption. As we become more attuned to how our actions as consumers affect the ability of others to survive well, the market becomes less a space of enchantment and unbridled pleasure and more a space of learning and collective responsibility.

If we can acknowledge the distant others that we encounter indirectly through our transactions, we might start to feel that we are encountering them more face-to-face. Perhaps before we make our next purchase we might take a moment to pause and consider the people and planet connections involved in the transaction. Perhaps if we can start to "see" distant others more clearly, it will change not just what but how much we consume. And to meet this challenge of living well together we might explore other ways of meeting our needs, ways that involve more direct forms of encounter. This is another concern of a community economy.

ENCOUNTERING OTHERS DIRECTLY: ANOTHER KEY CONCERN OF A COMMUNITY ECONOMY

When we look at how people survive well together we find that our quality of life is mainly provided by encounters that do not involve money or calculations of price. We rely on others close by to provide care for us, intensively at the beginning and end of our lives and less demandingly throughout life. These encounters are guided by obligations and rules (often unstated) that embody relations of care for each other. We "see" each other face to face and in the process negotiate the fine balance between need and satisfaction of need—the nonmarket equivalents of demand and supply.

The transactions or exchanges that involve encounters with others close by take two overarching forms: transactions that are reciprocal and those that are gift based. There is, of course, a fuzzy distinction between reciprocal and gift transactions. Perhaps the most famous writer on the gift, Marcel Mauss, is credited with saying that gifts *are* reciprocal, because there is always an expectation that the gift will be repaid (even if at some unspecified time in the future). We distinguish between the two by saying that reciprocal transactions involve equivalences that are negotiated between those involved, whereas gift transactions are more open-ended—if there is a "return," it can take a very different and even unexpected form than the original gift and can involve a quite different time frame than the immediate time frame in which we've come to expect transactions to occur.

We can illustrate these two forms of direct connection through the transactions that take place in households. Generally we don't think of the household as a transaction site, but everyday material and emotional exchanges take place that connect us deeply with each other and our environment. Meals are produced; gardens are nurtured; clothes are washed; homes are maintained, cleaned, decorated, and made comfortable; children are cared for; household accounts are kept; and the list goes on.

Reciprocal transactions involve negotiated equivalences. There might be an arrangement in which one household member prepares three evening meals a week and one weekend lunch and another household member prepares four evening meals a week. In another arrangement a wife might clean the inside of the windows and a husband the outside.

In gift transactions things are more open. For example, the gift may be the unexpected delight that comes when a young teenager takes the washing off the outdoor clothesline—perhaps because he wants to ask for a loan or simply because he saw that rain was on the way. The gift has an element of unpredictability. There is no guarantee that the gift will be returned, and there is no guarantee that it will be returned in the expected form. Parents, for example, care for and support their children—perhaps hoping that the gift will be returned in their old age, or perhaps because they delight in the immediate pleasure of seeing their offspring develop and thrive. Either way, the outcome and the "return" of the gift are indeterminate.

Both types of direct connection involve complicated and even contradictory feelings for self and others. Care and concern for others become entangled with feelings of indebtedness and obligation. Indeed, Ralph Waldo Emerson noted that gifts "invade our privacy and demolish our carefully constructed autonomy."[19]

A calculation of sorts may well be at work in these transactions. Such calculations are an important and explicit part of negotiating direct reciprocal relationships with others, but the calculations are very different from familiar market judgments. Let's look at two examples to see how this works, the first in the United States and the second in Japan.

In Portland, Maine, a time bank and a health-care center were concerned that low-income people could not access quality health-care services.[20] They developed a way to connect low-income groups to health-care services. Hour Exchange Portland is a nonprofit time bank in which everyone's labor is valued the same. Members of the bank offer their services to other members. Paola, for example, spends three hours translating a policy statement from English into Spanish for a local legal service that is a member of the time bank. The three hours of time are credited to her account. She then spends two hours of her credit having Petra clean her windows and one hour having Pauline walk her dog. In turn, two hours of credit are added to Petra's account and one hour to Pauline's.

Low-income members of Home Exchange Portland can use their credit to see medical practitioners at True North, a nonprofit health-care center. A doctor sees a patient for a one-hour appointment and earns one hour of credit that she can spend on any of the services members offer through the time bank. A one-hour medical appointment earns *the same amount of credit* as one hour of elder care or mechanical work or cleaning or teaching a painting class.

In Japan, a similar time-banking system has been developed specifically to provide in-home care for elderly and disabled people. The system is called Fureai Kippu, or caring relationship tickets, and it is a way of connecting people who can provide care with those who need care. Anyone can earn Fureai Kippu by helping to care for an elderly or disabled person. Tasks such as shopping or reading are valued at 1 Fureai Kippu for each hour of service; tasks associated with bodily care such as helping with bathing are valued at 2 Fureai Kippu for each hour of service. People who earn Fureai Kippu can save them for their own use in the future or transfer them to someone else, say an elderly parent who lives in another part of the country. Fureai Kippu emerged in 1995 after the devastating Kobe earthquake when the government was overstretched and could not help meet people's needs. Since then, Fureai Kippu has spread across Japan and into China.

The reciprocal transactions in these two examples involve face-to-face connection between members and the use of a time-bank system to track the hours of labor that members contribute and use. As part of the reciprocal relationship, the value of members' time has been negotiated and agreed. In Hour Exchange Portland all labor is given the same value (reflecting a commitment to equality in all forms of work), whereas in Fureai Kippu the two different types of labor are valued differently (with the work involved in intimate bodily care given special recognition).

Reciprocal transactions can also take place in ways that acknowledge the needs of the planet and its human stewards to flourish. Community-supported agriculture (CSA) is based on an ethic of care and concern for the environment and for people who support our most immediate needs for nutritious food. CSA was developed in Japan in the 1970s and has since spread across the minority world and is starting to be adopted in the majority world.

CSA is based on a reciprocal relationship between rural producers and urban consumers. Consumers provide a guaranteed market and income for the farmers, and the farmers reciprocate with fresh produce to meet the needs of the consumers. In a classic CSA scheme, a group of consumers sign up with a single farm and pay the farmer in advance

> **We ask our farmers the price that they need to continue farming sustainably, in a way that ensures the health of their land and their future on the land.**
>
> **Food Connect Brisbane**

for a share of the farm's produce. This means that the farmer has money when she needs it—at the start of the growing season when purchasing inputs. It also means that producers and consumers share the risk of farming—if it's a good growing season, consumers will receive larger shares of produce, but if it's a poor season, shares will be smaller.

Determining the value of a farm share involves a negotiated calculation between producer and consumer—how much does the farmer need to grow the produce, and how much can the consumer pay for a share? But there are other less tangible calculations based on trust between producer and consumer. The consumer trusts the farmer to provide him with a regular (usually weekly) supply of quality and varied produce; the farmer trusts that the consumer will come back each season or each year so she can adapt her farming practices to suit the CSA model.

There are also calculations between the farmer and the environment. The farmer has to calculate the health of the soil and the types of inputs (usually organic) needed in order to produce for the consumers. The farmer trusts that if the soil and all the species that it hosts are well treated they will reciprocate by supporting abundance. In return the farmer agrees not to place too high a demand on the giving earth.

One of the concerns about CSA is that it potentially excludes low-income groups because a lump sum is paid up front. Many CSA initiatives have developed strategies to address this concern. In some CSA schemes, low-income members can pay in installments. The total of the installments is more than the season subscription, and this means that low-income members end up with a sum of money set aside for the next season's payment. Other strategies are for higher-income members to pay more in order to subsidize lower-income members, for low-income members to earn credits toward their subscription by working on the farm, and for all members to carry out volunteer work to keep the cost down for everyone.[21]

Gift giving is the other major form of direct connection between people and between people and environments that provides well-being and helps us all to survive well. All over the world, people gift their labor to others as volunteers and give away their money and possessions.

One of Marcel Mauss's observations was that there is no such thing as a "free gift"—all gifts carry some expectation of a return. This was because Mauss, as an anthropologist, was interested in the ways that gifts build societal relationships. Even in the minority world today, gifting usually involves unsaid but socially agreed protocols and obligations, whether offering someone a lift in one's car or wrapping and giving a wedding present, whether volunteering for the beach patrol at the local surf club or serving meals at a Thanksgiving dinner for the homeless, whether giving money to save endangered species or to fund cancer research. Gifting, then, like reciprocal and market transactions, involves negotiation with others. In reciprocal transactions, generally the negotiation is direct, between those involved; in market transactions, the price is the means of negotiation (and we are arguing that this negotiation can include ethical matters); in gift transactions, the negotiation generally involves an internal dialogue about our own interests and desires and societal expectations.

The more I give to thee, the more I have.

Juliet, *Romeo and Juliet*, act 2, scene 2

Societal expectations around gift giving can even be enshrined in legislation. Today, in many countries gifts of money to not-for-profit organizations for benevolent ends can be claimed as tax deductions. Historically, many countries protected gleaning—the practice of allowing whatever was left over after the harvest to be gathered by or for the poor.[22] This transaction involved landowners recognizing the survival needs of those who could not access their own land or were too frail to participate in harvest labor and obtain their share as payment. In the latter half of the eighteenth century in England, as the Industrial Revolution began, it is estimated that one-eighth of the annual household earnings of laboring people was gained from gleaning, and the proportion was even higher for families of widows.

To be human for us is to be able to give, is to be able to recognize each other as human beings.

Coumba Toure on *dama* (the gift economy) in Mali, in *Reclaiming the Gift Culture*

Today the practice of gleaning has taken on new meaning. In the concrete jungle of Los Angeles, urban fruit-tree gleaning is being

Fallen Fruit's Rules for Urban Gleaning

Take only what you need.
Say "Hi" to strangers.
Share your food.
Take a friend.
Go by foot.

promoted as a new practice that connects people to each other and to their environment. Groups such as Fallen Fruit use wonderfully simple but colorful maps to publicize where to find the unexpected gifts from fruit trees that are growing along streets, in public parks, and around parking lots. The group provides explicit rules for gleaning that honor the needs of others (not just other people but the fruit trees themselves and nonhuman gleaners, such as birds).

In direct connections, whether through reciprocal or gift transactions, there is a governing ethic of taking only what we need and contributing or returning what we can. It seems that when needs are met directly there is less call for excessive consumption, for taking more than we need. When we encounter the other that is satisfying our need directly, is there a recognition of the other's need alongside our own? Could this offer a negative feedback response that tempers our appetite?

TOOLS FOR ENCOUNTERING OTHERS

Taking back markets for people and the planet means recognizing the variety of ways that we transact goods and services. There is a dominant conception that markets are the most efficient and equitable mechanism for securing what we need from others. Certainly markets are critical, especially in today's interconnected world. But there are other ways of transacting for goods and services that build connections and meet more than our own material needs.

In this chapter we have touched on some of the diverse kinds of transactions that people are using—alternative market transactions such as direct trade and fair trade, reciprocal exchange and community supported agriculture, as well as nonmarket transactions such as gift giving and gleaning. The Diverse Transactions Identifier can be used to distinguish these different kinds of exchanges. The identifier also includes a wider range of transactions than we have discussed. With each of these transactions we need to inquire into the type of encounter that is being fostered.

In a community economy we are interested in how various needs are met in the process of transacting for goods and services. More direct transactions enable us to encounter and care for the people and places that are helping us to survive well. It can, however, be difficult to consider the needs of others in our transactions. For example, we've seen how the supply chain can involve multiple steps, with each step in the process obscuring the previous step and further disconnecting us from humans and the environment that is providing for us.

Today it is just about impossible to survive only on the basis of direct connections in which we have a face-to-face relationship with others. And it can take time we don't have to participate in direct transactions such as reciprocation or gift giving. The supermarket and shopping mall are convenient. But convenience is a form of "selective seeing" whereby we choose to overlook the cost of our transactions to others. And when we consider the multiple aspects of well-being introduced in chapter 2, we're reminded that convenience can also come at a cost to our own well-being.

DIVERSE TRANSACTIONS IDENTIFIER
MARKET
ALTERNATIVE MARKET Fair trade and direct trade Reciprocal exchange Alternative currency Local trading system Community-supported agriculture Barter Underground market Informal market
NONMARKET Household flows Gift giving Gleaning State allocations Hunting, fishing, gathering Theft, poaching

Perhaps in a community economy we can experiment with increasing our direct connections through alternative and nonmarket transactions. We can shift to market transactions in which impacts and relationships are more visible or cut back on our market relationships if the face of the human or earth other is obscured.

Using the Ethical Interconnection Checklist to help navigate the various exchanges on which we rely, we can inquire into the ways in which our diverse transactions connect us with each other and with the planet. We can start to build new habits of encounter.

ETHICAL INTERCONNECTION CHECKLIST		
THE ETHICAL CONCERN	THE ETHICAL QUESTIONS	THE PEOPLE AND PLANET CONNECTIONS
☐ Are both my needs and the needs of others being met?	☐ Am I connecting with others more directly? ☐ Am I taking only what I need? ☐ Are there ways I can give back to help others meet their needs? ☐ Are there other ways I can share or reciprocate?	**Animals** ☐ Are animals treated humanely? **Environment** ☐ Are the environmental impacts of production addressed? **People** ☐ Is well-being taken into account? **Politics** ☐ Are the politics just? **Sustainability** ☐ Does the product have a neutral or positive impact?

COLLECTIVE ACTIONS FOR ENCOUNTERING OTHERS

In a community economy we take ethical action by considering the well-being of others in encounters that meet our needs.

Others have gone down this pathway, and they have met the challenges. We can look to their collective actions for guidance on how we might ethically encounter others through our transactions.

Supporting Ethical Markets

Across the globe, people are finding ways to make markets work more ethically. This means shifting to market transactions in which there are more direct connections with the others who are helping to meet our needs. In terms of the supply chain, this can mean reducing the number of steps from raw material to end consumer (as fair trade does, for ex-

Questions to consider as you read about these collective actions

- Whose needs are being met?
- How are the needs of others (human and nonhuman) being considered?
- Are familiar patterns of consumption being tempered and adjusted? In what ways?
- What types of encounters are being fostered?
- What boxes are being checked in the ethical interconnection checklist?

ample), or it can mean finding out more information about all those involved in each step of the supply chain—and acting on that information.

ETHICAL ACTION: *Supporting markets in which the well-being of others is built into the encounter*

Expanding Fair-Trade Networks

Fair trade is an overarching term for a range of alternative transaction practices that shorten the supply chain and provide a fairer deal for producers. The most common fair-trade products are those that have been certified by international bodies such as FLO. The range of products now certified as fair trade is increasing, including everything from cotton and flowers to olive oil and rice. Increasingly, these products are available on the shelves of mainstream supermarkets.

Some fair-trade organizations are also finding ways for producers and consumers to have more direct contact. For example, in the United Kingdom Pa Pa Paa LIVE! uses the Internet to put the children of cocoa farmers in Ghana in direct contact with children in U.K. classrooms. This initiative is based on a partnership between Comic Relief (a U.K. charity set up by comedians), Trading Visions (a fair-trade educational organization), Kuapa Kokoo (a cooperative of more than 45,000 cocoa farmers in Ghana), and Divine Chocolate (a U.K.-based fair-trade chocolate company partly owned by Kuapa Kokoo).

Fair trade can also include direct-trade networks such as Alter Trade Japan Inc. These networks source produce directly from producers. Direct trade is most common in coffee, with coffee roasters in the minority world forming direct-trade relationships with coffee producers in countries like Nicaragua, Ethiopia, Indonesia, Papua New Guinea, and East Timor. For example, Intelligentsia Coffee, which is based in Chicago, Los Angeles, and New York, sources coffee from across the globe. The company's policies include paying growers 25 percent more than the international fair-trade price and sourcing only from farmers or cooperatives engaging in sound environmental and social practices.

Equal Exchange in the United States started in the mid-1980s with fairly traded coffee grown by small-scale farmers in Nicaragua. From its small beginnings, Equal Exchange has now grown large and trades in a range of products (including bananas), and in 2011 it achieved annual sales of nearly US$47 million. Equal Exchange trades with small farmer cooperatives; in keeping with this ethos, Equal Exchange is also a worker-run cooperative, with over one hundred worker-owners. As discussed in the previous chapter, this means that the workers are the owners of the enterprise and democratically make decisions about how the enterprise operates.

> **Fairness to farmers. A closer connection between people and the farmers we all rely on.**
>
> Equal Exchange motto

More informal fair-trade networks can develop through personal connections. Las Cruces-Chiapas Connection sells weavings from Mayan women's cooperatives in Chiapas, Mexico. From an initial stall at a U.S. farmers' market in Las Cruces, the Connection has expanded to the point that its products are now available online. It uses volunteer labor (including the volunteer labor of a U.S. university-based anthropologist who initiated the scheme). The money from sales goes back to the Mayan women's cooperatives. This operation helps members to survive well, earn a living on their own land, and maintain their cultural practices. The Connection also provides scholarships for schoolchildren and grants for women and children to study weaving designs.

Joining or Starting a Consumer Cooperative

A consumer cooperative is a group of consumers who join together to multiply their buying power. Some consumer cooperatives focus on getting the best prices they can for the products they want, but most have a strong ethical commitment to getting a fair deal for both producers and consumers. We started this chapter by discussing Alter Trade Japan Inc., an organization that acts as a broker between consumer cooperatives in Japan and producers in other parts of the world, making sure that the cooperatives are getting produce that is ethically produced and that producers are getting a fair price (and environments a fair deal).

The Co-operative Group in the United Kingdom is owned by over six million consumers, but it has its roots in The Co-operative, formed in 1844 by a small group of weavers and their supporters in Rochdale, northern England. It is the United Kingdom's fifth-largest food retailer, but it also has convenience stores, pharmacies, banking and insurance services, funeral services, and clothing and electrical goods labels. Because it is a cooperative, consumer-members are involved in making decisions about how the cooperative operates. One of the concerns of consumer-members is that along with meeting their needs, the cooperative should also meet the needs of its suppliers and producers—and the environment that supports them. As a result, the cooperative has developed an ethical operating plan and an impressive list of initiatives, which range from programs to support bees and other essential pollinators to programs that reuse and recycle mobile phones (with enough funds raised to support Oxfam's HIV and AIDS projects in Malawi for twelve months). As we might expect, fair trade and animal welfare are central to the cooperative's ethical policy.

In the previous chapter we discussed worker cooperatives. Sometimes smaller consumer cooperatives are also worker cooperatives, with the workers also serving as consumer-members. Larger consumer cooperatives tend to employ staff to run the operations, while the consumer-members make decisions about how the enterprises should operate.

Supporting Buy-Local Campaigns

In cities and towns across the minority world there is considerable interest in buy-local campaigns. Usually these involve independent, locally owned businesses getting together to promote what they do and to help support each other. Often this is in response to a large chain or big-box store's move into an area. The argument is that local businesses should be supported because they have a direct connection to the cities and towns they call home and they put more money back into their home places. Civic Economics has shown that this is indeed the case.[23] For every $100 spent at a locally owned business, $68 stays in the area, while $32 leaves, whereas for every $100 spent at a non-locally-owned business, $43 stays and $57 leaves.

In the United States, two main organizations help towns and cities with their buy-local campaigns—the American Independent Business Alliance and the Business Alliance for Local Living Economies.

In recent years, localism has featured in discussions of food. People talk of the hundred- or fifty-mile diet and of the number of food miles that produce has traveled to get to their tables. The concept is that if food is transported over shorter distances, fewer greenhouse gases will be emitted into the atmosphere. But we have to be careful. The amount of gases can depend on the type of transport used. Planes carrying perishable produce like fresh seafood or flowers emit considerably more greenhouse gas emissions (GGEs) than ships carrying stored apples or onions. It also depends on the type of fuel used (e.g., petrol versus diesel). Researchers are also finding that how the food is produced, stored, packaged, and even disposed of is critical. And, after all that, it turns out that the greatest impact on GGEs may come from food-related energy use in the consumer's home, from things like the energy efficiency of the refrigerator used for storage or the source of energy used for cooking.[24] If we want to buy local food to support local farmers, food miles are a good indicator of how local the farmers are. But food miles are an unreliable indicator of the GGEs related to the food we consume.

A series of studies have addressed the issue of food miles by examining the quantity of GGEs produced by apples imported into the United Kingdom from New Zealand compared to locally grown U.K. apples.[25] Overall, the research has found that there are probably fewer GGEs from locally grown U.K. apples eaten fresh or stored for no more than four months. But once apples have been stored for longer, it's likely that there are fewer GGEs from apples imported from New Zealand. The GGEs produced by transportation to the United Kingdom will be offset by the shorter shortage time (New Zealand apples come into season six months after U.K. apples) and the efficiencies in production that New Zealand apple farmers have achieved.

Promoting Ethical Consumer Guides

As discussed already, ethical consumer guides are readily available, and they can give us information about the ethics of the products on supermarket shelves and the companies that produce them. Based on information in these guides, we might decide to switch to companies that are more ethical and to products that are more ethically produced or to avoid some products altogether.

On its Web site, the Ethical Consumer Group provides all the information that a group of friends or a family needs for a self-guided supermarket tour to find out more about the products they purchase and their effects on people and the environment. The group also suggests that instead of selling chocolates for school fund-raisers, groups sell the ethical consumer guide.

Supporting New Markets

New markets are being developed to address climate change. Carbon offsets that can be purchased as part of an airline ticket are one way of acknowledging the impact of our travel on the environment and paying for an activity that will compensate for our impact (say, tree planting). "Cap-and-trade" markets operate at a national level, with a cap (or ceiling) placed on the level of greenhouse gases that can be emitted nationally. Permits to the level of the cap are put on the market, and polluters have to buy permits to cover their GGEs. Over time, the cap is reduced, and the shrinking supply of permits drives up the price that polluters pay, thereby encouraging them to reduce their GGEs—say, by introducing new technologies.

Cap-and-trade schemes are highly contentious, particularly because of concerns that the cost for the polluter is passed on to the consumer. One alternative is "cap-and-dividend" schemes in which the money raised by selling off permits is passed on to consumers as a monthly or annual dividend.[26] Even though all consumers receive the same dividend, the argument is that this benefits low-income households more because they spend less on energy requirements.

Preventing Trade Based on Violent Regimes and Inhumane Practices

Sometimes the conditions under which products are produced mean that they should not be bought. An early example of a boycott dates from the 1790s, when the Anti-Saccharine Society organized a boycott of sugar as a way of protesting against slavery (which the sugar industry in places like the Caribbean relied on).[27] Campaigns have continued to boycott products and companies involved in the worst forms of people and planet abuses—and they have helped to generate social change. The Boycott Movement was initiated in the United Kingdom in 1959 to refuse to buy goods imported from South Africa (such as fruit and tobacco). Within a short period of time, the Boycott Movement had become the much broader Anti-Apartheid Movement.[28] More recently, boycotts have been put in place on products and companies that include bluefin tuna (because of its status as an endangered species), Nestlé products (because of concerns that Nestlé's marketing of baby formula infringes the International Code of Marketing of Breastmilk Substitutes), battery-hen eggs (because of the inhumane conditions in which the hens live and die), and L'Oreal (because of continued animal testing of cosmetics). An Internet search for "consumer boycotts" for your country or region will give you details of current boycotts.

We are not being called upon to make much of a sacrifice. We are not being called upon to go hungry and court imprisonment. That is the lot of our brothers and sisters inside South Africa. We are being asked to substitute other goods for South African goods.

Julius Nyerere (first prime minister and president of Tanzania, 1961–1985), "On the Boycott of South Africa," 1959

Expanding Ethical Reciprocity

Reciprocal transactions involve direct contact and negotiation between the parties involved. These can include the humans and nonhumans who are helping to provide for our needs. Reciprocity means that we are more likely to take their needs into account.

ETHICAL ACTION: *Developing more ways of reciprocating to meet our needs and the needs of others*

Community-Supported Organizations

We've seen how community-supported agriculture (CSA) involves direct and negotiated connections between producer and consumer and between producer and earth provider. The model has met with such success that it is now being replicated across different food sectors.

Inspired by Port Clyde Fresh Catch, there are now more than seventy community-supported fisheries (CSFs) in the United States. Subscribers sign up in advance for a share of a catch. As well as guaranteeing that fishers receive a fair price for the catch, CSFs encourage fishers to fish sustainably and be good stewards of the ocean's resources.[29]

Meat and egg CSAs such as Stillman's in Massachusetts or Yeehaw Farm in Pennsylvania particularly respond to the environmental and humanitarian concerns that have been raised about the treatment of animals in confined feedlot-style operations.[30]

To bring agriculture into cities, there are several neighborhood or urban CSAs in which urban farmers grow produce on vacant city blocks, in backyards, and in schoolyards—anywhere a few plants will flourish. Fresh Roots Urban CSA in East Vancouver even delivers produce to subscribers by bicycle-trailer.[31]

Community Supported Coffee is a new initiative created by Pachamama Coffee Cooperative, an international farmer-owned cooperative that is based in California and made up of around 140,000 small-scale coffee farmers from Peru, Nicaragua, Guatemala, Mexico, and Ethiopia.[32] Consumers prepay for a one- to twelve-month subscription to one farmer's coffee that is delivered monthly. This helps farmers plan their growing season with certainty.

In grain and legume CSAs consumers pay for a share of the crop before it is planted. This guarantees that farmers receive a fair price in advance and that they have an income while the crop is growing. Usually the produce is delivered only once, at harvest time, and consumers take their grain to commercial millers or mill it themselves. The first grain CSA in Canada, the Kootenay Grain CSA, has even used sailboats to transport the harvest across Kootenay Lake and deliver it to consumer-members on the other side. Some grain CSAs like Pioneer Valley Heritage Grain CSA specialize in heritage grains to preserve genetic diversity.

Signing Up to Use Complementary Currencies

Earlier in this chapter we discussed two time banks: Home Exchange Portland and Fureai Kippu. These are organizations in which complementary currencies in the form of units of time (usually hours) allow members to trade services with other members. When they are established, members decide how people's time will be valued and whether all time will be valued equally (e.g., in Home Exchange Portland) or differently (e.g., in Fureai Kippu).

Local exchange and trading systems (LETS) extend the time bank idea in that members earn and spend credits by giving and receiving services *and* goods. Credits and commitments (the LETS equivalent to debits) are recorded in members' accounts. Some systems give names to their units of credit—everything from gems to sapphires and nuts to shells. In this direct people-to-people network, success is measured by the amount of turnover—the more members are spending and earning, the more the system is enabling people to give and receive services and goods. This is particularly important for people who may not have ready access to cash (and may not be able to participate in market transactions). LETS are a means for people who are talent rich but money poor to exchange their skills and abilities for the things they need.

Despite the name, LETS are not necessarily tied to a local area. The Community Exchange System (CES) is an international network that LETS can join so that members can trade internationally. Currently 330 LETS from every continent are members of the CES.[33]

Local currency systems provide another form of complementary currency. Groups print and issue their own currency for use between individuals and businesses. The main purpose of a local currency system is to maximize transactions in a local area (hence local currencies and buy-local campaigns can be interlinked). BerkShares is the local currency used in the Berkshire region of western Massachusetts. People can go into participating local banks and for US$95 buy US$100 BerkShares. The $100 BerkShares can then be spent in any participating local business—at the time of this writing there were over four hundred. Businesses can take their BerkShares back to local banks and exchange them for U.S. dollars.

There is also a range of initiatives that use currency substitutes, particularly to directly benefit people who do not have ready access to paid jobs. In Curitiba, Brazil, for example, the City Council paid slum *(favela)* residents in bus tokens for collecting rubbish. This means that the risk of disease in the *favelas* is reduced and that cash-poor residents can use the city's world-renowned public transport system to access the social and economic opportunities that are available across the city.

In all these complementary currency systems people are connecting more directly with each other than in the mainstream market with its anonymous pricing system. They are negotiating in a transparent and reciprocal way how best to meet their needs and the needs of others.

Exchanging What I Need for What You Need

Complementary currencies are different from barter. Barter involves a direct negotiation or swap between two people. For example, I'll work in your vegetable garden for one hour, and in exchange you'll repair a torn coat for me. The difference is that complementary currencies allow members or users to transact for goods and services with different people.

Gifting

Gifting generally involves direct contact; however, unlike in reciprocal transactions, the "return" is not directly negotiated. As we've said, there are no guarantees as to whether and when there will be a return or what form the return might take. Nevertheless, gifting can be an important way of helping to contribute to meeting the needs of other people and the environment.

ETHICAL ACTION: *Gifting well-being to others*

Participating in Principled Discarding

A form of giving is principled discarding. Take the case of Freecycle, an online network on which people offer items free to others. From its beginnings in 2003 among a small group of friends and nonprofit groups in Tucson, Arizona, the network has spread to eighty-five countries, gathering a membership of nearly nine million people.[34] Freecycle estimates that in 2010 it was keeping over five hundred tons of items a day out of landfills (and that if these items were put in garbage trucks that were then stacked one on top of the other, the trucks would extend to five times the height of Mount Everest). So Freecycle is certainly promoting care

> Changing the world one gift at a time.
>
> —Freecycle motto

for the planet through reusing items rather than buying new ones. Freecycle is also emphasizing people-to-people connections by asking people to consider sharing with others what they no longer need and through the Freecycle etiquette, which asks members to simply "be nice" and respect other members.[35]

Bringing Gleaning into the Twenty-first Century

It is perhaps an irony that one of the most rapidly expanding areas of people-to-people connection takes advantage of excessive overconsumption and oversupply. It is a form of gleaning that deals with waste in innovative and equitable ways. Food banks, often run by volunteers, accept "gifts" of unsold food and arrange for it to be distributed to those who need it rather than seeing good food just past its "use-by" date thrown out by large supermarket chains.

Dumpster diving is a more contentious form of modern-day gleaning. Like medieval gleaners sifting through leftovers and discards, adventurous dumpster divers put good food to good use—no matter where they find it. This doesn't stop some companies that see this as a form of theft from putting their "valuable" waste under lock and key to keep them out.

WHERE TO FROM HERE?

In this chapter we've introduced groups and organizations that are finding ways to take into account the people and environments that are helping them to meet their needs. We've presented only a few examples of the ingenious ways that have been developed to encounter others ethically in the course of the transactions that sustain us.

What would it take to participate in these ingenious schemes? What methods for ethical encounters can you devise with those who provide what you need? To get started, you might consider the following questions:

1. What types of market transactions do you engage in to meet your needs? To what extent do these market transactions take into account the needs of the people and environments that are

providing for you? Could you shift to more ethical markets in which the well-being of others is built into the encounters? Is fair trade an option? What about consumer cooperatives—are there any nearby? Can you buy local? Could you use an ethical consumer guide? Are there products you think should be boycotted? Is reuse an option?

2. What sorts of reciprocal relationships play a role in meeting your needs? How do the arrangements work? What sorts of things have you taken into account in establishing these relationships? Could you expand your reciprocal relationships by participating in initiatives like farmers' markets or CSA (and related initiatives like CSFs)? Are complementary currencies an option, whether in the form of time given through time banks or LETS, local currencies, substitute currencies, or barter arrangements?

3. Does gifting play a role in your well-being? In what way? Do you both give and receive gifts? Are there other things you could gift? Could an online initiative like Freecycle help you to give more? When you receive a gift, do you feel that you need to give a "return" to the giver? When you give, what's your return; do you expect one?

In a community economy we think about satisfying not just our own needs but also the needs of the people and environments that are providing for us, and we look to the variety of economic encounters that can help us and others to survive well together.

If markets have assumed a peculiar power in today's world, so too has private property. But just as markets can be reshaped to take account of people and planetary well-being, so too can private property. In the next chapter we examine what property might look like through the community economies frame, and we also consider a variety of ways that property can be "owned," with implications for how we manage and care for the natural and cultural resources that are essential to our own and others' survival.

5.
Take Back Property
Commoning

WHAT *IS* PROPERTY?

Property usually refers to all the things we own and use in order to survive well. If we're lucky we own a home and a car, as well as an array of other material bits and pieces—the "stuff" that gives us comfort, status, identity, and pleasure. If we're businesspeople, our property might include all the things our business needs to operate successfully—whether it's the merchandise we sell or the land, plant, and equipment that make up a production facility.

When we think of property we inevitably think of private property, the legal mechanism that gives us the right to use and control what we own and to reap the rewards that come from ownership. Private property gives us a sense of security. Take housing, for example. All over the world, people aspire to own their own home so they have a space that's "theirs"—a space they can decorate and change as they like, a space in which they can invest their time and labor, a space from which they can derive enjoyment and pleasure.

But private property also means exclusion. The sign "Private Property—Keep Out!" puts this message bluntly. Private ownership designates who has rights of access and use and who can derive benefit from the property.

Private property is seen as one of the founding pillars of modern democracies. Property-owning individuals are seen as independent sovereign beings, no longer obligated to landlords or attached to a clan, who can freely exercise their democratic rights. Of course this vision traditionally excluded the rights of women and slaves, who, until not that long ago, were considered forms of private property and denied a democratic vote.

Private property is also seen as one of the foundations of modern economies. The argument goes that land and other resources are best placed in the hands of private owners who will look after them and use them productively. Of course this ignores the countless ways that this productivity rests on shared assets like the common law and the earth's gifts.

The prominence that is given to private property overshadows other forms of property that are also essential to our well-being. Public property, for example, is owned by a government or authority and managed on the behalf of citizens and residents for their benefit. And when it comes to our most basic well-being, survival depends on many things that are not formally owned—our atmosphere, for example, or our water sources, sunlight, the resources of the sea, and our shared intellectual property. These are forms of open-access property that can benefit all. But often there are no formal rules of ownership and use, and, as a result, these essential resources are all too easily degraded and abused.

Today there is a push for the privatization of public property. Governments and organizations are portrayed as unwieldy, inefficient managers of public property who should step aside and let private owners take charge. Everything is up for grabs, from roads and water supplies to parklands and libraries.

Private ownership is also presented as the most efficient means of managing open-access resources. Privatization is occurring via a sell-off of rights to familiar resources such as water, fisheries, forests, and minerals, as well as new "resources" such as carbon emissions. It is also occurring via the taking of resources that are supposedly "idle." The long-standing knowledge resources of Indigenous communities are being pirated and commercialized by private companies in a new wave of colonization. The deep-sea floor is being privately mined for copper and gold, and the Arctic Circle is being mined for iron ore and other resources.

This period of privatization is beginning at the very time that our global circumstances demand not just collective thinking and acting but a move away from the boundary making that separates mine from yours and you from me. Can we take back property and better care for the resources that sustain all who inhabit this planet? We think we can, but we need to reconsider the ways we relate to the things around us, and we especially need to reconsider the privileging of private property.

In the Northern Territory of Australia, Aboriginal people are caring for "their" land not just for their immediate benefit as "owners" but for the good of the wider Australian population. They are creating an "us" that acknowledges the interdependence between humans in very different circumstances and between humans and the environment. Through their example we can see how we might relate to property in ways that take us beyond distinctions between yours and mine and you and me.

RECLAIMING A COMMONS OR LOCKING UP WEALTH?

For up to fifty thousand years, Aboriginal people have occupied and shared the Australian continent, living through major climate change events and species extinctions.[1] Throughout this long history they have both adapted to and shaped their environment. Colonization was to change all this. In remote northern Australia, Aboriginal people were moved off their traditional lands to live in government settlements and missions and were instructed to "assimilate." When they moved, the habitats they had nurtured for tens of thousands of years suffered.

Without the customary practice of fire-stick farming—the lighting of small-scale fires to replenish native vegetation and manage animal populations—the land became vulnerable to invasive exotic weeds and feral animals. Fast-spreading wildfires became a perennial threat to the profits of commercial pastoralists who enclosed and privatized land for cattle grazing. Displaced from their property, Aboriginal people could no longer continue to breathe life into their land and share this vital force with past, present, and future generations. When they lost access to "country" (as Aboriginal people refer to land), they lost much of what contributed to their spirituality, community, and economy.

Assimilation policies were replaced by support for self-determination in the mid- to late twentieth century, and, in a controversial move in the early 1970s, the Australian federal government granted Aboriginal people the legal right to their customary land in the Northern Territory. Suddenly Indigenous Australians were large property owners. Many settler-Australians resented this giveback, seeing it as the beginning of a threat to "their" backyards and beaches, paddocks and parks—a threat that would lock up access to the wealth to be gained by some from the land. While the furor raged, Indigenous people quietly started moving back onto remote outstations and resumed their time-honored practices of caring for country.

Scientists interested in land management began to take notice of what Indigenous people were doing and how it maintained and replenished vulnerable landscapes. The West Arnhem Land Fire Abatement project was hatched, bringing scientists and Aboriginal people together to systematically reinstate customary fire regimes in an area roughly the size of the U.S. state of Vermont. The Northern Land Council (an Indigenous organization) now employs people from five different Indigenous groups as rangers to conduct controlled burns in accordance with customary practices.

Recognition of the value of this work is going some way toward reclaiming the connections between people and place that Aboriginal people had lost as colonization in its various forms destroyed their life-world. Indigenous people are benefiting from restored access to their sources of spiritual and physical sustenance, and landscapes are being repaired.

We burn and we encourage our environments, our ecosystems, to come alive again.

Dean Yibarbuk, *Native Title Report 2007*

Importantly, Aboriginal people are forging new relationships between people and environments with respect to "their" property. Fire abatement on Aboriginal land helps pastoralists on adjacent properties, who no longer face the threat of feed loss from wildfires. It also regenerates ecologies and enhances the survival of plants and animals native to the region. In Darwin, asthma sufferers usually affected by smoke inhalation are benefiting from the decline of wind-borne particulate matter. And there has been a reduction of 450,000 metric tons of greenhouse gas emissions over three years—a significant contribution to planetary health and to Australia's commitment to international obligations. By gaining a form of private land title, Aboriginal people have created interdependencies and connections that extend across the white settler–Indigenous and the human–nonhuman divides. They have reestablished a commons.

But making and sharing a commons in a community economy is not a straightforward matter. The much-needed paid employment offered to Aboriginal people by the fire abatement project is partly funded by a payment of A$1 million per year from Darwin Liquefied Natural Gas Pty Ltd (Proprietary Limited) to offset its carbon emissions. Recently Indigenous groups became part of a seventeen-year agreement with this company and the Northern Territory government, which receives the payment and then passes it on to the Northern Land Council. The payment allows a "dirty-energy" company to offset both the running of its operation and the loss of monsoon forest cleared to build its plant on the outskirts of Darwin. There are no straightforward rights and wrongs here. As in all ethical negotiations, there's a weighing of the practical opportunities and possibilities available in the situation with our longings as to how the world might be.[2]

This is not an isolated dilemma. Across the globe, communities are faced with the development challenges that arise from mining, tourism, agriculture, and urbanization. In the case of Aboriginal people in a country such as Australia, the dilemmas are perhaps particularly acute. In the relatively short time frame of eight generations they have experienced the interruption of colonization, the degradation of country and custom, and now a form of collective land privatization that is helping with repair. Aboriginal people in West Arnhem Land are helping us rethink property in a community economy. They are breaking down the distinction between yours and mine and you and me by making and sharing a commons. How might this idea of commons serve people and the planet in the years ahead?

COMMONS: A KEY CONCERN OF A COMMUNITY ECONOMY

What are commons? And what does it mean to make and share a commons? A commons is a property, a practice, or a knowledge that is shared by a community. Our survival depends on many different kinds of commons:

- biophysical commons like rocks, soil, sunlight, water and air, and plant and animal ecologies;
- cultural commons like language, a musical heritage, sacred symbols, and artworks;
- social commons like educational, health, and political systems; and
- knowledge commons like Indigenous ecological knowledge and scientific and technological advancements.

Commons are continually made and remade, drawn down and replenished, maintained or degraded. What happens to commons depends on whether a community cares for and shares the thing that sustains it or whether it exploits or neglects it.

All too often the commons that sustain us come to our attention only when they are being extinguished, polluted, or otherwise debased—when the air around us has become thick with smog, when the last speakers of a language pass from us, when the final few specimens of a species are preserved only in zoos, when the parkland our children play on is covered with concrete by a private urban development. With the realization of this loss comes the recognition that a community has failed to take responsibility for caring what supports it. A loss of a commons is a loss of a community.

A community economy makes and shares a commons—without a commons, there is no community, without a community, there is no commons.

Stephen Gudeman, *The Anthropology of Economy*

In many people's minds, the loss of commons is inevitable. This misunderstanding has come from an influential article written in 1968 by Garrett Hardin.[3] Hardin introduced the phrase "the tragedy of the commons" through the example of a pasture that is used by a number of herdsmen. Each herdsman keeps adding more and more animals to his own herd in order to maximize returns. But as each herd gets bigger and bigger, the commons becomes more and more degraded until it collapses. According to Hardin, the tragedy of the commons is inevitable, because people act in their own self-interest without regard to the impact of their actions on others.

But it turns out that this presumed inevitability is far from the case. Researchers like the late Elinor Ostrom (the first woman awarded the Nobel Prize in Economic Sciences, in 2009) have shown that across the globe commons have existed for thousands of years without collapsing. These commons have been successfully maintained and managed by the communities they support. Rules of use and access and protocols for care and responsibility have been devised to ensure that people act responsibly with regard to each other and the environment. It is only when these rules and protocols are absent that tragedy results. Indeed, Hardin revised his original paper in a statement he made in 1998 pointing out that he had omitted a key adjective and that the tragedy of which he had previously written is one of an *unmanaged* commons.

For thousands of years people have self-organized to manage common-pool resources.

Elinor Ostrom, Joanna Burger, Christopher B. Field, Richard B. Norgaard, and David Policansky, *Revisiting the Commons: Local Lessons, Global Challenges*

Nevertheless, the idea of the tragedy of the commons has stuck. And the phrase has been used ever since to legitimize privatization and the ideology that resources are best placed in the hands of private owners who will manage them wisely so the owners can reap the rewards.

If we want to take back the economy for people and the planet, we need to reconsider property as a relationship between people with respect to things. All forms of property can be potential commons.

So what is it that characterizes a commons? Commons and community go hand in hand. And it is because of this intimate interconnection that rules and protocols can be developed to manage the commons. To be a commons,

- *access* to property must be shared and wide,
- *use* of property must be negotiated by a community,

- *benefit* from property must be distributed to the community and possibly beyond,
- *care* for property must be performed by community members, and
- *responsibility* for property must be assumed by community members.

The question of who "owns" a commons is open. Commons can be created with any type of property—private property (that might be owned by an individual owner, a family, a corporation, or a collective), state-owned property, or open-access property. In other words, ownership of property is largely a legal matter and does not deter land or other resources from being managed as a commons.

For example, the West Arnhem Land Fire Abatement (WALFA) project area is a form of private property with traditional owners recognized through Aboriginal land tenure. But the land is managed as a commons. *Access* to the WALFA project area is shared among five Indigenous ranger groups: the Adjumarllarl Rangers, the Djelk Rangers, Jawoyn Association, the Manwurrk Rangers, and the Mimal Rangers. The *use* of the project area for fire abatement is negotiated among the five groups, with each group taking *responsibility* to manage and *care* for the fire regime in their area. Each year there is a meeting of the groups and the WALFA project coordinator to plan and map the season's burning. The season's burn *benefits* the immediate community—the Indigenous rangers, who get to care for country through traditional practices of mosaic burning, and the area's ecosystem, which is rejuvenated through regular burning. The season's burn also *benefits* communities well beyond the immediate areas, including pastoralists on adjacent properties, asthma sufferers in Darwin, and Darwin Liquefied Natural Gas. We summarize what makes the WALFA Project Area a commons in a nearby figure.

The WALFA project area might seem a long way from the places where many of us live our daily lives, but if we take a moment we will find that commons are not as remote as we might think.

We can explore our experience of commons—and community—with the aid of

A COMMONS ANALYSIS OF THE WALFA PROJECT					
ACCESS	USE	BENEFIT	CARE	RESPONSIBILITY	PROPERTY
Shared by five Indigenous groups	Negotiated by five Indigenous groups and the WALFA project coordinator	To Indigenous and non-Indigenous people nearby and at a distance	Shared by five Indigenous groups	Shared by five Indigenous groups	Privately and collectively owned under Aboriginal land tenure

1. a *Time–Property Geography* in which our activities in space are recorded over a twenty-four-hour period and
2. a *Commons Identi-Kit,* which we can use to identify whether the activities involve the use of a commons.

The Time–Property Geography categorizes the movements of an individual according to the types of property he or she comes into contact with over a twenty-four-hour period. Property types are divided into

- individually owned private property (including individual, family, and corporate property),
- collectively owned private property (such as the WALFA project area),
- state-owned property, and
- open-access property (both managed and unmanaged).

Let's look at the Time–Property Geography of a real-life couple—Bill, a coal miner, and his wife, Sue, who is a nurse. Bill's activities are recorded in black and Sue's in gray. Bill spends most of his time between the home that he and Sue rent from the mining company he works for and the coal mine, which is also privately owned by the same mining company. He travels to and from work on state-owned roads. On this

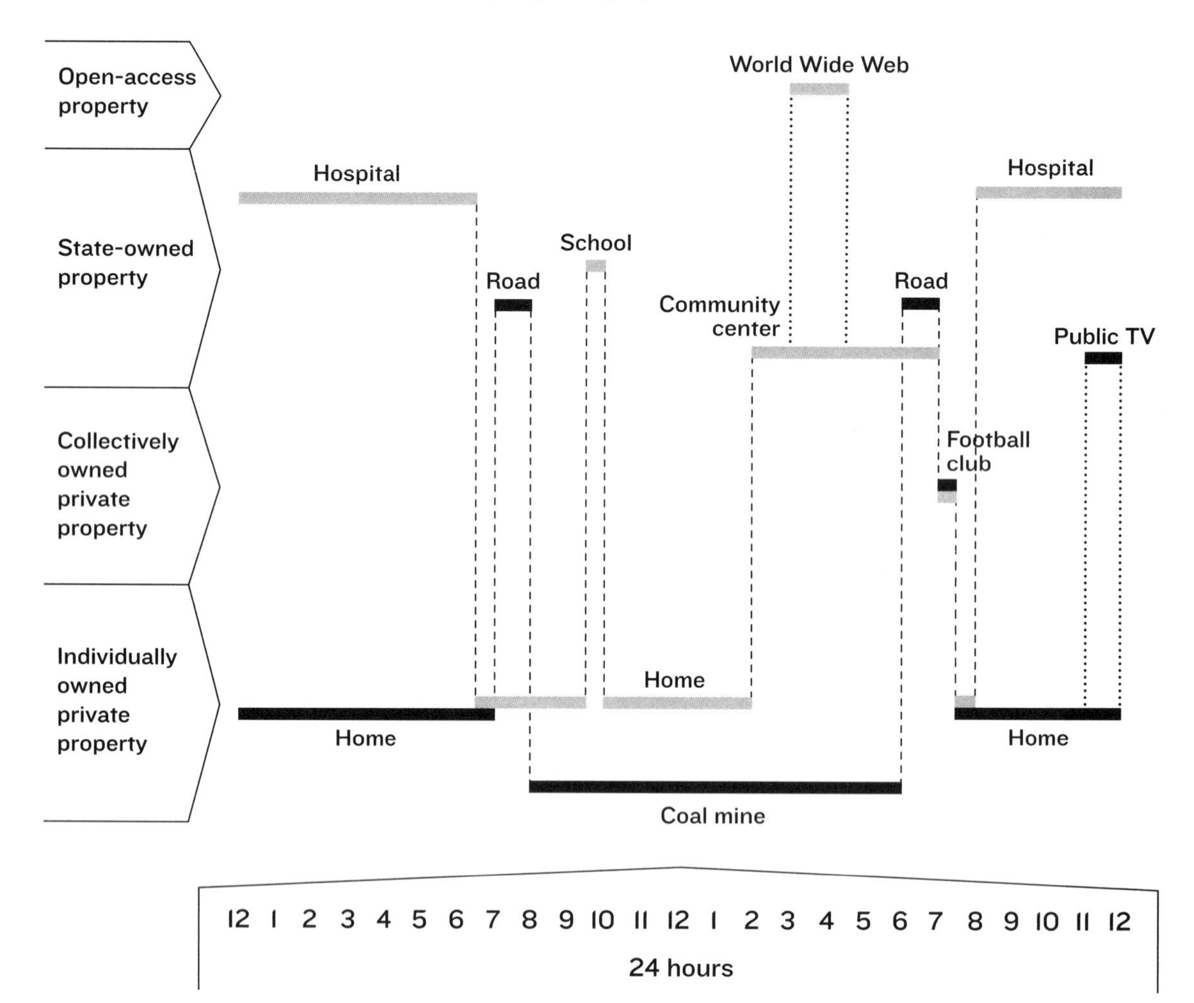

particular day he, Sue, and their children have a family dinner at the local football club. When they return home, Bill and the children watch television via the public broadcaster, while Sue heads off for her night shift at the hospital. On this particular day, Sue managed to squeeze in a few hours of sleep after she took the kids to school and volunteered for half an hour in the class reading program and half an hour in the school kitchen garden. When school was over for the day, Sue met the

COMMONS IDENTI-KIT

ACCESS	USE	BENEFIT	CARE	RESPONSIBILITY	PROPERTY
Shared and wide	Negotiated by a community	Widely distributed to community members (and beyond)	Performed by community members	Assumed by community members	Any form of ownership (private, state, or open access)

kids at the local community center, which offers after-school care, craft activities, and Internet access. After a few hours there, Sue and the kids joined Bill at the football club for dinner.

The Time–Property Geography identifies all the different types of property that Bill and Sue encounter in one day. With the Commons Identi-Kit we can identify where they associate with others throughout the day to make and share commons and community.

Bill, Sue, and their family are involved with four commons in their typical day. Although they access and use three kinds of state-owned property (the roads, the hospital, and the school), it is only at the local primary school that they participate in a community to make this resource a commons. The school is accessed and used by schoolchildren, teachers, and parents, and these groups shoulder some of the responsibility for its upkeep and improvements. Parents such as Bill and Sue raise money for extra books and equipment, assist with reading programs, and help with the school kitchen garden. The school community forms a living commons in which rules of use and practices of care are actively negotiated and the benefit is shared. As users of the roads and hospital, Bill and Sue are positioned as consumers (or employees in the case of Sue at the hospital), not active shapers of or carers for a commons and a community.

It is easy to see how collectively owned private property, such as the football club and state-owned property like the community center, are commons. They are the focus of a community that enjoys access and rights of use, derives benefit, and assumes care and responsibility. Each property is associated with a "we" that identifies itself as a community that maintains and shares the resource. At the football club where Bill is a member, he has access to and use of collectively owned property and takes his role of a carer for these facilities seriously, often volunteering to do maintenance work, mowing, and even bartending.

Sue and her kids spend time in the afternoons at a state-owned community center that offers after-school care and a range of hobby facilities for community members to use. This is where she and her children access the Internet for information to help them with schoolwork and craft projects and to play computer games. Sue is a member of committee that manages the center, and it is here that she maintains her closest nonfamily social connections.

At the community center, Sue and her children are avid users of the Internet. This is an open-access resource that hosts multiple communities of users. Sue has a particular interest in photography and is a photomontage artist in her spare time. She accesses images and exhibits her photographs on the Internet using Wikimedia Commons, a free online repository for media files. This activity brings her in contact with a growing creative commons community with its own rules that are outlined in its license agreement (which encourages users to share and remix material as long as they attribute the material in the way that the creator specifies and then "onshare" the work under the same conditions).

Of course, Sue and the children access the Internet through a provider. This provider is a privately owned corporation, and Sue and other users are customers who have to pay to access the service. So although applications like Wikimedia Commons can function as a commons, the community of users must navigate to the application through a privately owned service.

We summarize the commons that Bill and Sue and their children are part of in the nearby Commons Identi-Kit. From this brief analysis we see that they are engaged in making and sharing a number of important commons that contribute to the well-being of their town (the local primary school, the football club, and the community center) and the world (Wikimedia Commons). In contrast to the antagonisms that often pervade private workplaces or the apathy that can accompany the

COMMONS IDENTI-KIT FOR BILL, SUE, AND FAMILY

	ACCESS	USE	BENEFIT	CARE	RESPONSIBILITY	PROPERTY
Primary school	Teachers, children, parents	Teachers, children, parents	Teachers, children, parents	Teachers, children, parents	Teachers, children, parents, state government	State-owned public property
Football club	Members and families	Members and families	Members and families	Paid employees, members	Football club committee of management	Privately and collectively owned by members
Community center	Community members	Community members	Community members	Paid employees, community members	Committee of management, local government	State-owned public property
Wikipedia	Open	Anyone who follows the license agreement	Anyone	Volunteer administrators	All users	Open access

use of public resources, in these communities Bill and Sue forge respectful and convivial connections with others, learning and teaching how to negotiate living well together.

As we've seen with the example of the WALFA project, people are also maintaining commons alongside and in collaboration with other species and natural forces. The "we" that makes and shares these commons is not only an association of humans but a collective of human and nonhuman beings, including rivers and water bodies, plants and forests, fish and animal species—what are often referred to as natural resources. These commons have been created by developing respectful relationships with the soil, water, and animal and plant life.

Making and sharing a commons is not as simple as it sounds. It involves questions about who and what make a community and what kinds of actions are involved in sharing the commons on which community survival rests. The ethical decisions involved in "commoning" are an important focus for any collective process of taking back property for people and place.

COMMONING: ANOTHER KEY CONCERN OF A COMMUNITY ECONOMY

Commoning refers to the ongoing production and reproduction of commons. The practice of commoning is key to building community economies and for negotiating ways of surviving well with each other and with other species on this planet, especially as we face the dual challenges of a climate-changing world and the powerful pull of privatization as the best means of managing our resources.

Commoning claims resources for a collective or community of more than one. It involves defining who is the "we" that establishes protocols for sharing access to and use of this property, as well as shouldering its care and how benefits are to be distributed.

The practice of commoning is motivated by an ethic of care for what nourishes and sustains people and the planet both now and into the future. In some Indigenous societies this ethic is codified according to the seven-generations philosophy, which asks us to consider everything we do today in light of how it will affect our children and our children's children for seven generations.[4] This is surely a guideline for sustainability. Might it also be a guide for ethical decision making around our relationships to property—and thus to each other and the environment that sustains current and future generations?

There are no commons without incessant activities of commoning, of (re)producing in common.

Massimo De Angelis, *The Commoner*

Perhaps we could record our relationships to commons over a time period that places our present in the kind of temporal context that climate change requires us to consider. Many of us can remember our grandparents and the stories they told about their lives and those of their parents, so most of us can imagine back three generations. Can we try to imagine forward, not just three generations but seven? Using a *Commons Yardstick* we can start to locate ourselves in this generational time frame. If we consider a generation to be twenty-five years, we can locate commoning (and uncommoning) activities in the past, present, and future. Perhaps this might help us to see more clearly what kinds of ethical actions we need to take when it comes to making and sharing commons that will ensure survival.

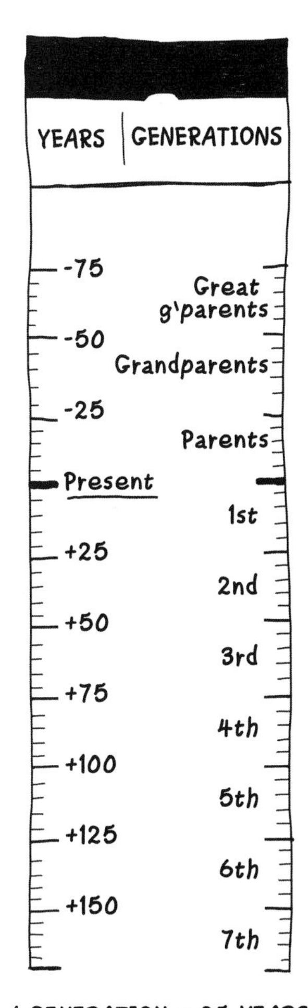

Some private landowners are starting to take this temporal time frame into account when managing their properties. In so doing, they are reworking the treasured tenet that within the bounds of private property the owner is sovereign. These landowners are showing how private property can become part of a commons in which broader community concerns come to the fore. In countries like the United States and Australia, landowners can put restrictions on their properties through conservation covenants and easements. These voluntary agreements are legally binding and permanent: even if the property is sold, the covenant or easement remains. Concerned landowners enter into these agreements because they want to protect the land for future generations. They are willing to forgo the financial benefits that might come from more intensive forms of development in order to contribute to the conservation of the planet.

Agreements are tailored for each property to protect its specific conservation value, whether protecting water quality in aquifers and watersheds, maintaining scenic vistas, establishing corridors for migratory species, linking isolated remnant forests, or even keeping landscapes in traditional uses, such as farming. Generally agreements prohibit the land from being subdivided or developed and require the owner to manage and maintain the property (say, by clearing weeds or controlling feral predators or keeping livestock away from streams).

Let's look at an example of one private property that has become commoned. The Spooner family began extensive cattle grazing on their property, Avocet, in the brigalow scrub of central Queensland in the 1930s.[5] As one of Australia's last frontiers, brigalow country is a vast region populated by hardy acacia bushes that have proved particularly resistant to clearing for pastureland. Large-scale land clearing did not take place until discarded army tanks and Bren Gun Carriers left over from World War II were turned into bulldozers dragging anchor chains that could rip out the scrub in vast arcs.[6] By the 1970s, most of the brigalow scrub had been "conquered." In recent years, greater scientific understanding of the role the scrub plays in maintaining soil fertility and reducing water runoff led to its listing as an endangered ecological community in 2001.

In the meantime, the Spooner family had already rallied to protect remnant brigalow scrub on their cattle property for future generations. They did this in 1999 by entering into a voluntary conservation agreement with the state government, which designated one-fifth of their property as the Avocet Nature Reserve. The reserve is just over 2,700 acres (1,500 hectares). Other private landholders in the area were strongly opposed, and the family was largely isolated from the rest of the community.

In 2001 the Spooner family was approached by the Queensland State Department of Environment and Resource Management. Would the Spooners be prepared to help save an endangered species? Bridled nailtail wallabies are small wallabies also known as flashjacks. They were thought to be completely extinct until 1973, when a small, isolated population was discovered on private property in central Queensland.

My father before he died in 1996 wanted a part of the property . . . preserved from development. After he died we looked into it and had that area declared a nature refuge. That meant that we had to protect that area.

Hugo Spooner,
Avocet Nature Reserve

The Avocet Nature Reserve is perfect for flashjacks. It has the appropriate brigalow habitat and offers protection from the flashjacks' feral predators.[7] As part of the conservation agreement the Spooners entered into, they must control the numbers of feral animals. To do so they have teamed up with sporting shooters' clubs, whose members are happy to volunteer their services to keep down the feral pig population. The Spooners subsidize the management of the nature reserve through their cattle business, and they are supported by researchers, government employees, volunteer community members, and donations from individuals and corporations (through the Bridled Nailtail Wallaby Trust).

Starting in 2001, around 160 wallabies have been released into the nature reserve, and Hugo Spooner estimates that now there are probably 140 to 180, around half the total number of flashjacks in the wild. Unfortunately, this still makes the flashjack one of the most endangered mammals in the world.

By ceding their private property rights to others—including endangered animals and the people who want to care for them—the Spooner family has commoned part of their property. One-fifth of Avocet is now "owned" by a community dedicated to the maintenance and flourishing of many different native species in their habitat. The community that has formed includes odd bedfellows—family farmers, conservationists, shooters, academic researchers, rangers, cattle, a particular species of wallaby, and the brigalow scrub. As the nearby Commons Identi-Kit shows, each member of this new flashjack commons has a relationship to the nature reserve and thus to each other.

I think Avocet is essential to the survival of the species. They have such a specific habitat . . . they really need to live in a brigalow forest and so the nature refuge at Avocet is essential.

Hugo Spooner,
Avocet Nature Reserve

If we use the Commons Yardstick, we see the potential for an even wider community to take shape—the future generations of flashjacks and other life forms that will appreciate them. The Commons Yardstick positions the Spooners' commoning move in its historical context. On the yardstick we highlight the 1870s as a period that marked the end of bloody and bitter struggle between Aboriginal groups and settlers in this part of the country and when European settlement was firmly established. Then, as a result of large-scale land clearing and the

COMMONS IDENTI-KIT FOR THE FLASHJACK COMMONS

ACCESS	USE	BENEFIT	CARE	RESPONSIBILITY	PROPERTY
Spooner family, sporting shooters, community volunteers, researchers, rangers, cattle, and native species of plants and animals	Rules set by the conservation agreement and researchers and rangers to protect brigalow habitat and flashjacks and eradicate weeds, feral animals, pests, and fire	Flashjacks, cattle, brigalow scrub, and future generations	Spooner family, sporting shooters, community volunteers, community organizations, researchers, and rangers	Spooner family, researchers, volunteers, and Bridled Nailtail Wallaby Trust	Individually owned private property gifted by the Spooner family

introduction of feral animals, flashjacks were thought to be extinct until a small population was discovered in 1973. We then highlight the late 1990s and early 2000s, when the Avocet Nature Reserve was established and the flashjacks were first released.

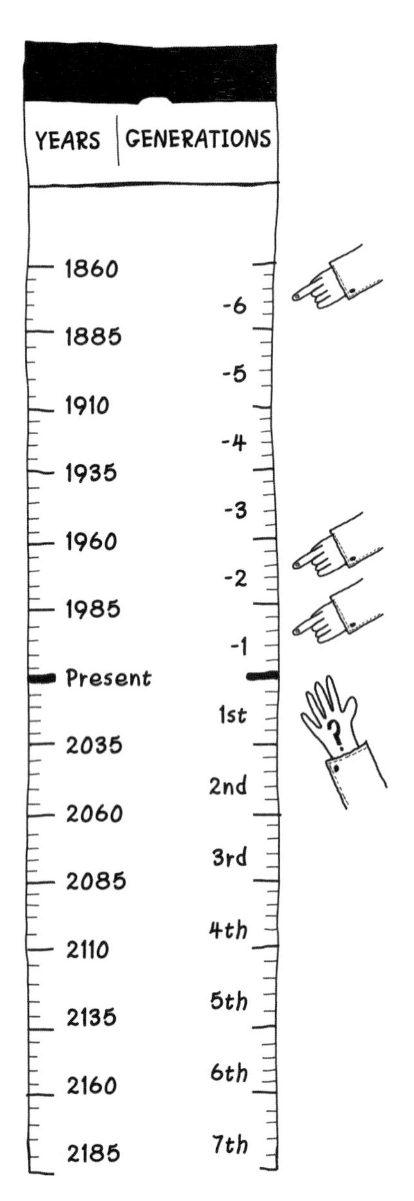

It would be nice to think that the future of the flashjack commons is secure, but all over central and southern Queensland, as in many other areas of rural Australia, a new form of enclosure is on the agenda. Because the right to explore for minerals and gas transcends any private, public, or collectively owned surface-property right, the future of many species and ecosystems is currently being threatened by the coal seam gas industry. Farmers and other landowners are locked in a battle to keep gas drilling off their properties. And many farmers who have allowed gas extraction are now up in arms about the pollution of their groundwater supplies, truck traffic through their properties, and fire hazards. The Flashjack Commons Yardstick helps locate this recent threat to the natural environment in context. What type of future is this form of resource extraction creating for generations to come?

The flashjack commons at Avocet Nature Reserve is a relatively recent endeavor that has grown out of the initiative of one family, but commoning can take many forms. It's not just material resources like land that can be commoned; virtual resources such as language, music, and ideas can also be commoned.

With the explosion of information that is readily available on the Internet and the rapid pace of scientific, medical, and technological developments, the issue of intellectual property (IP) and the "ownership" of these commons has become critical. There is considerable debate about who should own IP—its creator or society? Usually creations of the mind are deemed property privately owned by the creators. This entitles the creators not just to obtain recompense for their initial efforts but to control how their creations continue to be used and how the creators benefit from subsequent use. In the United States, an inventor owns the patent for an invention for up to 20 years. An author maintains copyright for his or her lifetime plus 70 years.[8] We highlight these time frames on the IP Commons Yardstick, showing how inventions are patented for up to 20 years and how a copyright can last for around 150 years (six generations), assuming that the author lives out the average U.S. lifespan of 78 years.[9]

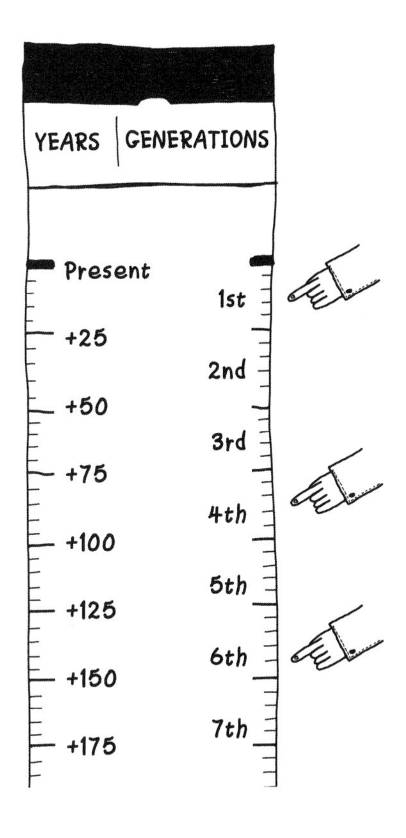

These property rights are justified on the basis that creation and innovation will take place only if those doing this work are adequately protected from free riders—those who would prematurely take and profit from others' work.[10] But there are concerns that developments in IP protection are going well beyond adequate protection for creators toward absolute protection. More and more time, energy, and money are being spent establishing and enforcing IP and less and less on innovating and creating. In addition, more and more "downstream" creators are being stymied and deterred by the thicket of protection.[11] Overall, this means that society is paying the cost of IP—in terms of both the costs of the creations we have and the cost of forgone creations.[12]

How do we account for the fact that many creations of the mind build on an existing intellectual commons, on what many minds over time have produced? Musicians from folk artists like Woody Guthrie to hip-hop artists like DJ Spooky (Paul Miller) explicitly acknowledge that their music is possible only because of the contributions of earlier musicians.[13] The risk with overly protective IP protection is that it hides the debt that all creators owe to the contributions of others in their field—to their commons.

Others share these concerns, and, particularly in the area of information technology, there is a flourishing of experiments with private-property and open-access resources that prioritize the relationships between people over our relationships to things and, in the process, build new online communities. Initiatives include the Creative Commons, open-source software (like Linux and Firefox), and free software (like GNU) and its associated innovations, General Public License and Copyleft. Far from losing out, businesses are finding that open-access collaborative design practices can increase their market share and ensure loyalty and vibrant innovation.[14]

If our love affair with technology has given rise to open-access commons, it is a love affair that is also eroding our commons. So much of the technology that we take for granted today relies on our planet's nonrenewable resources—whether resources in the component parts of our technological devices or those used to power the production and operation of these devices.

Currently we seem willing to trade our coastlines and our weather systems for patterns of development and growth that rely on burning nonrenewable fossil fuels. Can the practice of commoning be applied to climate change as a way of taking back the economy and contributing to, rather than undermining, our planet's survival?

We know that our climate has been warming since the 1860s (for six generations).[15] As an earth community we are shitting in the nest, to use a common expression, and largely failing to care for our most precious commons. How we have mistreated our atmosphere is a global tragedy of an *unmanaged* open-access resource. There are, however, glimmers of hope that this neglect will not continue.

Over the past two generations at least, people have been involved in commoning the atmosphere by arguing for protocols of behavior that maintain and replenish its life-giving properties. This action has often been prompted by scientific discoveries about the complex systems that make up our atmosphere, including the mix of life-giving and life-destroying gases and liquids produced on earth.

Take, for example, CFCs (chlorofluorocarbons), which were invented in 1920 and became widely used in air conditioners, refrigerators, and aerosols until their use was banned in minority-world countries from

1996 and in majority-world countries from 2010. As a global community we have decided to cease production of the CFCs that have thinned the ozone layers of the stratosphere, allowing damaging rays to reach earth and cause cancer.[16] But, as we show on the Ozone Commons Yardstick, it will not be until 2070 at the earliest—that is, two generations from now!—that the ozone hole will be repaired and we will not need to be so protective of the skin of future children or quite so worried.

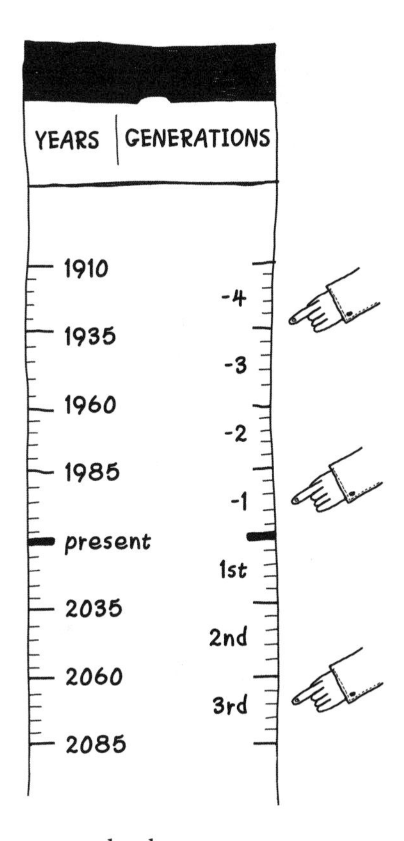

Clearly we cannot know what the future will hold, but we can try to make assessments based on the scenarios offered by scientists who work on climate change. Many vocal commentators are convinced that humans need not worry about global warming, that our inventiveness has, in the past, overcome grave challenges like global oil and food shortages and the threat of millennium bugs and nuclear winters. Some say that the newest threats (if indeed real) will surely be overcome by whiz-bang technological fixes—nuclear power or geoengineering of ocean and atmospheric conditions. Invariably, when these types of technosolutions are put forward, the agenda is to find ways for "business as usual" to continue. The focus of attention too often shifts to the efficacy of the various fixes, and we lose an opportunity to reflect on whether the planet can sustain business as usual or how fixes in one area will inevitably flow on to other commons.

With our Commons Yardstick in mind, perhaps we can more clearly identify the issues and time frames that confront us. On the Atmospheric Commons Yardstick we identify the 1860s as the period from which average temperatures have been rising several degrees Fahrenheit. It was not until the 1950s that scientists started to systematically study global warming (helped by increased U.S. government funding in the sciences because of the cold war). Even though the scientific evidence was mounting, it was almost two generations later, in 1997, that the Kyoto Protocol was signed by most minority-world governments, agreeing to reduce greenhouse gas emissions to 5.2 percent below the 1990 levels for the period 2008–2012. Ten years after that, in 2007, the Nobel Peace Prize was awarded jointly to the Intergovernmental Panel on Climate Change and Al Gore for their efforts in generating and disseminating knowledge about human-induced climate change.

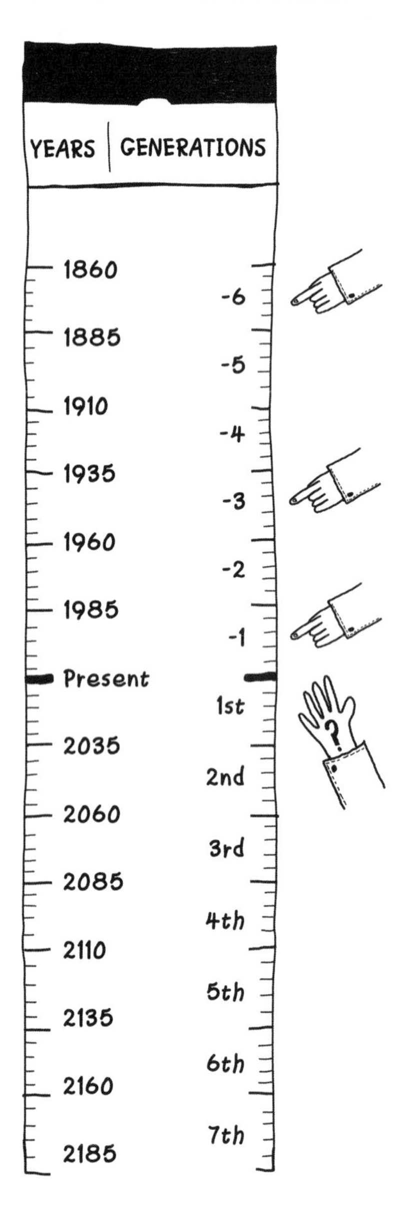

What of the future? Might we be able to act now as a global community to care for our atmospheric commons? A number of pathways are available. For one thing, we could take more remedial action to absorb the greenhouse gases that have already been released into the atmosphere. Ways of working with our planetary commons are emerging that recognize the interconnectedness of biological, hydrological, and climate systems. For example, scientists are beginning to better understand the role of trees in the water vapor cycle and the much greater-than-expected impact that reforestation and forest conservation might have on slowing global warming.[17] Others are measuring the extent of carbon that could be sequestered through methods such as organic farming.[18] The Ecuadorian people have acknowledged that we need to see ourselves as part of a planetary community with "earth others," making and sharing a commons together. In 2008 they approved a new constitution that recognizes the inalienable right of the Andean people's goddess Pachamama (loosely translated as "mother nature") to an unspoiled existence.

We could also care for our atmospheric commons by taking preemptive action to prevent the addition of more greenhouse gases. We need strategies to intervene in our polluting economies to ensure survival seven generations from now. If we place ourselves in a community of present and future generations of humans and other species, perhaps that will help provoke the types of ethical thinking and acting that we are elaborating in this book.

TOOLS FOR COMMONING

Taking back property for people and the planet involves recognizing that it is the relationships between people with respect to property that matter in the making and sharing of commons. There are diverse property ownership forms that coexist and interact in our economies, as we see in the Diverse Property Identifier. Property in all these forms of ownership is a potential source of commons. Certainly some might be more conducive to commoning, such as state-owned property and collectively owned private property. Nevertheless, as we've seen in this chapter, commons cut across different types of property.

We are continuously sustained by biophysical, social, cultural, and knowledge commons. If our commons are to survive and flourish, they need to be maintained and managed. It is critical that there be a "we," a community that establishes how commons are to be managed. Without a commitment of care, we are likely to lose our commons. We need to become commoners and to see ourselves as active contributors to shaping the ways in which we are accessing, using, benefiting from, caring for, and taking responsibility for commons. The Commons Identi-Kit can be modified into a Ways of Commoning tool to help us identify opportunities for commoning, whether by maintaining existing commons and building new ones or by transforming unmanaged open-access resources and enclosed private property.

There are significant obstacles to managing or expanding our commons. There are the disheartening tragedies of resource depletion, species extinction, vegetation denudation, and global warming that

DIVERSE PROPERTY IDENTIFIER
PRIVATE
ALTERNATIVE PRIVATE State-owned Tenanted Ninety-nine-year lease Customary Community-managed Community trust
OPEN ACCESS Atmosphere Water Open ocean Ecosystem services

	WAYS OF COMMONING					
	ACCESS	USE	BENEFIT	CARE	RESPONSIBILITY	OWNERSHIP
Commoning enclosed property	Narrow	Restricted by owner	Private	Performed by owner or employee	Assumed by owner	Private individual Private collective State
Creating new commons	Shared and wide	Negotiated by a community	Widely distributed to community and beyond	Performed by community members	Assumed by community	Private individual Private collective State Open access
Commoning unmanaged open-access resources	Unrestricted	Open and unregulated	Finders, keepers	None	None	Open access State

our agricultural and industrial "advancements" have wrought on our earthly commons. And there is the confusion of navigating tricky arguments about innovation and intellectual property. In the face of these challenges, it is important to recognize the interconnectedness of different commons and their communities. For example, in order to repair our atmospheric commons we need to ensure that scientific knowledge is available through our knowledge commons.

In a community economy we begin to take responsibility not just for individual commons but for how one commons is interconnected with another and how one specific "we" is interdependent with differently constituted we's. These considerations must be part of any actions to take back property and common it for the benefit of all.[19]

COLLECTIVE ACTIONS FOR COMMONING

In a community economy we share what sustains us with current and future generations.

In this section we look at the ways that people are taking back the economy by maintaining and building commons and community.

Questions to consider as you read about these collective actions

- Who are the commoners? Who makes up the community involved in commoning?
- What new communities are being constructed? In what ways are humans and nonhumans present in these new communities?
- How are current and future generations (human and nonhuman) being considered?
- Over what period of time (past, present, and future) is the commons yardstick being applied?
- How are interdependencies between humans and between humans and nonhumans taken into account?
- What might threaten these commons? How might commoners respond?

Resisting Enclosure

In many parts of the world, people are fighting to maintain the commons that have already been established on various forms of property (whether private, state-owned, or open-access property). Resisting enclosure means that groups are contesting attempts to limit access and use and to minimize who benefits, cares, and has responsibilities. Instead these groups are working to ensure that access is shared, that benefits flow to a wide range of people, and that use, care, and responsibility are negotiated by the community that is connected to the commons.

ETHICAL ACTION: *Protecting the commons we already share*

Protecting Open and Accessible Spaces in Urban Areas

The World Communal Heritage is a European movement that draws attention to the benefits and potential of shared urban space created around modernist tower apartment blocks (especially in post-Soviet states). Such space includes the pedestrian walks, bike paths, open green spaces, and alleys where people bump into each other and interact.[20] This alternative heritage listing seeks to identify and protect these spaces. If this communal space is not protected, used, and cared for, it is under threat of being redeveloped by private interests. This will take space out of public use and reduce the opportunities for the less wealthy to enjoy living in the city. The World Communal Heritage is resisting enclosure and keeping urban spaces as open and accessible commons.

Protecting the Basis of Community

The Nandigram dispute in West Bengal, in India, arose in response to a move by the leftist state government to forcibly acquire land from entire villages and establish a chemical hub as a special economic zone.[21] The village land included fertile common lands where cattle were grazed, private land worked by the landowners or landless peasants, and schools, mosques, and temples. Without land, villagers would lose their livelihoods and be forced to move to cities such as Kolkata, where they would have no option but to eke out a living on the streets like so many other displaced rural people. The villagers formed the Bhumi Ucched Pratirodh Committee (Resist Land Eviction Committee, or BUPC). Bloody battles in 2007 between tens of thousands of villagers and police resulted in deaths and many casualties. Struggles continued through 2008 until the government backed down. This dispute is widely recognized as influencing the 2011 elections in West Bengal in which the Communist Party of India (Marxist) was defeated after more than thirty years in power, and it has inspired similar struggles throughout India. The Nandigram villagers fought against the privatization and secured their lifeblood—their agricultural and village lands.

We will never be parted from our land, it is our life, the dearest thing to us.

The cry of hundreds of Muslim women in Nandigram after the battles in 2007

Protecting Human Genes

One important area in which struggles over commoning and enclosing have life-or-death consequences is in the field of cancer research. In the United States, Myriad Genetics (and the University of Utah Research Foundation) has patents on the breast and ovarian cancer genes BRCA1 and BRCA2 and exclusive rights to conduct diagnostic tests on these genes. If patients want to know whether they have the cancer genes (and therefore an increased risk of breast or ovarian cancer), they have to be diagnosed through Myriad Genetics. This arrangement prevents other researchers from studying these genes and developing other diagnostic tests.

In 2009 the American Civil Liberties Union (ACLU) filed a suit against Myriad Genetics (on behalf of some 20 individuals and institutions representing some 100,000 doctors and researchers).[22] In March 2010, a U.S. District Court ruled in favor of the ACLU, finding that the BRCA1 and BRCA2 genes were indeed products of nature—part of our shared commons—and therefore not patentable. Myriad Genetics appealed the decision, and in July 2011 the Court of Appeals for the Federal Circuit reversed the ruling. The ACLU appealed to the Supreme Court, and in March 2012 the Supreme Court ordered the Court of Appeals to reconsider its decision. At the time of this writing there was no decision from the Court of Appeals. Meanwhile, two researchers at the University of Washington have recently developed and made available a do-it-yourself screen by using publically available resources.[23] They have commoned the IP needed to explore cancer risk and have thereby contributed to a sharing of knowledge with the community of cancer sufferers and their descendants, as well as the wider medical research community.

Protecting New Frontiers

The pressure for enclosure reaches even into star wars territory. Currently the 1967 UN Outer Space Treaty establishes that outer space is *terra communis* (communal land—in other words, common property that cannot be privatized).[24] The first treaty principle is that "the exploration and use of outer space shall be carried out for the benefit and in the interests of all countries and shall be the province of all mankind." But there is pressure from corporations to have outer space declared *terra nullius* (no man's land—in other words, property belonging to no one), in which case it could be not just colonized by nations but also privatized by corporations. This would lead to the enclosure of what is currently a commons. For the moment, *terra communis* prevails, and it is being protected by the one hundred nations that are party to the treaty and by the twenty-six nations that are signatories (as of 24 November 2011).

Commoning Private Property

As a result of neoliberal economic policies all over the world, state-owned property, particularly public services, has been privatized. In some cases communities have mobilized to reclaim privatized resources and transfer them into collective or public ownership. In other cases, communities are overturning centuries of tradition to claim private property and create commons.

ETHICAL ACTION: *Reclaiming and expanding commons to share the things that sustain us*

Remunicipalizing Water and Sewerage Systems

Grenoble, France, is a small mountain town near the border with Switzerland. In 1989 its water and sewage treatment utilities were privatized. Immediately the prices for these utilities soared. Even conserving water was no help to citizens, because the company could charge more per unit once water usage dropped below a certain level.[25] The outraged citizens demanded an investigation. The investigation and subsequent prosecution uncovered a culture of political corruption and incompetence. The city council "remunicipalized" the water and sewage treatment systems in the late 1990s. Forty other municipalities, including Paris in 2010, have followed suit. The remunicipalizing of water and sewage treatment systems is making sure that these resources are managed for the benefit of the citizenry and not for the benefit of private corporations.

Collectivizing Private Housing

The Alliance to Develop Power (ADP) is an organization whose members and leaders come from low-income communities in western Massachusetts. The ADP's focus when it started in 1994 was to preserve affordable housing. Decades earlier, private developers had taken out low-interest loans from the federal government, agreeing to build affordable housing. When the loans came to term in the 1990s, many of these developers tried to convert the housing into high-rent student apartments. The ADP sourced loans and grants to buy the housing so it could remain affordable housing. Each housing development is managed by its own tenant association, thereby transferring what was once privately owned and managed affordable rental housing into "cooperatively controlled, community held assets."[26]

Commoning Abandoned Private Land

In the 1980s, residents formed the Dudley Street Neighborhood Initiative (DSNI) to try to stop the illegal dumping of toxic and solid waste on the empty but privately owned blocks that made up about one-third of this poor inner-city neighborhood in the Roxbury area of Boston.[27] As part of its campaign, DSNI came up with its own plan for the neighborhood and successfully petitioned the city for the power of eminent domain so it could acquire the vacant land. Since 1988, DSNI has built four hundred high-quality affordable houses on these vacant lots. DSNI has been able to shift land from individual private ownership to collective private ownership with an emphasis on producing benefits for the Dudley Street community. In the process, DSNI has built not just a housing commons but a powerful community organization, community centers, parks, and other amenities.

Commoning Traditionally Held Private Lands

Until recently, two-thirds of all land in Scotland was owned by just 1,200 landowners.[28] Then in 2000, the first Scottish Parliament was elected in nearly three hundred years, and one of its first acts was to repeal Scottish Feudal Law (which originated in the eleventh century) and introduce a new land reform act. One part of the new act essentially gives tenants of rural estates (crofters) the right to form what are called community bodies and to buy estates (and other assets) when they are put up for sale. Like DSNI, the land reform act has transformed individual private property into collectively owned private property with an emphasis on managing the resources for community benefit. For example, community bodies in places like the Isle of Eigg and the Isle of Gigha have established new businesses, renovated housing, invested in infrastructure, and generally been able to reverse the fortunes of what were frequently deteriorating estates with absentee owners.

In the very different setting of Brazil, another legal document is providing a vital means for people to gain livelihoods and lead secure and settled lives. Article 184 of the Brazilian Constitution states that "land not serving its social function to produce goods of economic value and provide employment under proper legal safeguards of workers" can be expropriated from the landowner and used for agrarian reform.[29] The Landless Workers Movement (Movimento dos Trabalhadores Rurais Sem Terra or MST in Portuguese) was started in 1984, and it uses this article in the constitution to help groups of landless rural workers take ownership of unused (or misused) estates. Over 350,000 families now live on land that the MST has expropriated. Again, enclosed lands are being transformed into commons for community benefit.

Commoning Aspects of Private Property

Private property all over the world is being commoned by allowing nonowners to have access to and use of privately owned property, thus ensuring that the benefits are more widely distributed. This is happening especially in response to the need to care for the environment, and it involves private property owners accepting that care and responsibility for the earth can be shared.

ETHICAL ACTION: *Sharing aspects of private property to distribute benefits more widely*

Carving Out Conservation Areas from Private Property

Gondwana Link is a work in progress that involves protecting an arc of bushland almost 650 miles long in Australia's southwestern corner.[30] The arc stretches from tall, wet forests to desert landscapes and is Australia's only globally recognized biodiversity hot spot. To protect this land, a variety of conservation groups are working with scientists, private landholders, and Aboriginal communities. A key to establishing the continuous arc is that private landholders are establishing conservation covenants for parts of their properties so that, rather than being cleared and developed, the land can be restored and conserved and made accessible to scientists, Aboriginal groups, and even tourists who want to visit parts of the arc. Like the Spooner family, other private landholders are turning parts of their privately owned land into an environmental commons.

Temporary Use of Underutilized Private Property

In Cagayan de Oro City in the Philippines, the local government has opened up negotiations with private landowners to let groups of poor urban residents use unoccupied land to grow vegetables. There is interest in establishing agreements that would give tax breaks and other incentives to landowners who make their land available for these gardens to be allotted to poor urban dwellers. Even such temporary commons are of vital importance to poor urban residents.[31]

Splitting the Land from the Home

Across the minority world there is a growing community land trust movement. In a land trust the land is owned by a nonprofit group.[32] The land can never be sold but is managed by the trust for a social purpose, such as providing affordable housing for low-income groups. The housing on the land is owned by individual owner-occupiers or sometimes by another group (say, a housing cooperative). In the case of individual private home ownership, the house can be sold and resold, and it remains affordable because the value of the land is not included in the value of the house. This is particularly important in areas where land values are increasing and housing is becoming unaffordable for those on low incomes (for example, in inner-city neighborhoods that are being gentrified). By combining collective land ownership with individual home ownership, groups are ensuring that access to housing remains open to low-income groups.

Creating New Commons

New commons can be created by forming a community to share unmanaged open-access property. Sharing involves setting up rules of access and use where there were previously none. This means that benefits flow to those who care for and maintain the resources rather than just to those who found it first.

ETHICAL ACTION: *Managing open-access resources wisely and sustainably with others now and into the future*

Commoning Urban Resources

In chapter 4 we discussed Fallen Fruit, a group in Los Angeles that encourages people to access fruit that is readily available in the urban landscape, growing along streets, in public parks, and around parking lots. The group helps to maintain this urban commons with explicit rules and protocols to ensure that the fruit can be shared with others (not just other people, but the fruit trees themselves and nonhuman species, such as birds).

Community gardening is another way that groups are commoning urban resources. The most adventurous are guerilla gardeners, who turn unsightly and underused sites into urban spaces of creativity and productivity. One group of residents on an inner-city street in Sydney decided to common the area covered by concrete pavement outside their homes. They hired a concrete cutter and ripped up the pavement. They brought in soil and planted vegetables for the neighborhood. They even invited the local mayor to come and open their gardens![33]

Commoning Natural Resources

In the late 1980s, prawn (or shrimp) fishermen in the Spencer Gulf of South Australia experienced the lowest catch on record and realized that they needed to better manage the seafood resource. The fishermen have developed a management system based on trust and cooperation. There's no preset quota. Instead the fishermen voluntarily take surveys of the gulf before the season opens, and then a committee of fishermen decides which areas can be fished (just as the ranger groups of the West Arnhem Land Fire Abatement project sit down to plan and map the areas for seasonal burning). Once the fishing season starts, independent observers on the boats survey the catch. When there are concerns that fishing is having a detrimental impact, the area is closed—this can happen within an hour of the survey results being radioed in. The Spencer Gulf fishermen demonstrate how what was once an unmanaged resource can become a well-managed commons for current and future generations.

My father was a fisherman and I'm a fisherman and one day my son may be a fisherman, so we want to make sure something is left for the next generation.

Nathan Hood, prawn fisherman

Commoning Intellectual Resources

The publically funded Human Genome Project (1990–2003) mapped the entire human genome sequence. In 1996 the scientists involved agreed that the results should be made publically accessible as quickly as possible (even before data were published). An open-access online database, GenBank, was established, and scientists had to submit each genome sequence within twenty-four hours of its discovery. Early data sharing has become the "default" option in this area of scientific endeavor. This means that information about our human makeup has become a commons openly available to anyone with access to the Internet, an advance that is particularly important for medical researchers.

Without GenBank everything could have ended up in the hands of an American corporation.

Sir John Edward Sulston,
joint winner, 2002 Nobel Prize
in Physiology or Medicine, *Nature*

WHERE TO FROM HERE?

What would it take to contribute to the work of commoning? Can you be a commoner? To get started, you might use the Commons Yardstick to situate yourself and your community in relation to past and future generations and consider the following questions:

1. What resources (e.g., land, natural resources, cultural practices) does your community depend on? Are any of these resources threatened by processes of enclosure (e.g., privatization)? What sorts of actions could you undertake to preserve commons? Would the approach used by the World Communal Heritage movement or the Nandigram villagers or the ACLU or even nation-states concerned about access in outer space be suited to your issue? What other strategies could you use?
2. How might community well-being be improved if efforts were made to common private property (or aspects of it)? In this chapter we've looked at examples of how groups have done this in places as diverse as France, the United States, Scotland, Brazil, Australia, and the Philippines.

3. Some communities recognize the benefit they derive from open-access resources (whether physical, intellectual, or cultural), and they are working to make sure that these open-access resources are well managed. Are there resources of this sort in your community that you could care for, whether you are part of a neighborhood community (like Fallen Fruit), a business-based community (like the Spencer Gulf fisherman), or an intellectual community (like the researchers of the human genome sequence)?

In this chapter we introduced the Commons Yardstick to help us connect our current actions to those of past generations and to the world in which future generations will dwell. A key concern for community economies is our interdependence not just with future human generations but with the future of the planet itself. In the next chapter we delve more deeply into how we might invest in futures that will provide well-being for all.

6.

Take Back Finance

Investing in Futures

WHAT *IS* FINANCE?

The finance sector with its flighty financial markets has become our oracle of economic health. Every night on the TV news, graphs and figures showing currency fluctuations or the Dow Jones index are deciphered by economic commentators who tell us what we can and cannot expect of the future.

Since the beginning of the global financial crisis (GFC) in 2007, people all over the world have had to confront the fact that our lives are touched by an economic reality called finance. Some have lost jobs and houses because of the GFC, and others have seen their pension savings evaporate. Capitalist corporations have gone begging to governments for financial bailouts. And governments have initiated domestic austerity programs and scaled back international aid in its wake.

But what is finance really? And why does it have such a grip on our lives?

The term "finance" variously refers to money, savings, investment, taxation, budgets, debt, and risk management. It is associated with institutions like banks, insurance companies, credit unions, stock markets, and brokerage houses and with a whole host of "financial instruments"—hedge funds, interest rates, equity bonds, pension funds, exchange rates, and derivatives.

Many of the financial institutions we know of today began by offering specific financial services linked to groups of people who needed a way to manage their wealth. The merchant banks of the seventeenth and eighteenth centuries assisted traders to provide outlays of funds for ships and crews in the hopes of future rewards when their goods-laden ships came in. Bankers charged interest on their loans and accrued huge wealth, while traders took most of the risk. The insurance companies and consumer banks of today have their origins in mutual assistance funds organized by working people who put away their meager savings to tide them over in case of unemployment, sickness, injury, or death.

With the growth of capitalist industrialization in the nineteenth century, financial institutions became intimately linked with marshaling funds for the production economy. The finance industry grew to take charge of society's savings, "socializing" individual wealth by making it available in large bundles as credit and arranging for the repayment of loans in a timely manner. In return for private interest payments, financiers facilitated the turnover of savings, getting them out from under the mattress or from being sunk in machinery and plants, allowing them to work for the "greater good."

Over time the finance sector has grown disproportionately to the rest of the economy. Its relationship of service to target groups is no longer evident. Indeed, it appears to have developed its own modus operandi. Now the finance sector operates more like a giant casino than like society's guardian of wealth. Money begets money, so the mantra goes. And any way of doing so is condoned in today's world.

Almost any contract that has monetary value is now prey to "financialization." On the advice of forecasters and economists, financial institutions trade what are called financial derivatives of home loans, pension funds, stock indexes, machinery leases, and government treasury bonds. As we have seen with the unfolding of the GFC, individuals, corporations, and government regulators got caught up in the thrill of the gamble. They approached the risks involved in these markets with extraordinary naïveté, sometimes willing ignorance, and certainly no sense of broader social obligations. The ethos among financial traders was

I am a trader. If I see an opportunity to make money, I go with that. For most traders, it's not about . . . we don't really care that much how they're going to fix the economy, how they are going to fix the whole situation. Our job is to make money.

Alessio Rastani, financial market trader, *BBC World News*, 2011

IBGYBG—"I'll be gone, you'll be gone"—so why worry about the long-term catastrophe that financialization might induce?[1]

The GFC is an ongoing event in which the gamblers began to go bust at the same time. International investors from Iceland to India exchanged their savings for fractions of thousands of U.S. mortgages, only to have their fortunes dashed as the subprime mortgage market crashed. Private equity managers bought and sold distressed firms, stripping their salable assets or using the newly acquired business as collateral to take out larger loans. One U.S. company, Simmons Mattress Pty Ltd (Proprietary Limited) was bought and sold seven times in twenty years. Investors made money, while Simmons's debt ballooned from US$164 million in 1991 to US$1.3 billion in 2009. The last private equity firm that bought Simmons couldn't find a buyer, and the firm went bankrupt.[2]

Now in its fifth year, the GFC is not going away. A lucky few have, in the jargon of the financial world, made a killing.[3] But many institutions in the corporate and public finance sectors have been badly damaged or destroyed. Communities and nations are suffering, and the life chances of current and future generations have been put at risk.

If we want to take back the economy for people and the planet, we must reclaim finance as an enabler of futures not as an end in itself that is liable to self-destruction. We must consider how individual interest and social interest can be combined as funds are stored and circulated. And we must connect monetary investment with all the other kinds of nonmonetary investment that build secure futures.

One of the few financial institutions to have weathered the GFC relatively unscathed is Spain's La Caja Laboral (the Working People's Bank). This institution is part of the Mondragón worker-owned cooperative network introduced in chapter 3. La Caja is committed to serving its region and abides by the core cooperative principle of putting people over capital, that is, of the subordinate and instrumental character of finance. We can learn a lot from how La Caja Laboral ensures that the stored wealth of the community is safeguarded and directed into generating widespread well-being now and into the future.

"Why bother about winter?" said the Grasshopper. "We have got plenty of food at present." But the Ant went on its way and continued its toil.

"The Ant and the Grasshopper," *Aesop's Fables*

REDEPLOYING SAVINGS TOWARD A COMMUNITY'S FUTURE

In the late 1950s, the Basque region of northern Spain still felt the devastating effects of the Spanish Civil War. With the continued repression under Franco's rule, many families saw international migration as the only option for surviving well in the future. What small amount of wealth the region possessed drained away with every migrant. The proud Basque people who had stopped the Roman occupation centuries before were in danger of becoming an overseas diaspora.

As people drifted away, the priest whose teachings had inspired the formation of the first worker-owned manufacturing cooperatives in the town of Mondragón, Don José María Arizmendiarrieta, grasped the magnitude of the problem.[4] As he saw it, the future was either "savings or suitcases." Father Arizmendi had the idea of starting a bank. In the establishment phase of the cooperative businesses, the cooperators' dividends, or surplus, were allocated to individuals to use as they chose. Don José María convinced the reluctant cooperators to start La Caja Laboral and deposit this money so that it could be used collectively.

La Caja opened in 1959 as a "second-degree" cooperative, that is, a cooperative owned by the production cooperatives that would service these "first-degree" enterprises. Father Arizmendi further convinced the cooperators of the benefit of accessing only the interest earned on their saved surplus during their working lives. Their accumulated holdings would be available upon their retirement, but in the meantime the bank could use these consolidated funds.

Once established, the bank had as its central mission the facilitation of opportunities for workers' ownership in the Basque region. In theory, La Caja Laboral could have invested the cooperators' surplus elsewhere in the world where a high rate of return was promised. But, because it was a cooperative committed to the principle of putting people over capital, the bank directed its capital holdings back into thickening the network of cooperative enterprises and generating more regional employment.

La Caja Laboral hosted a business development agency that offered business and financial support to start-up cooperatives. Soon this was spun off as a separate research and development cooperative. The bank also invested in the social and cultural fabric of the region, helping to set up second-degree cooperatives involved in social insurance (offering health care, life insurance, and social security) and in education and training (from preschool to university).

La Caja has been a crucial conduit for investing in a secure future for the Basque region. From a handful of people employed in a single factory in the 1950s, the Mondragón Cooperative Corporation (MCC) has grown to currently employ nearly 85,000, a third of whom are located in the home region of Euskadi. La Caja Laboral is now one of the major banks in Spain, with 1.2 million clients, of which only 120 are the MCC cooperatives.[5]

Unlike most European and U.S. banks, La Caja Laboral was barely touched by the GFC.[6] For one thing, its finance managers earn extremely modest incomes pegged to the narrow salary range of all cooperators. For another, its commitment to reinvesting in the MCC meant that it had limited exposure to the U.S. subprime mortgage market, whose collapse precipitated the spread of financial catastrophe. Losses were incurred when U.S. bonds acquired to hedge against long-term interest rate decreases collapsed, but they did not affect the bank's asset and equity holdings.

When cooperators in Mondragón invest their surplus in La Caja Laboral, they are consolidating savings so as to secure a decent future for themselves, their children, and the region they are so proud of. Their Working People's Bank offers a safe and secure repository that redeploys funds toward people's well-being and toward regional sustainability. An ethic of solidarity regulates any temptation to heed the lure of quick returns and risky speculation.

Unlike the post-GFC zombie banks of Wall Street, which have been put on government life-support to the tune of hundreds of billions of US taxpayer dollars, Mondragón stands on its own feet and sponges off nobody.

John Ballantyne, *News Weekly*

INVESTING IN A FUTURE: A KEY CONCERN OF A COMMUNITY ECONOMY

What does it mean to invest in the future? It means taking action now to ensure that our descendents can survive as well, if not better, than we do. It means building up our commons and circulating new wealth so that it supports sustainable modes of living with each other and with our earth. It also means attending to the survival chances of others who are less fortunate than we, whose futures will be ever more entangled with ours as our earthly home adjusts to major environmental challenges.

In a community economy, investment comes in many forms, and money is just one way in which it is stored, circulated, and magnified. We invest our time, energy, and imagination into human memory, arts, culture, and social networks. These investments can also be circulated, maintained, and magnified. And the earth is one big investment that continues to give returns to all, despite our frequent mismanagement and destruction of its natural gifts.

How we marshal our wealth and put it to use is a matter of great importance, especially when the consequences of destroying it or distributing it unfairly are so devastating for people and environments.

As we hurtle along together on spaceship earth, it seems that concern for the very future of our planet can easily be eclipsed by preoccupations with fluctuating interest rates and asset values in a finance sector that services only a fraction of the world's population but manages almost the entirety of its stored monetary wealth. But how do we step away from our individual worries about money to think about the kinds of investing practices that will ensure a livable future?

Let's return to the simple idea of our economy as a community garden that was presented in the Introduction. What secures the future of this garden—and many real gardens across the globe—is investment in replenishing the nutrients taken out of the soil and investment in the relationships between those who toil to make the garden flourish. Maintaining soil nutrients and social networks is one side of the equation; the other is accumulating a richer soil profile and knowledge bank.

Most industrial agriculture ignores the accumulation side of this equation, relying on more and more chemical inputs to maintain soil fertility and ignoring or discrediting the place-based knowledge that farmers build up over generations. The long-term effect is depletion of the soil structure along with traditional know-how—and ultimately loss of arable land and cultures of stewardship. By contrast, systems like permaculture and agroecology offer an entirely different approach. With each cycle of production and consumption, compost is added to the soil and farmers

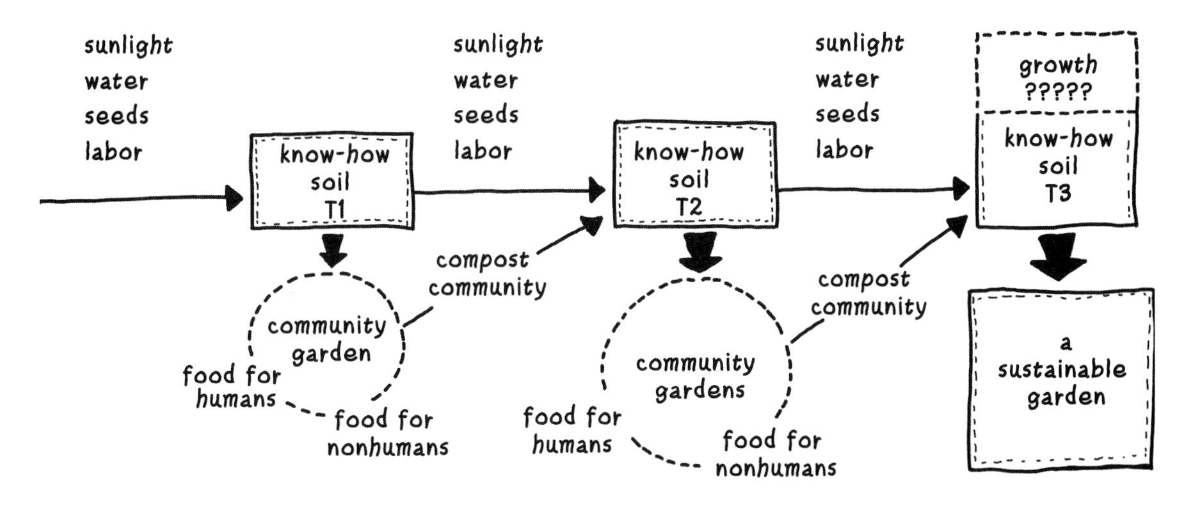

Stocks and Flows of a Community Garden

increase their understanding of how to interact sustainably with plants, animals, insects, soil, and water. Depending on the earth's ability to support more life and the group's ability to govern itself sustainably, the garden can either grow more food and take on more members or maintain itself in a steady state, as shown in the nearby figure.

In this figure sunlight, water, seeds, and labor "flow" into the garden, where they combine with the "stock" of soil and gardeners' know-how at Time 1 (T1). The first cycle of production and consumption produces food for the gardeners, birds, insects, and other life forms associated with the garden. It produces compost (made up of food and plant waste) and new knowledge about the productive interactions between all living beings in the garden. Compost is then invested in the soil bank and the soil stock regenerates or possibly grows in quantity by Time 2 (T2). Community relationships thicken, and new knowledge is added to existing know-how by T2. The gardeners can decide whether to sustain their output with maintenance investments or to grow their garden by investing in more land, richer soil, or more intensive methods, like gardening vertically. As the cycle is repeated for Time 3 (T3), these decisions regarding growth will affect the future.

This simple figure of stocks and flows helps us to understand the potentiating force of La Caja Laboral. In the next figure, cooperators' surplus and local consumers' savings flow into the stock of bank holdings at T1. Funds are used to finance new producer cooperatives, social services, and cultural institutions, all of which produce more employment.[7] Over time these new businesses generate surpluses, a proportion of which flows into individual cooperators' accounts, which they, in turn, deposit in the bank. The bank's holdings expand at T2, and the capacity to reinvest in the MCC grows. As part of its commitment to supporting the well-being and viability of Basque communities, the bank expands its financing of health insurance, social security, and education cooperatives, as well as expanding the network of cooperative and non-cooperative companies throughout Spain and the world.

We're a small community garden and we decided to keep it this way. For us, with the group that we've got, and the size of the garden, we manage fine.

Nellie Hobley, *A Community Garden Manifesto*

The next cycle shows that as the bank becomes more established and extends its consumer banking functions throughout Spain, it invests some funds in mainstream financial services such as the fixed-interest U.S. bonds whose value evaporated upon the collapse of Lehman Brothers. This brings about a decline in the stock of value of the bank but doesn't affect its ability to service its primary clients—the cooperatives and individual consumers.

From the individual cooperators' point of view, the security of their future, as safeguarded by La Caja Laboral, is offset by a comfortable present in which their survival needs are more than adequately met by a combination of their cooperators' wage income and the provision of public goods.

Our ability to invest in the future is closely linked to the conditions under which we live today. When there is no need to squirrel away funds in fear of unexpected personal emergencies and when there are respected institutions that can offer security for those savings, it is possible to mobilize wealth for socially valued ends.

As we saw in chapter 2, public goods such as transport infrastructure and social services such as health care provide a direct subsidy for the survival of all people. Public investment in these areas builds up the

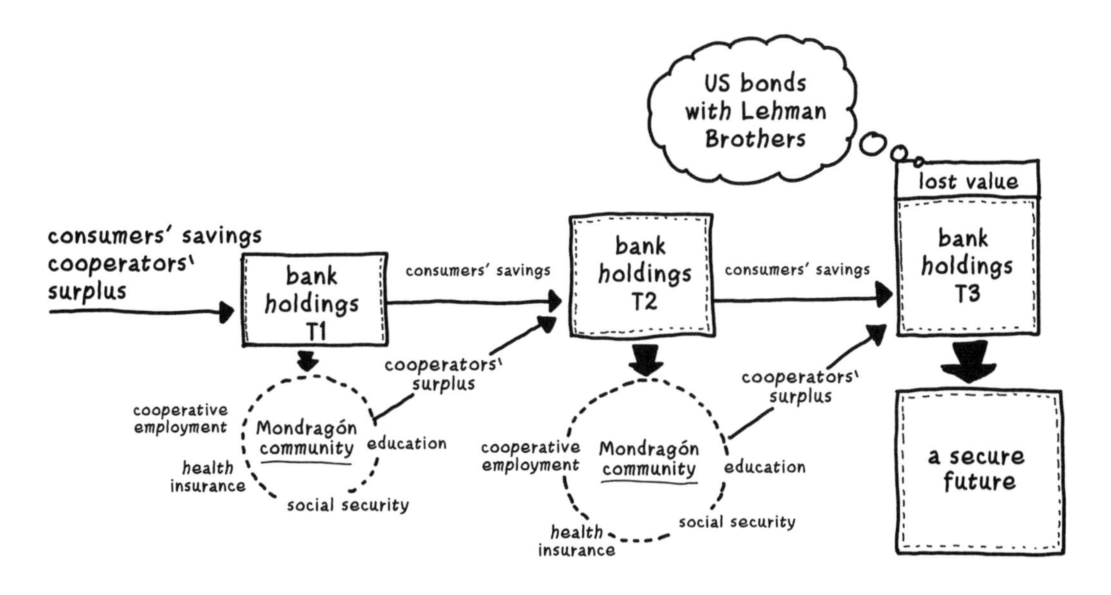

Stocks and Flows of La Caja Laboral

stock of a societal commons. On this collective base we can work hard to save for our own futures, to accumulate personal finances, and to contribute funds to the futures of others.

National and regional governments have big roles to play when it comes to investing social wealth. Taxation systems can be used to ensure that there are adequate public goods and social safety nets to allow citizens to survive well enough in the present to be concerned for a collective future. Far too often, however, taxes on trade, property, and income are used for nearsighted or destructive purposes.

Since the GFC and the bailouts offered by governments to failing banks and corporations, the evaporation of public funds in many nations has been acute. Even in "wealthy" countries like the United States, people are told that the public coffers are too empty to maintain public infrastructures

Most of us were simply lucky enough to be born in a prosperous country. Whether or not we inherit money as individuals, from our parents or other benefactors, we all inherit societal capital, in the form of effective government, law and order, a power supply, systems of transportation and communication, and so on.

Peter Singer and Tom Gregg, *How Ethical Is Australia?*

like schools and hospitals.[8] The negative flow-on effects on daily well-being are already being felt with rising unemployment and deteriorating public goods. What's more, we see growing resistance by a vocal minority to any attempt at sharing society's wealth and extending health care and social security to a greater number of people. In this context, the ability to think about our collective future is being compromised.

Not all communities and governments are so myopic. Indeed, there are individuals, organizations, and governments that are taking a far-sighted approach, investing now for future benefit.

Marshaling Diverse Investments for a Different Kind of Growth

The southern Indian state of Kerala presents an amazing example of long-term investment in improving well-being for all.[9] Kerala is a state of thirty-three million people with a mixed population that is 60 percent Hindu, 20 percent Muslim, and 20 percent Christian. Although it is poor by standard measures of per capita cash income, the population is rich by other measures. The average life expectancy is seventy-three years for males and seventy-five years for females, comparable with that of the United States (and some ten years greater than for India as a whole). Some 94 percent of births are attended by health professionals, and the infant death rate is lower than that for African Americans in Washington, D.C. The total fertility rate is two births per woman, and the population growth rate is below replacement level. Compare this to the 1950s, when Kerala had the highest population growth rate in India.

These demographic changes have been achieved *without* the coercive state practices pursued in China or the rest of India, which have reduced population growth but seen the rise of abnormal sex ratios of females to males. In India as a whole, this ratio is 91 women to 100 men. In Kerala, for every 100 men there are 109 women.

Kerala has solved one-third of the equation that drives environmental destruction the world over. And, defying conventional wisdom, it has done so without rapid economic growth—has done so without becoming a huge consumer of resources and thus destroying the environment in other ways.

Bill McKibben, *The Enigma of Kerala*

Since the State of Kerala was formed in 1956,

state governments, many of them communist led, have prioritized land reform, food security, health, and education. Importantly, there has been concerted investment in mass literacy and the education of boys *and* girls. Since the late 1950s a much higher proportion of state government expenditure has consistently been spent on education in Kerala than in all the other Indian states.

An important social investment in Kerala has been in the strong library and adult education movement aimed at eradicating illiteracy.[10] Early on, this movement was led by P. N. Paniker, a champion who popularized the slogan "Read and grow." Since the 1970s it has been supported by state investment in printing primers, reference books, and guidebooks and paying organizing and field staff. Massive investments have also come in the form of volunteer labor and nongovernmental organizing power. In 1989–91 the Total Literacy Campaign recruited 350,000 volunteer teachers to target rural illiteracy. Volunteers learned from doctors how to match 50,000 pairs of donated eyeglasses to recipients with bad eyesight. The effect of this concerted effort is an official literacy rate of 90 percent today. Throughout the decades, women's literacy has been particularly targeted—for a number of very good reasons. When women are literate, it is more likely that *all* children, not just boys, will also be literate. And when women are educated, the transition from high to low population rates is much more likely to occur.[11]

The experience of the state of Kerala shows that it is not just financial investment that reaps benefits but investment in people *by* people. Many challenges still face this region. An unfortunate consequence of the better wages and conditions achieved by workers in Kerala is that factories move to cheaper regions in India. There are high rates of unemployment and underemployment. Many educated Keralites seek employment overseas. And although physical health across the board has improved dramatically, mental health problems remain, including high suicide rates.

Though mainstream economists are unhappy with Kerala's low rate of economic growth, others are intrigued by the experiments with a nonmainstream kind of economic growth that are being pursued there. The stabilized population and commitment to fairness and redistribution could well be ingredients for a low-wage future built around a good life.[12]

In Mararikulam, one of Kerala's poorest areas, women are taking the lead.[13] Some fifteen thousand neighborhood savings groups, each made up of between twenty and forty women, are transforming themselves from credit associations into production cooperatives. Small amounts of money saved by seventeen thousand women have yielded enough to capitalize a range of producer cooperatives making soap, school items, coconut coir products, and food. In 2002, thirty thousand women took the pledge to buy locally produced Maari soap rather than imported brands. And in 2008, three hundred representatives from a hundred local governments in Kerala signed the "Mararikulam Declaration for Self-Sufficiency in Vegetable Production." They pledged to support women's participation in organic vegetable farming, to diversify crop production, and to achieve food security in the foreseeable future. Kerala shows us that there may be many ways of investing in a stable economy that serves people and the planet well.

From Nonrenewable Resources to Renewable Funds to Renewable Industries

Norway offers a different kind of example of a nation that is strategically considering how revenues from nonrenewable and greenhouse gas–producing resources can be used to leverage a renewable energy economy. The Norwegian people have ownership rights over extensive oil and gas deposits in the North Sea. A large part of the benefit flowing from the exploitation of these resources is claimed by the Norwegian government. When production began in 1971, money started rolling in to the government's coffers. Oil profits were taxed at 50 percent, and oil companies also paid the standard 28 percent business tax. For decades now, oil and gas companies have been paying a whopping 78 percent tax!

When nations are faced with "windfall gains" like this, many suffer what is called a "resource curse." National industries other than mining can decline as exchange rates appreciate and domestic goods become uncompetitive for export. Returns from mining are volatile as commodity prices fluctuate. And corruption and mismanagement of huge resource revenues is often rife. Inevitably, such a nation must confront the final rundown of the nonrenewable resource and transition to a postresource situation. Norway, after a short honeymoon period, has taken steps to avoid the worst aspects of the resource curse.

Less than a decade after its windfall boost in revenues, the Norwegian government realized that, like so many other countries with vast mineral resources, Norway had been treating these petroleum revenues as "easy money" (in the words of the secretary general of the Ministry of Finance). It had been reneging on its responsibility "to ensure that also future generations will benefit from the oil wealth."[14] In 1990 a sovereign wealth fund, the Government Petroleum Fund, was established to receive oil and gas revenues. In 2006 it was split in two, with the Government Pension Fund Global receiving 95 percent of the petroleum revenues. Currently this fund has holdings of US$513 billion and is the second-largest investment fund owned by a government. Clear principles of transparency are followed to ensure that the people of Norway are informed about their investment. Importantly, no more than 4 percent of the fund can be spent in the annual national budget. The rest is invested overseas and managed so that it can be drawn on in the future.

We cannot spend this money now; it would be stealing from future generations.

Eirik Wekre, Norwegian economist, *New York Times*

There are clear stipulations as to where the money in the fund can be invested. It is *not,* for example, to be invested in companies that violate human rights (e.g., by manufacturing cluster munitions, using child labor, producing tobacco goods, or seriously degrading the environment). It *can* be used to lobby U.S. firms in its portfolio that oppose climate protection laws. Importantly, in 2009 it was decided that over five years US$3.3 billion would be invested in companies developing energy-efficient and cleaner technologies.

Norway offers an example of how states can invest responsibly to help the survival of all the species that live on this planet. There is, of course, a sad irony in using windfall gains made from exploiting nature's fossiliferous fuels to deal with the problems generated by burning these same fuels. And there is something quite problematic about transforming nonrenewable resources into investment funds that continue to grow in perpetuity by exacting interest payments and placing bets in the global finance casino.

In terms of global climate protection, the significance of the Norwegian sovereign welfare fund until now has been certainly limited but should not be underestimated.

Danyel Reiche, *Energy*

Poorer countries with access to resource windfalls often have more need for current improvements in their living standards than does Norway, and they view sovereign funds in a different light. They are drawn toward spending now rather than investing for the future. How to do so without inducing the resource curse is a challenge. The small Pacific island state of Kiribati, for example, uses returns from its sovereign wealth fund to finance government business and reduce reliance on development aid.[15] Venezuela, in an attempt to reduce its oil dependency, has used its Macroeconomic Stabilization Fund to support the growth of a social economy made up of microcredit banks, microenterprises, state–worker comanaged companies, and social production enterprises (what we have called social enterprises).[16] However, like Norway, Venezuela takes the risk of relying on an international finance market with a casino temperament to safeguard its sovereign wealth.

There are no simple answers as to how best to invest in improving present conditions and collective futures. But we can learn from La Caja Laboral's commitment to the principle of people over capital. In a community economy, ethical commitments can guide how we invest in futures that will be worth living in.

INVESTMENT STOCK TAKING: ANOTHER KEY CONCERN FOR A COMMUNITY ECONOMY

The flows of monetary and nonmonetary wealth in our world derive from different sources—from enterprise surplus, taxes, natural resources, personal savings, and volunteer efforts. When this wealth is pooled, it takes on a different life, becoming investment funds that have a huge potentiating force. In a community economy we are interested in marshaling wealth, safeguarding it, dispersing it to worthwhile ends, and making a social return that can be shared in a transparent and ethical manner.

Investing is not an end in itself but a means to a better end. Our investments lay down the preconditions for a different future. But how can we be sure that our investments *are* building desirable futures for people and the planet? We need to regularly take stock of what our investments are producing. And we need a way of foregrounding the ethical decisions we make as we negotiate investing now for future benefit.

Global financial systems seem unable to help bridge the gap between now and later and connect us to a desirable future. As we have seen with the GFC, recent returns on investments (ROI) managed by international finance markets have been negative for many investors. People today are extremely disgruntled with their lack of knowledge about where their investments go in the corporate finance sector. There is a demand for more transparency. Indeed the demand for "ethical" investments is getting stronger. Ethical investments involve a return that brings about a socially responsible or greener future.

When it comes to investing, the usual way of taking stock is to undertake a cost–benefit analysis. Here flows of investments (costs) and flows of benefits are expressed in terms of net present value. With the growing interest in social and environmental responsibility and in sustainability accounting, and with the rise in the number of social enterprises, there has been a call for a different kind of cost–benefit accounting. A new stock-taking tool, the calculation of social return on investment (SROI), has been developed. This tool allows for social and environmental returns created by monetary investment to be measured by means of financial proxy values (as we see in the figure below).[17]

To illustrate, let's take Homeboy Industries, discussed in chapter 3, and measure a hypothetical SROI. This social enterprise targets at-risk youth, aiming to keep them out of jail and help them build worthwhile lives in the community. In the equation given in the figure, the total investment in Homeboy might amount to $200,000 per year. Let's say that each year the enterprise keeps ten young people out of jail. The cost of keeping one person in prison per year may be something on the order of $70,000. So the monetary proxy for what is saved by keeping ten young people out of prison for one year is $700,000. When the total investment is deducted, the remainder is $500,000, and when this amount is divided by the total investment, the SROI that results is a figure of 2.5. This means

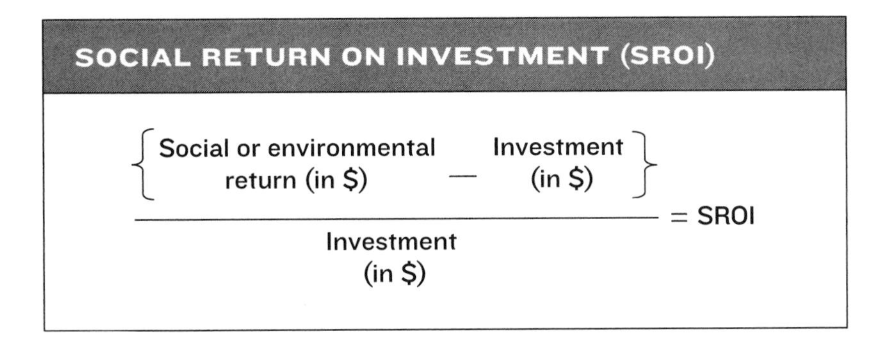

that for every dollar invested in Homeboy, society is saved the expenditure of $2.50.

As with any new measuring instrument, there is much discussion about the usefulness of the SROI measure. Some point to the difficulty and perhaps the undesirability of reducing all benefit to monetary values in the SROI. Others are suspicious that the tool can be used as a way of monitoring how to cut costs rather than how to increase social benefits.

For the purposes of taking back the economy as a space of ethical decision making, perhaps we can use a version of the ROI as a way of identifying the choices we have when it comes to investing in our future. Before we do so, though, we need to question the definition of growth that is attached to any measure of "returns."

The mainstream principle of investing is that individuals, corporations, and nations should maximize their returns in as short a time frame as possible. The desire for short-term returns commits us to following a path of continuous economic growth. Of late, the shortcomings of this approach have been revealed: the growth it produced was a series of bubbles that have popped in a spectacular fashion. Objectively this approach has paid off for a very few at the expense of almost everyone else.

The growth of some enterprises, particularly those that serve the broader interests of the community and the planet, may continue to be seen as ethically desirable. We see in this chapter, however, that communities can invest in other things that ensure a better future but that are not seen to grow in the narrow economic sense. Resources can be directed to ensure the growth of vital commons and ethical exchange relations in ways that improve quality of life while reducing waste. We might think of this as a no-growth or even a degrowth approach to investment. Alternatively, we could understand these investments as producing growth of a different sort. Adding these investments to our "portfolio" allows us to grow other things—intact ecologies, communities that share a common purpose, and more enriched, informed, and capable citizens.

Taking back investing for people and the planet involves thinking about all that sustains us and the well-being of those who will come after us. We can use the *Community Economy Return on Investment* (CEROI) to explore the investment pathways that are open to us in a community economy.

Community economy investments are those in

- social services that support health, education, child care, and elder care so that individually sourced survival payments do not need to be as large;
- technologies and commons that help us to consume less;
- initiatives to reduce our ecological footprint (such as expanding reuse activities, renewable energy industries, and public mass transport systems);
- democratically owned companies that generate employment and distribute surplus to the community and the environment;
- ethical trade and other types of transactions that help us to encounter others more directly; and
- repair, care for, and expansion of commons that help support life.

The community economy returns we might expect from these investments are

- increased well-being for people and environments,
- reduced ecological footprints,
- increased opportunities for surplus to be democratically distributed toward generating social and environmental well-being,
- increased ethical trade and more direct transactions, and
- expanded commons.

The CEROI is determined by a stock-taking formula that helps us think about the future and what actions we need to take now in order to help create that future for generations to come. La Caja Laboral, for example, has prioritized building a future in which the people of Spain's Basque region will have secure employment and dignified livelihoods—this is the return it is seeking. Investment is channeled into maintaining and expanding the cooperative network, capitalizing new cooperative ventures, and financing social insurance, health, and education services—initiatives that all reflect the cooperative principles of

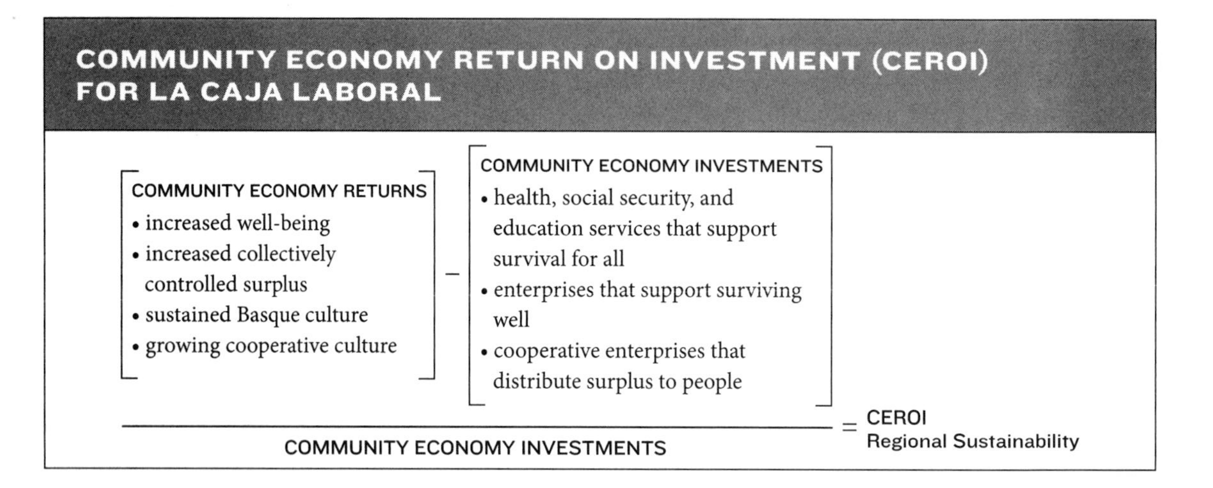

the Mondragón Cooperative Corporation. The CEROI for La Caja Laboral might look like that in the figure above.

In this chapter we have touched on three different examples of communities investing in their own future well-being. Each faces different challenges—rural poverty in Kerala, cultural sustainability in the Basque region, and an overabundance of "dirty" wealth in Norway. In each case we see people wrestling with how to direct their investment strategies—toward education, health, land redistribution, and a stabilized population; toward employment opportunities and regional and cultural sustainability; and toward a renewable energy future. These may be very different communities, but what they have in common is an approach to investment that is deliberate rather than haphazard and long-term rather than shortsighted—more like permaculture and less like slash and burn.

TOOLS FOR INVESTING IN DIFFERENT FUTURES

The old adage in finance is "Don't put all your eggs in one basket." Conventional financial planners typically tell individual investors to diversify their assets. In a community economy, diversified investment would focus on ways of investing for the benefit of the entire society and in ways that allow people to meet their present and future needs without further straining planetary resources.

The Diverse Finance Identifier can be used to distinguish the variety of ways of organizing investment. As in the case of other aspects of the diverse economy, there is much more to finance than the banks, brokerages, and insurance companies we associate with the sector's mainstream. A diversity of public-sector and community-based organizations are involved in the work of underwriting a better future. In addition, families, neighbors, community organizations, and whole regions can direct stored wealth and other resources through nonmarket mechanisms from interest-free lending to sweat equity and free labor inputs.

In a community economy we must keep our collective eye on how monetary and nonmonetary resources are directed toward ensuring a better, more sustainable future. We invest with the interests of future generations in mind, including the continued integrity of the natural systems that sustain life. Sometimes an investment decision will have flow-on effects that need to be accounted for in order to get a sense of the full return. For example, Norway's decision to invest some of its wealth fund in alternative energy technologies will yield both financial *and* ecological returns. At other times, emphasizing one desired outcome—such as increased jobs for community members—may come with the price of not being able to invest in other things that ensure well-being.

DIVERSE FINANCE IDENTIFIER
MAINSTREAM MARKET FINANCE
ALTERNATIVE MARKET FINANCE State banks Government-sponsored lenders Credit unions Microfinance Friendly societies Community-based financial institutions
NONMARKET FINANCE Sweat equity Community-supported business Rotating credit funds Family lending Donations Interest-free loans

The CEROI helps us to recognize the real diversity of options available to us as members of communities seek to ensure future resilience.

COLLECTIVE ACTIONS FOR INVESTING IN DIFFERENT FUTURES

In a community economy we use investment more transparently to build a future for all.

In this section we look at ways that people are taking back investment and connecting to new futures in the making.

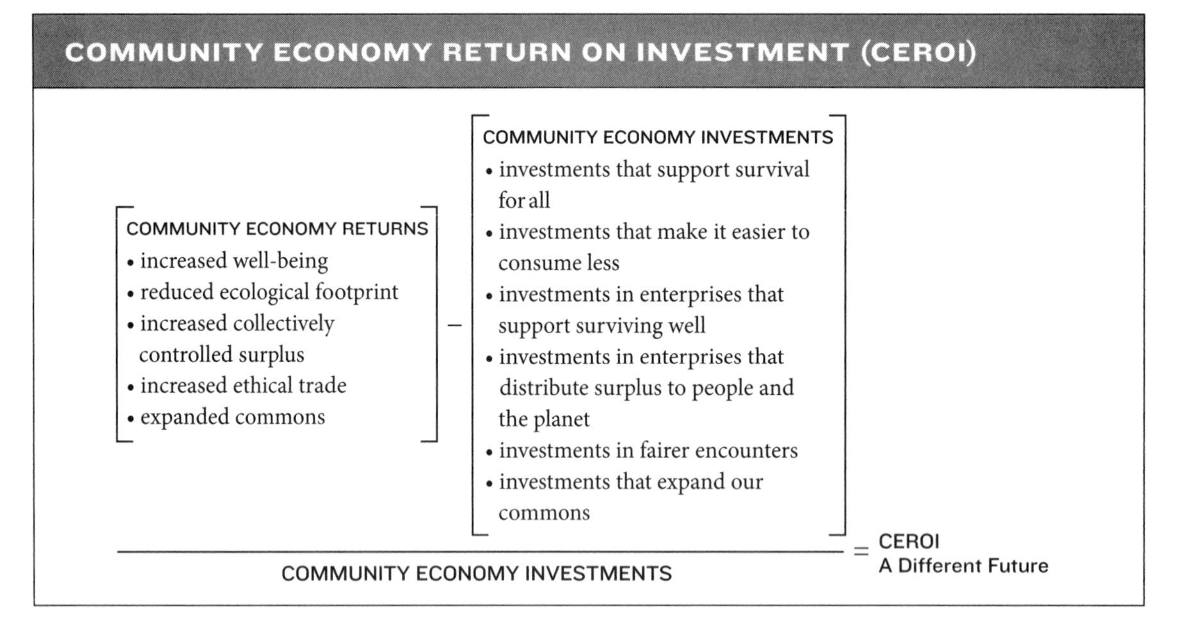

Participating in Peer-to-Peer Finance

Peer-to-peer financing allows people to directly connect with each other without going through an intermediary, like a bank, that might charge exorbitant fees or might not divulge where funds are being invested. Peer-to-peer finance provides direct support to those in need of funds. When there is an interfacing institution, it is usually a nonprofit people's organization.

ETHICAL ACTION: *Directly investing to help others build their futures*

Questions to consider as you read about these collective actions

- Who are the community of investors? How do they relate to one another?
- Whose wealth is being harnessed? How is it being stored?
- What futures are being constructed?
- What combination of monetary and nonmonetary investment is being marshaled toward building future benefit?
- What new forms of financial institution are being developed?

Peer-to-peer finance has a long history. For centuries, rotating savings and credit associations (ROSCAs) have been widespread across parts of Africa, Asia, Europe, and Latin America. They continue to be a critical financing tool in the majority world, and, despite the so-called modernization of countries like South Korea and Taiwan, they endure. One study found that at least 20 percent of households in Taiwan use ROSCAs (or *hui*) and that participation increases as household income increases.[18] ROSCAs have spread to other countries such as Australia, Canada, and the United States through migrant groups.

ROSCAs are based on a very simple arrangement. A ROSCA group meets on a regular basis (say, every month), and at each meeting all members put in the same amount of money (although it's reported that some groups in India put in rice or cows). At the meeting the pot of money is immediately given to one member. This is repeated at each meeting until everyone in the group has had their turn. The group may then start again or disband. Depending on the amount of money being contributed, members of ROSCAs use the funds for everything from helping to start small businesses to paying for health and educational expenses to buying small household items.

This type of simple but effective peer-to-peer financing arrangement has been taken up and modified for a digital world. Zopa is a financial institution founded in the United Kingdom in 2005. It is an online network in which people who have spare money offer to lend it directly to people who want to borrow. Zopa stands for "zone of possible agreement," highlighting the way that loans are negotiated—lenders set their terms, such as the interest rates and loan period, and borrowers find a loan with the terms that suit them. Lenders also specify what risk category they are willing to lend to (A*, A, B, C, or Young, for borrowers aged twenty to twenty-five). One way that Zopa manages risk is to make sure that lenders' money is spread across a number of borrowers (usually in small amounts of £10). As of May 2012, Zopa had lent over £205 million. The Zopa model has been copied in Germany (with Smava), Spain (with Communitae), and the United States (with Prosper). In Canada, P2P Financial, a Zopa-based network, has partnered with Newstart Canada, an organization founded in 1978 to help people establish or rebuild their credit histories.

Whereas peer-to-peer finance is changing the way that people invest and borrow in relation to personal finance, other organizations have focused on investing in projects and enterprises. Kickstarter, started in 2008, is a crowd-sourcing entity that allows people to invest in a variety of creative projects. In the United States there are still legal questions over who owns the crowd-sourcing approach, but it is an idea that is enjoying widespread support in an era when finance from conventional institutions is drying up.[19] Artists and creators pitch their ideas through the site, and in exchange Kickstarter collects a 5 percent fee out of funds successfully raised. Since 2009, more than twenty thousand creative projects have been funded through Kickstarter, with two million people pledging over US$200 million for projects (though most pledges are for only $25). Just two of the projects funded through Kickstarter that touch on the themes of this book are the short film *Portraits of the Solidarity Economy* (2011) and *A Guidebook of Alternative Nows* (2012).

While Kickstarter is giving artists and creators access to capital, other initiatives focus on making small loans to individuals and groups to help them survive well. Kiva started in 2005 and uses Internet technology to facilitate investment by the minority world in the majority world.[20] Kiva is a not-for-profit financial institution that works with microfinance organizations across the world. The organizations send Kiva information about individuals and groups that are looking for loans (usually to start or strengthen small enterprises in areas such as agriculture and retail). The information is posted online, and investors can sign up to finance the loan. Usually people invest in lots of $25, so a single loan will have a number of investors. Currently more than 770,000 people worldwide have lent more than US$317 million to projects in sixty-one countries. There is a remarkable repayment rate on the loans of almost 99 percent.

Whereas Kiva is an international organization, other peer-to-peer financial institutions have been developed directly by people in the majority world. Unlad Kabayan Migrant Services Inc., which started in 1996, is a Philippines-based community financing institution that spun off from the Asian Migrant Centre in Hong Kong.[21] The Centre helps migrant workers form savings groups and begin to accumulate small amounts from their meager wages. In 1994 the Migrant Savings for Alternative Investment program was founded to pool investment funds from overseas Filipino workers and use them to develop productive capacity in the Philippines, where unemployment rates are extremely high. Rather than only sending savings home to individual households where it is used for consumption items, workers put aside some funds in the Migrant Savings program, where they are combined and used by Unlad Kabayan to help start enterprises in rural communities. These businesses aim to meet local needs while generating employment opportunities. The ultimate goal is to invest in economic opportunities that will provide people with an alternative to outmigration.

Do-It-Yourself Finance

When we think of finance we usually think of monetary resources, but in do-it-yourself finance other resources can be mobilized to help build a better future for people and the planet. Do-it-yourself finance can be family based, with family members lending money and volunteer labor to help other family members with housing or to start businesses. But there are also groups, organizations, and businesses that are experimenting with ways of engaging in do-it-yourself financing.

ETHICAL ACTION: *Finding opportunities for groups to raise their own finances*

Worcester Energy Barnraisers in Worcester, Massachusetts, is a community group that uses volunteer labor and skill sharing in order to improve the energy efficiency of residential and community buildings in their city.[22] Worcester's building stock is older, and home heating costs in the winter can be a significant expense. Since 2009, community members, college students, and building contractors have been helping out with "simple fixes" that can dramatically reduce heating costs without big outlays. Although insulated windows are great, often caulking and other unglamorous fixes can go a long way toward reducing thermal loss during the winter months.

Members of Worcester Energy Barnraisers were central players in organizing the Making a Green Solidarity Economy Conference, which was intended as a community conference to raise awareness about social, environmental, and economic issues and possibilities. In

To see the Amish barn raising is a thing of beauty—with no cranes and high-tech gear, the community comes together, works hard, eats well, and raises a neighbor's barn!

Terry Daniels, Long Island Home Enterprises

the process, the conference became a fund-raiser for the group. The group plans to use the proceeds from the conference as seed money for a local loan fund that could be used to help defray the costs of financing larger weatherization projects. The group has studied similar successful initiatives elsewhere in the country. What's significant here is the way a group that is largely based on sweat equity is extending its reach by finding new ways of generating funds.

Long Island Home Enterprises (LIHE) on Long Island, New York, has come up with a novel approach to finance. Members invest either time or money to help renovate run-down housing.[23] Members have to leave their money or their time (measured in hours) in the enterprise for a minimum of two years. The original time and money investments are interchangeable, with one hour of time equivalent to $20. This means that after two years, members can withdraw their investment in a number of ways—as rental payments or down payments on houses the LIHE has renovated, as hours of refurbishment work on their own properties, or as cash.

Small businesses have also devised do-it-yourself ways of financing. In Great Barrington, Massachusetts, Frank Tortoriello wanted to move his deli into larger premises.[24] But the bank wouldn't lend him the $4,500 he needed. So Frank printed his own currency—Deli Dollars—that his customers could buy for $8 and then redeem later for $10 of deli food. It took Frank only one month to raise $5,000. Over time the Deli Dollars all came back to Frank, but not always from the same customers who had purchased them. The dollars were being passed around town—employers were giving them as Christmas gifts to their employees, parents gave them to children so they knew their kids would eat well, and, because the local minister ate at the deli, Deli Dollars started turning up in his collection box.

Frank's customers were backing his loan because they felt they were helping him beat the bank and he was paying them back in sandwiches.

David Boyle, *Funny Money*

Supporting Community Finance Institutions

In many countries people are innovating with local financial institutions that serve their needs and their communities' needs directly and transparently. This movement has been given added impetus by the GFC and people's loss of confidence in large mainstream financial institutions.

ETHICAL ACTION: *Investing in institutions that prioritize building others' futures*

Across the United States, people have been hit hard by the GFC, and, to add insult to injury, in 2011 the Bank of America announced that it would impose $5 monthly fees on customers for the "privilege" of having an ATM card. Bank of America eventually backed down in the face of consumer outrage, but it was too late—something had begun to happen.[25] Helped along by Occupy Wall Street organizers, an event called Bank Transfer Day was promoted, and on that day US$4.5 billion in new deposits were transferred from banks into credit unions. In the United States credit unions are nonprofit financial service providers that typically charge lower rates on loans and higher interest rates on deposits than banks because they are not saddled with the expectations of shareholders. The money that was deposited in credit unions on Bank Transfer Day added to the US$1 trillion that ninety million members already had in credit unions.

In the United States, along with credit unions, there is a range of different types of community-based institutions that specifically direct investments in ways that will benefit communities and environments. Just a few of these include the Maine Organic Farmers and Gardeners Association (which has a loan fund to help organic farmers establish a credit history for their farms), the Cooperative Fund of New England (which lends money to cooperative enterprises and community-based organizations, particularly those that work with low income communities), and the Natural Capital Investment Fund (which lends to natural resource–based businesses that are following principles of sustainable development).[26]

In the days before the GFC, banks in Australia sought to cut their costs and increase profits. Between 1993 and 2000, more than 2,050 bank branches were closed.[27] This was a 29 percent reduction in the number of bank branches, and it left many communities, especially small rural ones, without any banking facilities. In 1998 two rural communities fought back by developing a partnership with one of the smaller banks in Australia, Bendigo Bank (which later became Bendigo and Adelaide Bank). This partnership became the basis of Community Bank®. Bendigo and Adelaide Bank works with local communities to help them establish a Community Bank® branch as a locally owned and operated franchise. Once sufficient surplus is achieved, funds flow back to local shareholders as dividends and to community groups and projects as grants. Currently there are almost three hundred Community Bank® branches employing around 1,400 people. Whereas nearly A$20 million has been paid in dividends to more than 70,000 local shareholders, almost four times as much—A$75.5 million!—has been returned to community projects.

Other kinds of community-based financial institutions have taken things a step further by specializing in the delivery of financial services for social enterprises, charities, and community organizations. Charity Bank was launched in the United Kingdom in 2002.[28] The bank's funds are supplied by charitable trusts and other banks, as well as deposits from individuals who are willing to take a lower return on deposits in exchange for a chance to lend to worthy charitable causes. Charity Bank's management consists of people from the social services world as well as retirees from the mainstream financial services industry. The people from these two different worlds decide which charities to lend to by assessing both the charitable organization's ability to repay the loan as well as the organization's overall social impact. As of 2010, Charity Bank had £68 million under management and had helped finance more than one thousand social organizations.

Promoting Ethical Investment

Many people in the minority world have superannuation funds in order to prepare for retirement. The usual advice workers might be given in relation to these funds depends on their age: if they are young, they are told to be "aggressive" with their investments and tolerant of risk, but as they get older they are advised to become more "conservative" and take fewer risks. Some mutual funds and other investment brokers are adding another option that could be exercised at any age—to invest in socially responsible funds that adhere to social or environmental principles.

ETHICAL ACTION: *Investing in mainstream financial institutions that use ethical investment*

In 1980 Triodos Bank started operating in the Netherlands with the express purpose of supporting projects and businesses that were working for a sustainable future. As a result, Triodos lends only to those that are making a positive social, environmental, or cultural contribution, such as organic food and farming businesses, renewable energy enterprises, recycling companies, and nature conservation projects. And Triodos is having a major impact. For example, by the time of this writing it had invested in 361 climate and energy projects across Europe, and these projects generated enough renewable energy to meet the needs of 1.5 million households in 2011. Triodos also has a policy of total transparency and publishes details of all businesses and organizations that it lends to. Triodos currently has offices in five European countries, including the United Kingdom.

In the United States, the Calvert Fund is a mainstream investment management company that also helps investors put their money into companies that act in socially and environmentally sustainable ways. Founded in 1976, the firm was among the first to offer a sustainable and responsible investments product in 1982. Currently Calvert has 400,000 customers and over US$12 billion under management.[29] Although Calvert was a trendsetter, many have followed it. According to the 2010 *Report on Socially Responsible Investing Trends in the United States,* US$3.07 trillion is invested in socially responsible funds, and this type of investment is growing faster than mainstream investments, a trend that has continued even during the GFC.[30]

Redirecting Government Revenue toward Life-Sustaining Rather Than Life-Destroying Activities

Individuals and communities are investing in their own futures through both money and muscles. And as we've already seen in the examples of

Kerala state, Venezuela, and Norway, this is also something that governments can do to help create futures for people and the planet.

ETHICAL ACTION: *Supporting governments to use tax revenues for social infrastructure and environmental initiatives that will help build a future for all*

In the Canadian province of Québec, more than two decades of community activism has helped mobilize a range of institutions, including the provincial government, to invest in the social economy.[31] In 1983 the Fonds de Solidarité des Travailleurs (Workers' Solidarity Fund) was established as a pension fund fed by members of the Québec Federation of Labour and ordinary citizens. With the support of provincial and federal legislation, funds were invested in job-creating community initiatives that were emerging from community economic development corporations concentrated in low-income neighborhoods. Then in 1996 the second-largest labor federation in Québec established another labor solidarity fund, Le Fonds de Développement pour la Coopération et L'emploi (FondAction). This fund invests in enterprises with social and environmental objectives. These two funds have been critical in helping build a social economy that employs almost 170,000 people through hundreds of initiatives that include child-care centers, workers' cooperatives, and credit unions.

As a result of the efforts of these funds, there is a social economy movement that has been strong enough to develop a working relationship with the provincial government and even demand "the same kind of support for our collective enterprises that the government has given to the private for-profit sector."[32] Most important, the movement has secured government funds to cover the operating costs of their coordinating institution, Le Chantier de l'Economie Sociale, and a government grant to establish La Fiducie du Chantier de l'Economie Sociale, a financial institution that offers long-term "patient capital" (capital for which the investor is willing to forgo an immediate return in anticipation of more substantial returns down the road) for enterprise development. This will enable the movement to build a resilient and diverse future.

In 1993, in a very different context, Belo Horizonte, Brazil's fourth-largest city, with 2.5 million people, introduced a series of food programs to make sure that people were not going hungry.[33] The city developed dozens of initiatives. One simple measure was to give local family farmers a spot in a public space from which they could sell their produce directly to urban consumers. Another was the development of Restaurante Popular (People's Restaurants) that serve up to twelve thousand or more people each day using mostly locally grown food (for the equivalent of around 50 cents a meal). As a result, Belo Horizonte has cut its infant death rate by more than half and its infant malnutrition by half, and the consumption of fruits and vegetables has gone up. Local farmers and their families and communities are benefiting from the new markets that have opened up for them. The program costs around US$10 million each year, which is less than 2 percent of the city's budget—or just over 1 cent a day per person! Surely this would have to be one of the wisest investments a government could make in its people and future.

I knew we had so much hunger in the world. But what is so upsetting, what I didn't know when I started this, is it's so easy. It's so easy to end it.

—Adriana Aranha, former hunger program director, City of Belo Horizonte, Brazil

What if more governments the world over were following the lead of Québec and Belo Horizonte and directly investing in people's quality of life and in environmental initiatives such as green technologies?

WHERE TO FROM HERE?

Investment is our moment in the economy in which we both predict the future and create and ensure it. In many ways this chapter brings together all the concerns and ethical moments we have considered in the course of this book. And tools like the Community Economy Return on Investment help us think through the various investments we might make.

What would it take for you to invest in people and the planet?

1. In your community are there credit unions or other community-based institutions that could house your deposits? Are there ways of influencing where and how these institutions invest?

2. If you are a member of a union or a municipal government, how is your superannuation invested? Are there possibilities for shifting to ethical investments?

3. If you are involved in any level of government, are there programs you could be investing in to help improve people's quality of life and the quality of the environment?

4. What are the social, economic, or local environmental challenges in your community? Are there options for peer-to-peer finance or do-it-yourself finance initiatives that could address the challenges?

5. What about your extended community of people in far-flung places—are there initiatives you could be investing in to help them survive well and to help improve the quality of their environments?

As we've discussed in this chapter, all of us can make decisions to invest in growing community economies—ones that are attentive to our own and others' survival; support ethical enterprises, trade, and transactions; and care for our commons. Why, then, is it so easy to put off making the ethical decisions that are demanded of us today? In our concluding chapter we turn to what stands in the way of a different future and where we might turn for the inspiration and energy to take back the economy—any time, any place.

Any Time, Any Place . . .

In this book we have taken back the economy by reframing it as a space of ethical action rather than a machine that must be obeyed. We have taken back work, business, markets, property, and finance and shown how, together, we can act to make a different future.

We have opened up the possibility of building community economies shaped by negotiation around the key concerns of

- *surviving* together well and equitably
- *distributing surplus* to enrich social and environmental health
- *encountering others* in ways that support their well-being as well as ours
- *consuming* sustainably
- *caring for*—maintaining, replenishing, and growing—our natural and cultural *commons*
- *investing* our wealth so that future generations can live well

In conclusion, we turn to what might stand in our way as we carry on taking back the economy—any time, any place. And we explore how nature might offer inspiration for living with one another equitably, ethically, and within earthly bounds.

WHAT'S IN OUR WAY?

In order to build a community economy founded on an ethic of negotiated interdependence, we must reframe the economy to make it a space of possibility. We do not have to go along with a framing of the economy as a machine governed by immutable laws or mechanical principles. Indeed, if we do, it will be only states, industries, and rich and powerful individuals that can manipulate its regulations, markets, and values and make economic change. People like us are relegated to a role as mere consumers, unable to get our hands on its controlling levers. As shown in chapter 1, the reframing of a diverse economy presents a collection of activities and practices, ones that can be modified and changed. In a diverse economy there are many roles to assume and many opportunities for action. Yet the question remains: why are we so reluctant to assert a role for communities in reshaping the economy for people and the planet?

Ultimately, the belief that human self-interest—or greed—directs the economy along its inexorable course is a stubborn aspect of what we're up against. As consumers we are encouraged to compete and get a better deal than the next person. Although there are countless examples of self-sacrifice, mutual aid, or even enlightened self-interest, when it comes to reframing the economy, human "selfishness" remains the sticking point, the supposedly unchanging fact of the human condition. Often the name we give to this fixed pursuit of self-interest is freedom.

Ironically, what follows from belief in the freedom to pursue self-interest is an almost slavish commitment to a vision of the economy as so powerful that it is beyond reproach. Even when presented with the devastating ecological and social consequences of following the path of continuous growth and increasingly privatized wealth, many readily acknowledge the problem but say that nothing is to be done.

In our view, these unexamined, fatalistic beliefs in a mechanistic economy and a fixed human nature are the principal impediments to taking back the economy for people and the planet. There may be no rational argument that can displace such ways of thinking. Experience might have a better chance. In this book we have invited you to suspend your disbelief long enough to act as if community economies were possible and to begin experiencing the economy as a space of ethical decision making.

The tools in each chapter help us as individuals to take account of our actual complicated economic lives. They enable us to imagine what might happen if we chose to experiment with taking back the economy, replicating what others are doing all over the world, right now. Our wager is that in the process of taking this initial ethical action—going through the exercises laid out in this book—a different understanding of the economy will emerge.

As a species, we need to be moved to action. It is in this area that turning to nature for inspiration can help. Though the economy is not natural, it does not follow that economies are purely ours to do with what we will. Biological human needs, the needs of other organisms, and the physical environment create possibilities and set limits. We can learn from nature in our efforts to refashion the economy in accordance with our ethical concerns. In natural systems

- diversity produces resilience
- maintaining habitats sustains life
- interdependence means that changing one thing creates changes in others

These observations about nature can guide us to think and act in ethical terms.

DIVERSITY PRODUCES RESILIENCE

The earth's biosphere is composed of many different climates, ecologies, and habitats in which life in all of its forms flourishes to a greater or lesser extent. The diversity of life forms ensures that there are ongoing relationships between organisms and species. Relationships of competition and cooperation and processes of natural selection and symbiosis over time build the complex diversity of natural systems that allows them to respond and recover from threat. The more complex these relationships and the more parallel functionalities there are, the more likely it is that any given individual or species or the web of ecological relations can survive disturbances—from ice storms to hurricanes. Diversity produces resilience.

Economies may not be natural, but it strikes us that vital economies, the economies we wish to live in, have a similar relationship in terms of diversity and resilience. When we reframe the economy as diverse—as something much more than just individuals and enterprises acting out of self-interest, mistrust, and fear—we become alive to all the relationships that make up our web of economic life. A pathway toward economic resilience opens up.

All of us have working lives that are more complex than just our paid jobs. We work at home, in community spaces, on a voluntary basis, or as part of a practice of mutual aid. The more diverse our working lives, the more likely we are to have all of our dimensions of well-being attended to and the more able we are to respond flexibly as change in one form of work occurs.

Our communities are sustained by enterprises that operate in the market for private profit as well as those that directly serve the interests of communities and care for the natural or social environment. Businesses that plunder the environment and show disregard for their workforces increase the vulnerability of people and places. The more diverse the forms of enterprise that direct their surplus toward sustaining environments and communities, the more secure our futures will be.

We sustain one another through encounters in the market but also in other settings in which we interact with one another in the form of barter, gifts, or mutual aid. The more variety there is in our encounters, the richer our connections with each other and our earth and the better able we will be to care for each other, especially in times of threat or scarcity.

As communities we make and share all sorts of commons that sustain our lives. Commons are not restricted to one kind of property ownership but can be built by people around a diverse range of property types. The greater the variety of commons, the more likely it is that they will be expanded and maintained.

We plan for our future not only through our investment in the market sector or by paying taxes to secure public goods like education or health care but also through investing in community initiatives, in the local environment, and in one another. The more instruments and mechanisms for investing there are, the better equipped we will be to ride the waves of fortune.

Taking back the economy any time, any place means deciding to increase economic diversity to ensure more resilient futures. In each chapter we have introduced a Diverse Economy Identifier based on the diverse economy described in chapter 1. This tool can be used to inventory economic activities in our daily lives or in our local, regional, or national economy. With the range of economic activities identified, we can work to amplify this foundational diversity.

MAINTAINING HABITATS MAINTAINS LIFE

Nowhere in nature does an organism exist by itself in isolation. All live in habitats that either sustain their lives or undermine their vitality. Many organisms are sensitive to subtle shifts in the climate, chemical composition, or ecologies that make up their habitat. For instance, frogs and other amphibians are hypersensitive to every kind of change—from changes in temperature to those related to the presence of toxins. Some yeast species are quickly poisoned as their habitat is changed in the process of wine making, while others survive the increasing alcohol content much longer to produce higher-proof concentrations of alcohol. In the end, though, all yeasts, no matter how hardy and insensitive to alcohol, end up at the bottom of the vat.

Humans are a generalist species that can survive in almost all habitats and thrive in a great many. But this very insensitivity to change in our environment may lead to the undoing of our species. It is possible that by continuing to expand industrial activity powered by fossil fuels we may end up destroying the very habitat in which human life has flourished.

As a species we need to be less like the yeast in the wine vat and more like amphibians. We could learn to become more sensitive to the changes we are inducing in our economic and ecological habitats and adjust our habits accordingly. The explosive growth of autoimmune diseases is one way in which we seem to be registering sensitivity to an environment and a food system that do not work to sustain life. But can we adjust our habits before it's too late?

Registering change is a crucial first step to change. The tools in this book are designed to help us develop greater sensitivity to our economy and its life-sustaining, life-damaging, or life-destroying effects. Each tool draws attention to a different way that our economic activities place us in relation to others and the earth. They connect our habits to our environmental and economic habitat and help us tune in to the interdependent consequences of change.

Beginning with chapter 2, on survival, we ask you to look at your working lives and use the Well-being Scorecard to become more aware of how you are balancing or trading off your different survival needs. We suggest that you measure the ecological footprint of your working life and look into how your survival habits are affecting our earthly habitat. Increasing our sensitivity to our ecological footprint may change the trade-offs we make to survive well.

The People's Account of enterprise in chapter 3 directs us to identify who makes decisions about where to direct surplus and how this will affect the survival chances of other people and the health of the environment. Increasing our sensitivity to where new wealth flows and its potential to shape worlds may encourage a bolder approach that demands that we have a say in surplus distribution.

The Diverse Economy Dandelion and Ethical Interconnection Checklist in chapter 4 help us to pinpoint how our consumption habits affect others near and far and what we can do to support their well-being without further damaging their ecologies. Developing sensitivity to the range of encounters that enrich our lives may lead to more direct connections of care between people and species.

The Commons Identi-Kit in chapter 5 attunes us to what we share and with whom we work to look after our habitat. The Commons Yardstick connects us with past and present actions of stewardship and destruction. By placing our actions in an intergenerational time frame, we can sensitize ourselves to the vulnerability of our earthly habitat and common heritage and may feel called to repair, maintain, and expand our common wealth.

The Stocks and Flows diagram in chapter 6 and the Community Economy Return on Investment tool help us see the big picture of how we direct funds in our economy and contribute to building futures. They allow us to identify different investment pathways that might lead toward the futures we desire.

All of these tools invite us to become more aware of the impact our decisions have on ourselves, one another, the biosphere, and the physical environment. By using these tools we can develop habits that, over time, construct new life-sustaining economic habitats.

INTERDEPENDENCE

We learn from nature how plants, insects, and animals have coevolved, how one life form's development is dependent on another's. In a diverse economy we see how interdependent different kinds of economic activities are with each other. For example, unpaid domestic labor in a household supports the well-being of household members and helps to stretch wage payments that flow into the family. When employers squeeze wages or intensify work rosters to extract more surplus value, it's not just members of the paid workforce who are affected. The pressure on household workers also mounts. Productivity rises in the business sector are likely to be offset by the social costs of family breakdown. Alternatively, when fair-trade networks ensure that poor majority-world farming families are guaranteed a livable income, school fees can be paid, and girls are sent to school. Increased educational opportunities for young women are likely to lower birth rates and slow population growth. These interdependencies are what we have to work with in a community economy. Initiatives for change can reverberate and resonate, having a much greater impact than initially thought.

From nature we also learn to expect the unexpected. Small mutations can spawn whole new species, and anything is possible within broad guidelines. Change is both path dependent (i.e., directed according to preexisting conditions) and capable of unexpected and uncertain swerves. The economy is not a lone ship on a predestined course. But although we can adjust the trim tab and set it on another course, this does not necessarily ensure that we will reach our desired destination. Currents, cyclones, mutinies, or refugee boats can put the ship off its new course. Changing one thing certainly changes others, but we can never avoid unexpected events and unintended consequences. All we can do is keep monitoring, adjusting, and revising our actions to keep moving toward our goals.

Communities and economies are not static; our challenges and concerns keep changing. A community may decide on a certain strategy for maintaining a common resource or investing for the future. This may work for a time, but eventually the same community may need to rethink its approach. Ethical concerns must be continually raised and considered, metrics reevaluated, and habits adjusted. The tools we have developed are designed as the basis for ongoing collective thought, action, monitoring, and modifying.

Nature keeps several records of living organisms as they continuously adjust to changes great and small in their habitats. The "files" can be found in the shifting genetic composition of species, the long history of symbiosis and coevolution, and the archaeological record of species that were unable to adapt. To take a page from nature's book, we can see the importance of making a record of our efforts as we engage in experiments to address ethical concerns. We should take note of our efforts and their consequences—intended, unintended, and surprising.

We can take a page from our own history, too. The gross national product (GNP) measure was invented in the minority world at a specific point in history and with a particular intention—to help with wartime production planning.[1] Long after its original application, the GNP remains an economic indicator that demands the repeated gathering and analysis of a certain data set that has come to represent the national economy. The habits associated with this measure have constructed an economic habitat that prioritizes growth and the prerogative of business.

As we work toward taking back the economy, we are sure to encounter unexpected obstacles, unlooked-for gains, and unintended consequences. Our hope is that the metrics we have introduced to help us take ethical action will, as they are used and their results recorded over time, allow us to create very different economic habitats.

BUILDING A COMMUNITY ECONOMY

Constructing community economies centered on ethical concerns is not about producing communities that are the same everywhere or that respond in similar ways to the concerns we have raised in this book. Ethical practice is about being open, sensitive, and adaptive. Each reader and each community, is free to come up with their own answers and even their own concerns.

There is, however, a certain freedom that comes from acknowledging that any individual or community is part of a "we," an "us," and an "ours." It is in thinking *together* about our working lives, our collective efforts, the places in which we encounter others, the commons we constitute through our care, and the future we collectively invest in that will allow us to build an economy worth living in with one another.

Learning from nature may help us to assume more collective agency in taking back the economy. Learning nature's lesson begins by recognizing that diversity produces resilience. There is no one right answer; rather, there is a diversity of answers. The lesson continues with prioritizing choices in relation to these ethical concerns that connect our habits to the preservation and continuity of our habitat. The lesson concludes, each time, with the understanding that there are more consequences to our actions than we can anticipate—changing one thing changes another. We can record and remember the results of our economic experiments, our failures and missteps, our triumphs and successes, and in doing so move together toward a more sustainable, equitable, and just economy.

Notes

I. Reframing the Economy, Reframing Ourselves

1. The Phillips curve charts the relationship between inflation and unemployment, and it remains a core principle in macroeconomics. See Tim Ng and Matthew Wright, "Introducing the MONIAC: An Early and Innovative Economic Model," *Reserve Bank of New Zealand Bulletin* 70, no. 4 (December 2007): 46–52, http://www.rbnz.govt.nz/research/search/article.asp?id=6006. Other material on the Phillips machine is from Steven Strogatz, "Like Water for Money," *New York Times,* 2 June 2009. For more on the Phillips machine, it's worth watching "How the Economy Is Controlled," a YouTube.com video from the BBC documentary *Pandora's Box,* episode 3 (1992), http://www.youtube.com/watch?v=bXBuWUQZ4vU; and a video of Allan McRobie demonstrating one of the machines: "Bill Phillips Moniac Analog Economic Computer," a YouTube.com video, filmed at Cambridge University (2004), http://www.youtube.com/watch?v=rVOhYROKeu4.

2. Jeffrey Sachs, quoted by Jonathan Perlman in "Rocking the World," *Sydney Morning Herald,* 12 July 2008.

3. The GPI measures national well-being by including metrics such as the value of unpaid household work, the national cost of crime, and the extent of environmental degradation. For information on the GPI, see John Talberth, Clifford Cobb, and Noah Slattery, *The Genuine Progress Indicator 2006: A Tool for Sustainable Development* (Oakland, Calif.: Redefining Progress, 2006). The state of Maryland is using the GPI to identify how development activities and policy decisions are impacting long-term well-being; see http://www.green.maryland.gov/mdgi. The nation of Bhutan has developed a survey of Gross National Happiness to assess the contribution of programs and policies to well-being. The survey (http://www.grossnationalhappiness.com) includes measures of standard of living, health, and education. The Happy Planet Index (http://www.happyplanetindex.org) has been developed by the New Economics Foundation and looks at the relationship between environmental inputs and well-being outcomes in nations across the globe.

4. Duncan Ironmonger, "Counting Outputs, Capital Inputs, and Caring Labor: Estimating Gross Household Product," *Feminist Economics* 2, no. 3 (1996): 37–64. See also Marilyn Waring, *Counting for Nothing: What Men Value and What Women Are Worth,* 2nd ed. (Toronto: University of Toronto Press, 1999); and Colin Williams, *A Commodified World? Mapping the Limits of Capitalism* (London: Zed Books, 2005).

5. Information about this initiative comes from The Uniform Project, http://www.TheUniformProject.com; and "Sheena Speaks at TEDx Dubai," online video, http://

theuniformprojectblog.com/press/sheena-speaks-at-tedxdubai, accessed 26 November 2012.

6. Information in this paragraph about the fashion industry comes from Alison Benjamin, "Clothing Industry Joins Green Drive," *The Guardian,* 6 September 2007. See also Eco-Asia, "The Environmental and Social Impact of the Fashion Industry, Part 2," 2009, http://www.eco-asia.info/content/f-fashion-dark-side2–>website down; and Sean Poulter, "Women Waste £1.6 Billion on Clothes: Guilt Prevents Wardrobe Clearout," *Daily Mail,* 17 January 2011.

7. Information on SEWA and STFC is drawn from John Blaxall, "Collective Action by Women Workers: The Self-Employed Women's Association, India," in *Ending Poverty in South Asia: Ideas That Work,* ed. Elena E. Glinskaya (Washington, D.C.: World Bank Publications, 2006), 68–103; and Emma Hapke, "Organizing Women in India's Informal Economy: A Case Study of a Self-Employed Women's Association" (Policy Fellow Working Paper 1, no. 2, Institute for Health and Social Policy, McGill University, Montreal, 2010).

8. In 1970s Australia, Buga-Up, an underground movement of graffiti artists, pioneered tactics to reframe smoking, targeting prominent billboards advertising smoking products and skillfully changing words and images.

9. Russell Leong, "Majority World: New Veterans of Globalization," *Amerasia Journal* 34, no. 1 (2008): vii–xii. Of course not everyone in a minority-world country enjoys a minority-world lifestyle, and vice versa: in majority-world countries there are people whose lives are more in line with those of people in the minority world.

10. "The World of 7 Billion," *National Geographic,* http://ngm.nationalgeographic.com/2011/03/age-of-man/map-interactive, accessed 26 November 2012.

2. Take Back Work

1. According to the economist Richard Layard, countries like the United States and Japan may have dramatically increased their GDP, but their levels of happiness have decreased (in the case of the United States) or remained the same (in the case of Japan). Richard Layard, "Happiness: Has Social Science a Clue?" (Lionel Robbins Memorial Lecture, London School of Economics, London, 2003). For more on happiness, see Richard Layard, *Happiness: Lessons from a New Science* (London: Penguin, 2005); and Tim Jackson, *Prosperity without Growth: Economics for a Finite Planet* (London: Earthscan, 2009).

2. Layard, *Happiness,* 48–49.

3. Richard Wilkinson and Kate Pickett, *The Spirit Level: Why More Equal Societies Almost Always Do Better* (London: Allen Lane, 2009).

4. Richard Freeman, an economist from Harvard University, estimates that the world's labor force doubled in the 1980s and 1990s, to almost three billion people. Richard Freeman, "What Really Ails Europe (and America): The Doubling of the Global Workforce," *The Globalist,* 5 March 2010, http://www.theglobalist.com.

5. Clive Hamilton defines downshifters as those who have *voluntarily* made a long-term change in how they live their lives so that they are earning less money. Planned retirement is not included in this definition. Clive Hamilton, "Downshifting in Britain: A Sea-Change in the Pursuit of Happiness" (Discussion Paper 58, Australia Institute, Canberra, 2003). Other material on downshifting is from Michelle R. Nelson, Mark

A. Rademacher, and Hye-Jin Paek, "Downshifting Consumer = Upshifting Citizen? An Examination of a Local Freecycle Community," *Annals of the American Academy of Political and Social Science* 611 (May 2007): 141–56; Christie Breakspear and Clive Hamilton, *Getting a Life: Understanding the Downshifting Phenomenon in Australia* (Canberra: Australia Institute, 2004); and Jackson, *Prosper-ity without Growth,* 150–51.

6. Hamilton, "Downshifting in Britain," 15.

7. Australian Bureau of Statistics, "6306.0—Employee Earnings and Hours, Australia, May 2010," http://www.abs.gov.au/ausstats/abs@nsf/mf/63060. Other information on work and coal mining in Australia is taken from the Australian Coal Association Web site, http://www.australiancoal.com.au; Georgina Murray and David Peetz, "The Big Shift: The Gendered Impact of Twelve Hour Shifts on Mining Communities" (paper presented at the International Sociological Association, Barcelona, Spain, 2008); David Peetz and Georgina Murray, "'You Get Really Old, Really Quick': Involuntary Long Hours in the Mining Industry," *Journal of Industrial Relations* 53, no. 1 (2011): 13–29; and Natalie Skinner and Barbara Pocock, *Work, Life, and Workplace Flexibility: The Australian Work and Life Index 2008* (Adelaide: Centre for Work and Life, University of South Australia, 2008).

8. Skinner and Pocock, *Work, Life, and Workplace Flexibility,* Figure 15.

9. Katherine Gibson, *Different Merry-Go-Rounds: Families, Communities, and the 7-Day Roster* (Clayton, Victoria: Centre for Women's Studies and Department of Geography and Environmental Science, Monash University, 1993).

10. Recently, electricians working on oil rigs in one part of Australia won a 15 percent pay increase, bringing their wages up to between A$220,000 and $230,000 per year. Perversely, one of the justifications was that the long hours and days away from home meant that they had one of the highest divorce rates in the country. Ewin Hannan, "Oil-Rig Sparkies to Earn $260,000," *The Australian,* 8 February 2012.

11. Tom Rath and Jim Harter, *Wellbeing: The Five Essential Elements* (New York: Gallup Press, 2010), 4, emphasis in original.

12. We note that this list does not include spiritual well-being. We would argue that spiritual well-being (whether defined in terms of religion or a deep sense of purpose and commitment) results when the requirements for all forms of well-being are being met.

13. The progressive British industrialist Robert Owen is said to have coined the slogan "Eight hours labour, eight hours rest, eight hours recreation" in the early 1800s, but he never introduced an eight-hour working day into his factories. Groups of tradesmen in the colonies of New Zealand and Australia first attained an eight-hour day, starting with carpenters in New Zealand in the 1840s and stonemasons in Australia in the 1850s. For New Zealand, see Herbert Otto Roth, "Eight-Hour-Day Movement," in *An Encyclopaedia of New Zealand 1966,* ed. A. H. McLintock, http://www.teara.govt.nz/en/1966/eight-hour-day-movement/1. For Australia, see *History of the Eight Hour Day* (Melbourne: Arts Victoria, 2006), http://www.8hourday.org.au.

14. The term "multiactivity" is used by André Gorz to describe the transition that he sees as needed from a work-based society to one based on multiactivity. André Gorz, *Reclaiming Work: Beyond the Work-Based Society,* trans. Chris Turner (Cambridge, U.K.: Polity, 1999), 76.

15. Global Footprint Network, *The National Footprint Accounts, 2011 Edition* (Oakland, Calif.: Global Footprint Network, 2012).

16. To calculate Josef's ecological footprint, we used the personal calculator on the state of Victoria's Environment Protection Authority Web site, http://www.epa.vic.gov.au/ecologicalfootprint.

17. On living wage campaigns, see the Universal Living Wage Web site, http://universallivingwage.org; Greater London Authority, *Fairer London: The 2011 Living Wage in London* (London: Greater London Authority Living Wage Unit, 2011); and "Living Wage Campaign," Citizens UK Web site, http://www.citizensuk.org.

18. Clean Clothes Campaign, http://www.cleanclothes.org.

19. WHO, *The World Health Report* (Geneva: World Health Organization, 2010), 7.

20. The sources of these figures are Arachu Castro, "Barrio Adentro: A Look at the Origins of a Social Mission," *ReVista: Harvard Review of Latin America,* Fall 2008; and Jennie Popay et al., "Understanding and Tackling Social Exclusion" (Final Report to the World Health Organization Commission on Social Determinants of Health from the Social Exclusion Knowledge Network, Geneva, 2008), 99.

21. The sources of these figures are Luis Antonio Lindau, Dario Hidalgo, and Daniela Facchini, "Curitiba, the Cradle of Bus Rapid Transit," *Built Environment* 36, no. 3 (2010): 274–82; Joseph Goodman, Melissa Laube, and Judith Schwenk, "Curitiba's Bus System Is a Model for Rapid Transit," *Race, Poverty, and the Environment* Winter 2005–6, 75–76; and Lloyd Wright, "Bus Rapid Transit: A Public Transport Renaissance," *Built Environment* 36, no. 3 (2010): 269–73.

22. The amount of paid parental leave ranges from almost one year (in Germany and Sweden) to none (in the United States). The information on paid parental leave is from Rebecca Ray, Janet C. Gornick, and John Schmitt, "Who Cares? Assessing Generosity and Gender Equality in Parental Leave Policy Designs in 21 Countries," *Journal of European Social Policy* 20, no. 3 (2010): 196–216.

23. Pay for carers can be funded by money that would otherwise have to be spent in health care services. For example, in the United States it was estimated that in 1997 unpaid carers provided $197 billion of services, compared to national spending on home health care of $32 billion and nursing home care of $83 billion. Peter S. Arno, Carol Levin, and Margaret M. Memmott, "The Economic Value of Informal Caregiving," *Health Affairs* 18, no. 2 (1999): 182–88.

24. "Talkback: Frugalism Is the New Black," *Life Matters,* ABC Radio National, 15 August 2008, http://www.abc.net.au/radionational/programs/lifematters/talk-back-frugalism-is-the-new-black/3199372.

25. "Reinventing the Workday: Meet the Guru—Ron Healey, Founder of the 30/40 Workweek," *Livelyhood,* PBS, http://www.pbs.org/livelyhood/workday/reinventing/guru.html, accessed 12 December 2012. See also Amy Saltzman, "When Less Is More," *U.S. News and World Report,* 19 October 1997.

26. Anna Coote, Jane Franklin, and Andrew Simms, *21 Hours: Why a Shorter Working Week Can Help Us All to Flourish in the 21st Century* (London: New Economics Foundation, 2010).

27. Benjamin Kline Hunnicutt, *Kellogg's Six-Hour Day* (Philadelphia: Temple University Press, 1996).

28. For more on cohousing, see Greg Bamford, "'Living Together On One's Own':

Cohousing for Older People—An Example from Denmark and the Netherlands" (paper presented at the Queensland Shelter Housing Conference, Gold Coast, Queensland, Australia, 2004).

29. Akanksha Web site, http://www.akanksha.org.

30. "Habitat for Humanity Fact Sheet (Frequently Asked Questions)," Habitat for Humanity Web site, http://www.habitat.org.

3. Take Back Business

1. Wealth is here defined as marketable assets such as real estate, including owner-occupied residences, stocks, and bonds. James B. Davies, Susanna Sandstrom, Anthony Shorrocks, and Edward N. Wolff, *The World Distribution of Household Wealth* (Helsinki: World Institute for Development Economics Research, July 2007), 7.

2. This story draws on the following sources: Lavaca Collective, *Sin Patrón: Stories from Argentina's Worker-Run Factories*, trans. Katherine Kohlstedt (Chicago: Haymarket Books, 2004); Avi Lewis, "Zanon," *ZNet*, 2004, http://www.zcommunications.org/zanon-by-avi-lewis; Peter Ranis, "Argentine Worker Cooperatives in Civil Society: A Challenge to Capital–Labor Relations?" *Working USA: The Journal of Labor and Society* 13, no. 1 (2010): 77–105; Marie Trigona, "Zanon: Worker Managed Production, Community, and Dignity," *Toward Freedom*, 2006, http://www.towardfreedom.com/labor/855-zanon-worker-managed-production-community-and-dignity; Marie Trigona, "FASINPAT (Factory without a Boss): An Argentine Experience in Self-Management," in *Real Utopia: Participatory Society for the 21st Century*, ed. Chris Spannos (Oakland, Calif.: AK Press, 2008); and Marie Trigona, "FASINPAT: A Factory That Belongs to the People" (report for the Americas Program, Center for International Policy, Colonia Tortuga, Mexico, 2009).

3. Trigona, "FASINPAT (Factory without a Boss)."

4. Ibid.

5. Lavaca Collective, *Sin Patrón*, 57–58.

6. Thanks to Ethan Miller, "Some Notes on Surplus" (unpublished manuscript, 11 April 2011). See also Georges Bataille, *The Accursed Share: An Essay on General Economy*, vol. 1: *Consumption*, trans. Robert Hurley (New York: Zone Books, 1991); and Harry W. Pearson, "The Economy Has No Surplus: Critique of a Theory of Development," in *Trade and Market in Early Empires*, ed. Karl Polanyi, Conrad M. Arensberg, and Harry W. Pearson (Glencoe, Ill.: Free Press, 1957).

7. In the ensuing discussion we draw on Karl Marx's concept of surplus value and on the theorization of surplus value production, appropriation, and distribution within the enterprise by Stephen Resnick and Richard Wolff in *Knowledge and Class: A Marxian Critique of Political Economy* (Chicago: University of Chicago Press, 1987).

8. "Frequently Asked Questions," Small Business Association Office of Advocacy Web site, January 2011, http://www.sba.gov.

9. Ben Schneiders, Ari Sharp, and Katharine Murphy, "Work Heads Offshore as Pacific Brands Axes Jobs," *The Age*, 26 February 2009, http://www.theage.com.au/national/work-heads-offshore-as-pacific-brands-axes-jobs-20090225-8hxk.html.

10. The increase gained from working longer hours was what Marx called "absolute surplus value."

11. Marx called these increases "relative surplus value."

12. This is from an interview with eighty-eight-year-old Bob Copper: "Bob Copper," *Music Show,* ABC Radio National, 7 June 2003, http://www.abc.net.au/radionational/programs/breakfast/outback-survival-bob-cooper/4190280.

13. The information on Mondragón is from J. K. Gibson-Graham, *A Postcapitalist Politics* (Minneapolis: University of Minnesota Press, 2006), 117; and "Frequently Asked Questions," Mondragón Corporation Web site, http://www.mondragon-corporation.com.

14. The story of GM and Toyota draws on the following sources: Peter Dicken, *Global Shift: Mapping the Changing Contours of the World Economy,* 6th ed. (New York: Guilford Press, 2011); Richard Wolff, *Capitalism Hits the Fan: The Global Economic Meltdown and What to Do about It* (Northampton, Mass.: Olive Branch Press, 2011); Jerry Flint, "Pumping on the Breaks," *Forbes.com,* 2 January 2007; Nick Bunkley, "GMAC Gets $3.8 Billion More in Aid," *New York Times,* 30 December 2009; and David Teather, "US Bails Out General Motors–Related Company GMAC with Further $3.8 Billion," *The Guardian,* 1 January 2010.

15. The story of Interface Carpets draws on the following sources: "Ray Anderson—Interface Carpets," *YouTube.com* video, http://www.ted.com/talks/ray_anderson_on_the_business_logic_of_sustainability.html, accessed 28 November 2012; and "Our Progress," and "Interface Workplace Culture," Interface Global Web site, http://www.interfaceglobal.com.

16. On the distinction between social and community enterprises, see Jenny Cameron, "Business as Usual or Economic Innovation? Work, Markets, and Growth in Community and Social Enterprises," *Third Sector Review* 16, no. 2 (2010): 93–108.

17. Organisation for Economic Co-operation and Development (OECD), *The Non-Profit Sector in a Changing Economy* (Paris: OECD Publication Services, 2003).

18. Jan Johnson, "Jobs Not Jails: Homeboy Industries Embraces, Nurtures, and Trains Former Gang Members for the Workforce—and a Better Future," *Prism Magazine,* May–June 2011. See also Homeboy Industries Web site, http://homeboy-industries.org.

19. For information on ESOPs, see "ESOP (Employee Stock Ownership) Facts," National Center for Employee Ownership Web site, 2012, http://www.esop.org; J. Michael Keeling, "Employee Ownership in the United States: Focus on the Employee Stock Ownership Plan, or ESOP, Model" (speech given at a conference on employee ownership, Granada, Spain, 5 June 2008, http://www.esopassociation.org/about esop overview.asp).

20. "The WorldBlu List 2008," WorldBlu Web site, http://www.worldblu.com.

21. The information on the Landless Settlers Movement is from Martina Burberi, "Contemporary Forms of Enslavement: Slavery in Brazil, University of Florence" (unpublished manuscript, 2007), http://www.oit.org.br/sites/all/forced_labour; and Magali Moser, "Production in the Settlements Shows MST beyond the Stereotypes," Friends of the MST (Brazilian Landless Workers Movement) Web site, 14 March 2011, http://www.mstbrazil.org/news/production-settlements-shows-mst-beyond-stereotypes-3-14-11.

22. "About," Collective Copies Web site, http://collectivecopies.com, and Janelle Cornwell, "Worker Co-operatives and Spaces of Possibility: An Investigation of Subject Space at Collective Copies," *Antipode* 44, no. 3 (2012): 725–44.

23. The material on the Solidarity Group comes from Christine Gregory, "Dignity Is Not for Sale," *Oxfam News*, December 2006, http://www.oxfam.org.au; Junya Yimprasert, "Dignity Returns—A Workers' Brand Is Possible!," ELBAG: Economic Literacy and Budget Accountability for Governance Web site, 2006, http://www.elbag.org; and Junya Yimprasert, ed., "When Cats Become Tigresses in Thailand: A Story from Asia" (Case Studies in Women's Empowerment, International Gender and Trade Network, Rio de Janeiro, Brazil), http://web.igtn.org.

24. "History," Yackandandah Community Development Company Web site, 2011, http://www.yackandandah.com/ycdco.

25. Community Economies Collective and Katherine Gibson, "Building Community-Based Social Enterprises in the Philippines: Diverse Development Pathways," in *The Social Economy: International Perspectives on Economic Solidarity*, ed. Ash Amin (London: Zed Books, 2009), 116–38.

26. R. Ridley-Duff, "Communitarian Perspectives on Social Enterprise," *Corporate Governance* 15, no. 2 (2007): 382–92; and "Community Interest Companies," Department for Business, Innovation, and Skills (U.K.) Web site, http://www.bis.gov.uk/cicregulator.

27. "Community Energy Solutions," Department for Business, Innovation, and Skills (U.K.), http://www.bis.gov.uk/cicregulator.

28. Jenny Cameron and Jarra Hicks, "Grassroots Initiatives: Contributions to a Climate Politics of Hope" (unpublished manuscript, 2012).

29. Jonathan Rushworth and Michael Schluter, "Transforming Capitalism from Within: A Relational Approach to Purpose, Performance, and Assessment of Companies," Relationships Foundation, 2011, http://www.relationshipglobal.net/Web/Content/Default.aspx?Content=43.

30. The information is from the KereKere Web site, http://www.kerekere.org; and Mark Daniels, Social Traders, personal communication, 11 November 2011.

31. "Who We Are," and "About the Western Massachusetts Food Processing Center," Franklin County Community Development Corporation Web site, http://www.fccdc.org.

4. Take Back the Market

1. Lindy Edwards, *How to Argue with an Economist* (Cambridge, England: Cambridge University Press, 2002).

2. Annie Leonard has documented the backstory to all the stuff we buy in *The Story of Stuff*. Her online movie is available at http://www.storyofstuff.org. See also Annie Leonard, "The Story of Stuff: Referenced and Annotated Script," The Story of Stuff Project, 2011, http://www.storyofstuff.org.

3. Alter Trade Japan Web site, http://www.altertradejapan.co.jp.

4. Ibid.

5. The following supply-chain diagram is modeled on Andreas Wieland and Carl Marcus Wallenberg's "Supply and Demand Network," *Wikimedia Commons*, 20 July 2011 (Creative Commons Attribution–Share Alike 3.0 Unported licence).

6. The information on conflict minerals comes from Enough Project, *Getting to Conflict-Free: Assessing Corporate Action on Conflict Minerals* (Washington, D.C.: Center for American Progress, 2010); and John Prendergast and Sasha Lezhnev, *From*

Mine to Mobile Phone: The Conflict Minerals Supply Chain (Washington, D.C.: Center for American Progress, 2009).

7. "UN Official Calls DR Congo 'Rape Capital' of the World,'" *BBC News*, BBC, 28 April 2010.

8. The following is based on Prendergast and Lezhnev, *From Mine to Mobile Phone*.

9. For information on the full life cycle of the electronic stuff in our lives, see Annie Leonard, "The Story of Electronics: Annotated Script," The Story of Stuff Project, 2010.

10. On 29 November 2010, the UN Security Council unanimously adopted Resolution 1952, "On Extension of Measures on Arms, Transport, Financial and Travel against the Democratic Republic of the Congo Imposed by Resolution 1807 (2008) and Expansion of the Mandate of the Committee Established Pursuant to Resolution 1533 (2004)." For information on the EICC and GeSI program, see EICC-GeSI, "EICC®-GeSI Conflict-Free Smelter (CFS) Assessment Program: Frequently Asked Questions," revised 30 March 2012, http://eicc.info. For information on the Enough Project, see the Enough Project Web site, http://www.enoughproject.org.

11. "The Kimberly Process," Global Witness Web site, http://www.globalwitness.org/campaigns/conflict/conflict-diamonds/kimberly-process.com, accessed 15 October 2011; and the Kimberley Process Web site, http://www.kimberleyprocess.com.

12. Val Plumwood, "Shadow Places and the Politics of Dwelling," *Australian Humanities Review* 44 (2008): 139–50.

13. In 1995 the General Agreement on Trade and Tariffs (GATT) became the WTO. There had previously been complaints to the GATT from Latin American countries since 1991. World Trade Organization (WTO), "Lamy Hails Accord Ending Long-Running Banana Dispute" (press release 591, WTO, 15 December 2009).

14. Gavin Fridell, "The Case against Cheap Bananas: Lessons from the EU–Caribbean Banana Agreement," *Critical Sociology* 37, no. 3 (2011): 285–307.

15. This quote is from "Europe Sticking to Banana Deal Despite Protests," *Caribarena News*, 18 March 2010, http://www.caribarena.com/dominicanrepublic/news/economy/europe-sticking-to-banana-deal-despite-protests--201003187105.html.

16. This information is from the Max Havelaar Foundation Web site, http://www.maxhavelaar.ch; and Alistair Smith and the Fairtrade Foundation, "Unpeeling the Banana Trade" (briefing paper, Fairtrade Foundation, London, 2009), http://www.fairtrade.org.uk/includes/documents/cm_docs/2009/f/1_ft_banana_reportweb.pdf).

17. For example, see Patrik Rönnbäck, *Critical Analysis of Certified Organic Shrimp Aquaculture in Sidoarjo, Indonesia* (Stockholm: Swedish Society for Nature Conservation, December 2003).

18. Kiah Smith and Kristen Lyons, "Negotiating Organic, Fair, and Ethical Trade: Lessons from Smallholders in Uganda and Kenya," in *Food System Failure: The Global Food Crisis and the Future of Agriculture*, ed. Christopher Rosen, Hugh Campbell, and Paul Stock (London: Earthscan, 2012), 180–99.

19. Mark Osteen, "Introduction: Questions of the Gift," in *The Question of the Gift: Essays across the Disciplines*, ed. Mark Osteen (London: Routledge, 2002), 13.

20. The information in this section is from Eric Molinsky, "Bartering for Health Care: Yardwork for Treatment," *Morning Edition*, National Public Radio, 26 September 2011, http://www.npr.org; Hour Exchange Portland Web site, http://www

.hourexchangeportland.org; True North Health Center Web site, http://www.truenorthhealthcenter.org; Bernard Lietaer, "Complementary Currencies in Japan Today: History, Originality and Relevance," *International Journal of Community Currency Research* 8 (2004): 1–23; Bernard Lietaer and Gwendolyn Hallsmith, *Community Currency Guide* (Montpelier, Va.: Global Community Initiatives, 2006); and David Boyle, Julia Slay, and Lucie Stephens, *Public Services Inside Out: Putting Co-production into Practice* (London: National Endowment for Science, Technology, and the Arts, 2010).

21. One such CSA initiative is Beanstalk in Newcastle, Australia. For a discussion of this practice, see Jenny Cameron, "Business as Usual or Economic Innovation? Work, Markets, and Growth in Community and Social Enterprises," *Third Sector Review* 16, no. 2 (2010): 93–108.

22. The information on gleaning is from Sandrine Badio, "Understanding Gleaning: Historical and Cultural Contexts of the Shifts from Rural to Urban Models for the Improvement of Food Security" (report for the Food Security Research Network, Lakehead University, Ontario, Canada, 2009); and Peter King, "Customary Rights and Women's Earnings: The Importance of Gleaning to the Rural Labouring Poor," *Economic History Review* 44, no. 3 (1991): 474, quoted by Badio in "Understanding Gleaning."

23. Local First and Civic Economics, *Local Works! Examining the Impact of Local Business on the West Michigan Economy* (Chicago: Civic Economics, 2008).

24. Llorenç Milà i Canals, Sarah J. Cowell, Sarah Sim, and Lauren Basson, "Comparing Domestic versus Imported Apples: A Focus on Energy Use," *Environmental Science Pollution Research* 14, no. 5 (2007): 338–44.

25. Ibid. See also Caroline Saunders, Andrew Baber, and Greg Taylor, "Food Miles—Comparative Energy/Emissions Performance of New Zealand's Agriculture Industry" (Research Report 285, Agribusiness and Economics Research Unit (AERU), Lincoln University, Christchurch, New Zealand, July 2006); and Gareth Edwards-Jones, Llorenç Milà i Canals, Natalia Hounsome, Monica Truniger, Georgia Koerber, Barry Hounsome, Paul Cross, Elizabeth H. York, Almudena Hospido, Katharina Plassmann, Ian M. Harris, Rhiannon T. Edwards, Graham A. S. Day, A Deri Tomos, Sarah J. Cowell, and David L. Jones, "Testing the Assertion that 'Local Food Is Best': The Challenges of an Evidence-Based Approach," *Trends in Food Science and Technology* 19 (2008): 265–74.

26. For more on cap-and-dividend schemes, see Peter Barnes, *Carbon Capping: A Citizen's Guide* (Minneapolis, Minn.: Tomales Bay Institute, 2007); and James K. Boyce and Matthew Riddle, "Cap and Dividend: How to Curb Global Warming While Protecting the Incomes of American Families" (Working Paper 150, Political Economy Research Institute, University of Massachusetts, Amherst, 2007).

27. The term *boycott* did not originate until the 1880s; it came from the name of an English land agent, Charles Boycott. In 1880 in Ireland, Boycott tried to evict tenants who resisted by withdrawing their labor. Boycott was subject to widespread social ostracism, one of the tactics used by the Land League in their struggle for land reform. Boycott was not the only landowner or land agent targeted, but he became the most famous, with British troops used to protect workers who were brought in to harvest crops on the land he managed. See Joyce Marlow, *Captain Boycott and the Irish* (New York: Sunday Review Press, 1973).

28. The information on the Boycott Movement is from Christabel Gurney, "'A Great Cause': The Origins of the Anti-Apartheid Movement, June 1959–March 1960," *Journal of Southern African Studies* 26, no. 1 (2000): 123–44. The quote is from Julius Nyerere, "On the Boycott of South Africa," letter to the editor of *Africa-South,* October–December 1959, reprinted in Godfrey Mwakikagile, *Nyerere and Africa: End of an Era* (Dar Es Salaam: New Africa Press, 2007).

29. For information on CSFs, see http://www.localcatch.org. The first CSF was Port Clyde Fresh Catch in Maine, http://portclydefreshcatch.com.

30. "Community Supported Agriculture for Meat and Eggs (Fact Sheet)," Union of Concerned Scientists Web site, February 2009, http://www.ucsusa.org/food_and_agriculture/solutions/expand-healthy-food-access/community-supported.html.

31. For information on urban or neighborhood CSAs, see the Freshroots Urban Farm Web site, http://freshroots.ca; and "Nourishing Newcastle," Transition Newcastle Web site, http://www.transitionnewcastle.org.au.

32. CoffeeCSA Web site, http://www.coffeecsa.org.

33. For more information on the geographic spread of LETS that are members of CES, see http://www.community-exchange.org.

34. Freecycle Web site, http://www.freecycle.org.

35. Ibid.

5. Take Back Property

1. According to the Tropical Savannahs Cooperative Research Centre, people have lived in this area for between forty to fifty thousand years. See "40,000 Years of Culture," Tropical Savannahs CRC Web site, http://savanna.org.au/savanna_web/information/arnhem_culture.html, accessed 3 December 2012. The remainder of this story draws on the following resources: Jon C. Altman, "In Search of an Outstations Policy for Indigenous Australians" (Working Paper 34, Centre for Aboriginal Economic Policy Research, Australian National University, Canberra, 2006); Jon C. Altman, "People on Country, Healthy Landscapes, and Sustainable Indigenous Economic Futures: The Arnhem Land Case," *Drawing Board: An Australian Review of Public Affairs* 4, no. 2 (2003): 65–82; Jon Altman, G. J. Buchanan, and L. Larsen, "The Environmental Significance of the Indigenous Estate: Natural Resource Management as Economic Development in Remote Australia" (Working Paper 286, Centre for Aboriginal Economic Policy Research, Australian National University, Canberra, 2007); Jon Altman, Sean Kerins, Emilie Ens, G. J. Buchanan, and Katherine May, "Submission to the Review of the National Biodiversity Strategy: Indigenous People's Involvement in Conserving Australia's Biodiversity," *Centre for Aboriginal Economic Policy Research Topical Issue* 8 (2009); Andrew C. Edwards and Jeremy Russell-Smith, "Ecological Thresholds and the Status of Fire-Sensitive Vegetation in Western Arnhem Land, Northern Australia: Implications for Management," *International Journal of Wildland Fire* 18, no. 2 (2009): 129; Aboriginal and Torres Strait Islander Social Justice Commissioner, *Native Title Report 2007* (Canberra: Human Rights and Equal Opportunity Commission, 2008); "Case Study: West Arnhem Land Fire Abatement Project," *Greening the Territory*, 21 October 2010, http://virtualmeetingplace.com.au; Stephen T. Garnett et al., "Healthy Country, Healthy People: Policy Implications of Links between Indigenous Human Health and Environmental Condition in Tropical

Australia," *Australian Journal of Public Administration* 68, no. 1 (2009): 53–66; Fay H. Johnston et al., "Exposure to Bushfire Smoke and Asthma: An Ecological Study," *Medical Journal of Australia* 176, no. 11 (2002): 535–38; Deborah Bird Rose et al., *Country of the Heart: An Indigenous Australian Homeland* (Canberra: Aboriginal Studies Press for the Australian Institute of Aboriginal and Torres Strait Islander Studies, 2002); and Peter J. Whitehead et al., "The Management of Climate Change through Prescribed Savanna Burning: Emerging Contributions of Indigenous People in Northern Australia," *Public Administration and Development* 28, no. 5 (2008): 374–85.

2. John Armstrong provides a fascinating discussion of the necessary and complementary relationship between what's possible and what's desirable. Armstrong even talks of the grace, poetry, and beauty that can be found in commercial endeavors. John Armstrong, "Pragmatism, Idealism: The Perfect Partnership?" interview with Paul Comrie-Thomson, *Counterpoint*, ABC Radio National, 27 June 2011.

3. The information about the tragedy of the commons comes from Garrett Hardin, "The Tragedy of the Commons," *Science* 162, no. 3859 (1968): 1243–48; Elinor Ostrom et al., "Revisiting the Commons: Local Lessons, Global Challenges," *Science* 284 (1999): 278–82; and Garrett Hardin, "Extensions of 'The Tragedy of the Commons,'" *Science* 280, no. 5364 (1998): 682–83.

4. Rodney Nelson, Anishinabe elder from Canada, personal communication with Katherine Gibson, September 2011.

5. Brigalow scrub is the semiarid scrub vegetation that occurs in parts of Australia. The information about Avocet comes from "Where Nature Dictates," Bridled Nailtail Wallaby Trust Web site, http://www.bntwallaby.org.au/habitat_and_reserve/avocet_nature_reserve, accessed 3 December 2012; Jacquie Mackay, "Endangered Flashjacks Surviving," *ABC Capricornia*, ABC Radio National, August 2008, http://www.abc.net.au; N. D. MacLeod et al., "Conservation of Critically Endangered Wildlife Species: Scope for Private Landholder and Citizens' Action," in *Proceedings of the 16th Biennial Conference of the Australian Rangeland Society*, ed. D. J. Eldridge and C. Waters (Perth: Australian Rangeland Society, 2010); and Hugo Spooner, "Statement," *NaRLA News* (Nature Refuge Landholders' Association of Queensland), May 2010.

6. Clive McAlpine and Leonie Seabrook, "The Brigalow," *Queensland Historical Atlas* Web site, created 27 October 2010, http://www.qhatlas.com.au.

7. Researchers have now found that cattle and flashjacks happily coexist, because cattle help keep the grass at a height and density that suits the small wallabies. Hugo Spooner in Mackay, "Endangered Flashjacks Surviving."

8. Michele Boldrin and David K. Levine, *Against Intellectual Monopoly* (Cambridge, England: Cambridge University Press, 2008), 8.

9. According to the World Bank, this was the average life expectancy in the United States in 2010. "World Bank Life Expectancy at Birth, Total (Years)," World Bank Web site, http://data.worldbank.org/indicator/SP.DYN.LE00.IN, accessed 3 December 2012.

10. Mark A. Lemley, "Property, Intellectual Property, and Free Riding," *Texas Law Review* 83, no. 1031 (2005): 1031–75.

11. Some characterize this as the creation of anticommons. Michael A. Heller and Rebecca S. Eisenberg, "Can Patents Deter Innovation? The Anticommons in Biomedical Research," *Science* 280, no. 5364 (1998): 698–701.

12. This point is tellingly made by Boldrin and Levine in *Against Intellectual Property* in the opening discussion in their book regarding the impact of Watt's patenting of the steam engine.

13. David Bollier, in *Field Guide to the Commons: How to Save the Economy, the Environment, the Internet, Democracy, Our Communities, and Everything Else That Belongs to All of Us,* ed. Jay Walljasper (New York: New Press, 2010), 198–200.

14. Don Tappscott and Anthony D. Williams, *Macrowikinomics: Rebooting Business and the World* (New York: Portfolio Penguin, 2010), 64–68.

15. This is based on reliable recorded measurements. Spencer Weart, *The Discovery of Global Warming* (Cambridge, Mass.: Harvard University Press, 2011). See also Weart's Web site, www.aip.org/history/climate/index.htm.

16. Dianne Dumanoski, *The End of the Long Summer: Why We Must Remake Our Civilization to Survive on a Volatile Earth* (New York: Crown, 2009).

17. Walter Jehne, "Global Warming: Twenty Inescapable Facts about the Inconvenient Truth," *Nature and Society,* April–May 2001, 1–5. See also CSIRO (Commonwealth Scientific and Industrial Research Organisation) Sustainability Network Update 56E, 31 March 2007, http://www.newcastle.edu.au/.../CSIRO%20sustainability%20Network%20Index.doc-2011-03-24.

18. Carbon sequestration is the process of capturing and storing atmospheric carbon dioxide. For information on those measuring the potential effects of organic farming for this purpose, see Maria Müller-Lindenlauf, *Organic Agriculture and Carbon Sequestration: Possibilities and Constraints for the Consideration of Organic Agriculture within Carbon Accounting Systems* (Rome: Natural Resources Management and Environment Department, Food and Agriculture Organization of the United Nations, 2009).

19. This draws on Greig de Peuter and Nick Dyer-Witheford, "Commons and Cooperatives," *Affinities: A Journal of Radical Theory, Culture, and Action* 4, no. 1 (Summer 2010): 30–56.

20. "World Communal Heritage Manifesto," World Communal Heritage Web site, http://communalheritage.wordpress.com/about, accessed 12 December 2012.

21. Tanika Sarkar and Sumit Chowdhury, "The Meaning of Nandigram: Corporate Land Invasion, People's Power, and the Left in India," *Focaal: European Journal of Anthropology* 54 (Summer 2009): 73–88; Martha C. Nussbaum, "Violence on the Left: Nandigram and the Communists of West Bengal," *Dissent* 55, no. 2 (2008): 27–33; and Steven Kirschbaum, "Nandigram Says 'No!' to Dow's Chemical Hub," International Action Center Web site, http://www.iacboston.org/india/1207-nandigram-says-no-html, accessed 3 December 2012.

22. "Testing Time for Gene Patents," *Nature* 464, no. 957 (15 April 2010); Andrew Pollock, "Justices Send Back Gene Case," *New York Times,* 26 March 2012; and John Conley, Dan Vorhaus, and Robert Cook-Deegan, "How Will Myriad Respond to the Next Generation of BRCA Testing?" *Genomics Law Report,* 1 March 2011.

23. Steven L. Salsburg and Mihaela Pertea, "Do-It-Yourself Genetic Testing," *Genome Biology* 11 (2010): 404.

24. The information on outer space is from United Nations Office for Outer Space Affairs (UNOOSA), "Treaty on Principles Governing the Activities of States in the Exploration and Use of Outer Space, Including the Moon and Other Celes-

tial Bodies," http://www.untreaty.un.org/cod/aul/ha/tos.html, accessed 3 December 2012; UNOOSA, "Treaty Signatures," http://www.oosa.unvienna.org/oosa/spacelaw/treatystatus/index.html, accessed 3 December 2012; and Christy Collis and Philip W. Graham, "Political Geographies of Mars: A History of Martian Management," *Management and Organizational History* 4, no. 3 (2009): 247–61.

25. Alex Alech, "Background Information," *Water Makes Money* film Web site, http://www.watermakesmoney.com; and Julio Godoy, "Water and Power: The French Connection," *iWatchNews*, 4 February 2003, http://projects.publicintegrity.org/2003/02/04/5711/water-and-power-french-connection.

26. "Housing Co-Ops: Cooperatively Controlled Institutions," Alliance to Develop Power Web site, http://www.a-dp.org/community-economy/housing-co-ops#.

27. Holly Sklar, "No Foreclosures Here," *Yes! Magazine*, 31 October 2008; and "History," Dudley Street Neighbourhood Initiative (DSNI) Web site, http://www.dsni.org/history.

28. John Bryden and Charles Geisler, "Community-Based Land Reform: Lessons from Scotland," *Land Use Policy* 24, no. 1 (2007): 24–34; A Fiona D Mackenzie, "'S Leinn Fh èin am Fearann (The land is ours): Re-claiming Land, Re-creating Community, North Harris, Outer Hebrides, Scotland," *Environment and Planning D: Society and Space* 24 (2006): 577–98; and Bruce Macdonald and Fiona Simpson, *The Scottish Land Fund Evaluation* (Cambridge, England: SQW, 2007).

29. "MST Receives 2011 Food Sovereignty Prize," Friends of the MST Web site, http://www.mstbrazil.org/content/mst-receives-2011-food-sovereignty-prize, accessed 3 December 2012; and Angus Wright and Wendy Wolford, *To Inherit the Earth: The Landless Movement and the Struggle for a New Brazil* (Oakland, Calif.: Food First Books, 2003), 35.

30. "Gondwana Link: Bringing an Ancient Land Back to Life," Gondwana Link organizational brochure, 2007, http://www.greeningaustralia.org.au/uploads/Our%20Solutions%20-%20Toolkit%20pdfs/Gondwana_Link07.web.pdf.

31. Robert J. Holmer and Axel W. Drescher, "Allotment Gardens of Cagayan de Oro: Their Contribution to Food Security and Urban Environmental Management," in *Urban and Peri-Urban Developments: Structures, Processes and Solutions*, ed. Christine Knie (Cologne, Germany: Southeast Asian–German Summer School Program, 16–29 October 2005), 149–55; and Ann Hill, m.ann.hill@anu.edu.au, personal communication with authors.

32. John Emmeus Davis, "Origins and Evolution of the Community Land Trust in the United States," in *The Community Land Trust Reader*, ed. John Emmeus Davis (Cambridge, Mass.: Lincoln Institute of Land Policy, 2010).

33. Anonymous Australian government officer, personal communication with Jenny Cameron, Community Gardens Conference, Canberra, Australia, October 2010. For examples of guerilla gardens across the globe, see http://www.guerrillagardening.org.

6. Take Back Finance

1. Thanks to George DeMartino and Ilene Grabel for this insight and phrase.

2. Julie Creswell, "Profits for Buyout Firms as Company Debt Soared," *New York Times*, 4 October 2009.

3. In his book *Griftopia,* the investigative journalist Matt Taibbi claims that in the United States the top 1 percent have seen their share of wealth increase from 35 percent before the crisis in 2007 to over 37 percent in 2009. In this same period, the median U.S. household's net worth was almost halved, falling from US$102,500 to $65,400. Meanwhile, in the top 1 percent, net worth held relatively steady, dropping from $19.5 million to 16.5 million. Matt Taibbi, *Griftopia* (New York: Spiegel & Grau, 2011), 12.

4. The material in this section is drawn from Gibson-Graham, "Surplus Possibilities: The Intentional Economy of Mondragón," in *A Postcapitalist Politics,* chap. 5. See also Race Mathews, *Jobs of Our Own: Building a Stakeholder Society,* 2nd ed. (Irving, Tex.: Distributist Review Press, 2009).

5. Mondragón Web site, http://www.mondragon-corporation.com, accessed 4 December 2012.

6. Updates on how the bank fared in the global financial crisis are from Randeep Ramesh, "Basque Country's Thriving Big Society," *The Guardian,* 30 March 2011; Carl Davidson, "Mondragon Diaries: Day Four," *Solidarity Economy.net,* 19 September, 2010; "No Caja Laboral Customers Will Be Affected by the Collapse of Lehman Brothers," 22 September, 2008, http://www.mondragon-corporation.com/ENC/Press-room.

7. In Spain cooperators were seen as "self-employed" and were excluded from national social insurance systems. This provided an early challenge for the Mondragón community, which responded by setting up their own social security system administered via Lagun Aro, a social protection organization (Gibson-Graham, *A Postcapitalist Politics,* 116, 227).

8. Annie Leonard, "The Story of Broke," video, *The Story of Stuff Project,* 2012, http://www.storyofstuff.org/movies.

9. The Kerala story is drawn from a number of sources. The population figures for 2011 are from "Kerala at a Glance," *Expert-Eyes.org,* last updated August 2011. The religious breakdown is from Bill McKibben, "The Enigma of Kerala," *Utne Reader .com,* web specials archive, 1996, http://www.utne.com/archives/TheEnigmaofKerala .aspx. The life expectancy figures are from K. Ravi Raman, "Asian Development Bank, Policy Conditionalities and the Social Democratic Governance: Kerala Model under Pressure?" *Review of International Political Economy* 16, no. 2 (2009): 287. The fertility figures are from the United Nations, "International Cooperation at the Crossroads: Aid, Trade, and Security in an Unequal World," *UN Human Development Report* (New York: United Nations, 2005), 30, 58. The comparison with the 1950s is from Govindan Parayil, ed., *Kerala: The Development Experience; Reflections on Sustainability and Replicability* (New York: Zed, 2000), 4. The sex ratio figures are from K. M. P. Basheer, "State Makes Big Leap in Sex Ratio," *The Hindu,* 1 April 2011. The state education expenditure is from V. K. Ramachandran, "Kerala's Development Achievements and Their Replicability," in *Kerala: The Development Experience,* ed. Parayil, 104, 108.

10. The discussion of the literacy campaign and its effects is drawn from K. Sivadasan Pillai, "KANFED and the Adult Education Scene in Kerala" *Adult Education and Development* 60 (2003). The volunteer figures are from Richard W. Franke and Barbara H. Chasin, "Is the Kerala Model Sustainable? Lessons from the Past, Prospects for the Future," in *Kerala: The Development Experience,* ed. Parayil; and McKib-

ben, "The Enigma of Kerala." The literacy figures are from Kerala Information and Public Relations Department, "Education," http://www.prd.kerala.gov.in/education.htm, accessed 4 December 2012. The mental health information is from Centre for Development Studies, *Kerala Human Development Report 2005* (Thiruvananthapuram, Kerala: Government of Kerala, 2005), 30–31.

11. For example, see Emily Hannum, "Educational Expansion and Demographic Change: Pathways of Influence" (background paper prepared for the World Bank Workshop Asia's New Demographic Realities: Do They Matter for Economic Growth?, Bangladesh, April 1998).

12. McKibben, "The Enigma of Kerala."

13. The story of Mararikulam is taken from Gibson-Graham, *A Postcapitalist Politics*, 180–81. The information on the most recent pledge is from K. G. Kumar, "Self-sufficiency in Vegetables," *The Hindu*, 1 October 2008.

14. The story of Norway is drawn from the following sources. The tax rates are from KPMG, *Tax Facts Norway 2010: A Survey of the Norwegian Tax System* (Oslo: KPMG Law Advokatfirma Da, 2010), 20. The quoted comments are from Tore Eriksen, *The Norwegian Petroleum Sector and the Government Pension Fund—Global* (Oslo: Ministry of Finance, Government of Norway, 2006); and Landon Thomas Jr., "Thriving Norway Provides an Economic Lesson," *New York Times*, 14 May 2009. Details of the history of the Fund and its stipulations are from Danyel Reiche, "Sovereign Wealth Funds as a New Instrument of Climate Protection Policy? A Case Study of Norway as a Pioneer of Ethical Guidelines for Investment Policy," *Energy* 35 (2010): 3569–77. The figures on the current holdings are from Charles Duxbury, "Norway's Oil Fund Positive on Southern European Bonds," *Wall Street Journal*, 22 February 2011. The figures on investments into renewables are from Sigurt Vitols, "European Pension Funds and Socially Responsible Investment," *Transfer: European Review of Labour and Research* 17, no. 1 (2011): 37.

15. Michael Pretes and Katherine Gibson, "Openings in the Body of 'Capitalism': Capital Flows and Diverse Economic Possibilities in Kiribati," *Asia Pacific Viewpoint* 49, no. 3 (2008): 381–91.

16. Gregory Wilpert, *Changing Venezuela by Taking Power: The History and Policies of the Chávez Government* (London: Verso, 2007), 76–82.

17. New Economic Foundation, *Measuring Social Impact: The Foundation of Social Return on Investment (SROI)* (London, 2004).

18. Alec Levenson and Timothy Besley, "The Anatomy of an Informal Financial Market: Rosca Participation in Taiwan," *Journal of Development Economics* 51, no. 45 (1996): 68. Other sources of information on Roscas are Shirley Ardener and Sandra Burman, eds., *Money-Go-Rounds: The Importance of Rotating Savings and Credit Associations for Women* (Washington, D.C.: Berg, 1995); Mary Kay Gugerty, "You Can't Save Alone: Commitment in Rotating Savings and Credit Associations in Kenya," *Economic Development and Cultural Change* 55, no. 2 (2007): 251–82; and Markku Malkamäki et al., *The Role of Informal Financial Groups in Extending Access in Kenya* (Nairobi, Kenya: Financial Sector Deepening Trust, 2009).

19. Information on Kickstarter is from the organization's Web site, http://www.kickstarter.com; and Devin Coldewey, "Kickstarter Hit with Patent Claim over Crowd Funding," *TechCrunch.com*, 4 October 2011.

20. "About Kiva," Kiva Web site, http://www.kiva.org.

21. "Mission Statement," Unlad Kabyan Web site, http://www.unladkabayan.org. See also Community Economies Collective and Katherine Gibson, "Building Community-Based Social Enterprises in the Philippines: Diverse Development Pathways," in *The Social Economy: International Perspectives on Solidarity,* ed. Amin, 116–38; and "Stories from the Philippines," Community Economies Collective Web site, http://www.communityeconomies.org/stories.

22. "About Us," Worcester Energy Barnraisers Web site, http://www.energybarnraising.org.

23. Terry Daniels, "3DN Long Island Home Enterprises," AboutUs.org.

24. Helen Jones, "Deli-Dollar Offers Route to Business Funding," *The Independent,* 17 February 1999.

25. Mark Huffman, "Bank of America Cancels Its $5 Debit-Card Fee," *Consumer Affairs,* 11 January 2011; and Gar Alperovitz, "Move Your Money, Change the System," *Truthout,* 10 December 2011.

26. For information on a range of community finance institutions, see the Slow Money Web site, http://www.slowmoney.org.

27. "About Community Bank®," Bendigo Bank Web site, http://www.bendigobank.com.au.

28. Martin Buttle, "Diverse Economies and the Negotiations and Practices of Ethical Finance: The Case of Charity Bank," *Environment and Planning A* 40 (2008): 2097–2113; and Charity Bank, *Annual Review 2010: Chief Executive Statement* (Tonbridge, Kent, England: Charity Bank, 2010), http://www.charitybank.org/annual-reports-and-publications.

29. "Overview and History," Calvert Fund Web site, http://www.calvert.com.

30. Social Investment Forum Foundation, *Report on Socially Responsible Investing Trends in the United States* (Washington, D.C.: Social Investment Forum, 2010).

31. The information for this story is from J. K. Gibson-Graham, "Post-Development Possibilities for Local and Regional Development," in *Handbook of Local and Regional Development,* ed. Andy Pike, Andres Rodriguez-Pose, and John Tomaney (London: Routledge, 2010); Marguerite Mendell, "The Three Pillars of the Social Economy: The Quebec Experience," in *The Social Economy: International Perspectives on Solidarity,* ed. Amin; and Nancy Neamtan, "Chantier de l'Economic Sociale: Building the Solidarity Economy in Quebec," in *Solidarity Economy: Building Alternatives for People and Planet,* ed. Jenna Allard, Carl Davidson, and Julie Matthaei (Chicago: Changemaker, 2008), 268–76.

32. The quote is from Neamtan, "Chantier de l'Economic Sociale," 272.

33. Frances Moore Lappé, "The City That Ended Hunger," *Yes! Magazine,* 13 February 2009.

Any Time, Any Place . . .

1. U.S. Department of Commerce, Bureau of Economic Analysis, "GDP: One of the Great Inventions of the 21st Century," *Survey of Current Business,* 2000, http://www.bea.gov/scb/account_articles/general/01000d/maintext.htm.

Index